ONCE UPON A TIME IN

HOLLY WOOD

Acknowledgments

To my sparkling editor, Catherine Laulhère-Vigneau. I would like to thank her particularly for her incredible faith in me. Thanks to Flammarion and to all of the team who worked on this book. All of my gratitude goes to Michel Hazanavicius for his contribution. To the Rhett Butler of French cinema, Jean-Pierre Lavoignat. I owe him more than I could express here. To the great man of journalism, Jean-Paul Chaillet, with whom I spoke about "old films" on many a long-haul flight. To all of the enthusiasts at *Studio* where I cut my teeth. A special thank you to *Studio Magazine* for the publication of the interviews of Kirk Douglas and Shirley MacLaine. To Charlie Levi. For his advice, his support, and his wonderful artistic view of the world. Thanks to the Hollywood Foreign Press Association which made it possible for me to meet so many of the greats of American cinema. A big thank you to Melody Korenbrot and to Harlan Boll. I must thank Patrick Brion and Claude-Jean Philippe's film clubs which created many a movie buff, myself included. Did I also mention the television channel Turner Classic Movies?

This book contains interviews with nine exceptional, essential artists who are inseparable from the Hollywood myth: a very big and humble thank you to Julie Andrews, Kirk Douglas, Jane Fonda, Tippi Hedren, Shirley MacLaine, Mickey Rooney, and to the immortal Ernest Borgnine, Farley Granger, and Lillian Gish. The privilege of talking to these fascinating people who we all adore, to listen to them share their extraordinary memories in a very simple way, often in their own homes (this is how Jean-Paul Chaillet ended up in New York in the apartment of the first lady of Hollywood, Lillian Gish, or how I, with heart pounding, visited Shirley MacLaine's sanctuary in Malibu and Kirk Douglas's in Beverly Hills), remains an unforgettable experience. And proof, again and again, that the Hollywood myth is real.

Finally, I dedicate this journey into the golden age to the stars in my family who have helped me so much. This book belongs to them.

J. M.

Editorial Director: Catherine Laulhère-Vigneau

Editorial Coordination: Marc Feustel

Translated from the French by Barbara Mellor

Design and Typesetting: Marie-Laure Miranda

Copyediting: Chrisoula Petridis

Proofreading: Marc Feustel

Color Separation: Point 4, Paris

Printed in China by Toppan Leefung

Simultaneously published in French as *Il était une fois Hollywood*
© Flammarion, S.A., Paris, 2013

English-language edition
© Flammarion, S.A., Paris, 2013

editions.flammarion.com

13 14 15   3 2 1

ISBN: 978-2-08-020172-0

Dépôt légal: 10/2013

Juliette Michaud
Foreword by Michel Hazanavicius

ONCE UPON A TIME IN HOLLYWOOD

Flammarion

ONCE UPON A TIME IN

HOLLY WOOD

PHOTOPLAY

The
Beauty Who Sits Alone

Contents

Foreword

Michel Hazanavicius

When I was small, I had posters of actors on my bedroom walls. One of Steve McQueen in *The Great Escape* (1963) had pride of place. I'd spend ages just gazing at it, and in my head I'd be saying something like this: "Dear Steve, Thank you for being so brave and free. Thank you for never letting anyone mess with you, for being so calm, and for showing us all the way. You're the coolest guy in the world, make me be like you." I should have added an "amen" for good measure, but back then I didn't know what I was doing.

Years later, despite my best efforts, I am nothing like Steve McQueen but am lucky enough to have made movies. And I became aware that lots of us—actors, directors, producers, technicians—felt, without really saying it openly, that the fact that we were making films somehow raised us above ordinary mortals. It was as if there was a different set of rules that applied to us, as if we should be free of some of the constraints, as if—without really being able to explain why this should be so—we occupied by rights a special place in society. Some people might call this arrogance, self-importance, big-headedness, conceit—but I think it's something else.

In many ways, cinema works like a religion. Or like a pagan cult on the Greek or Roman model, at least. First and foremost, it's a matter of faith and belief. The stories that are told don't purport to be real, but merely set out to paint pictures of reality, in a way that might be solemn or outrageous, funny or tragic. It's a way of transcending reality, of using fiction to expose a sliver of truth, that gives us all—in religion as in the cinema—the feeling that we share a common destiny. Its stories remind us that we're all in it together, that we're not alone. And that feeling is crucially important in helping us deal with the blows that life deals us, and with the dizzily existential areas into which our questions sometimes plunge us.

The analogy can be pushed further: actors idolized like icons; movie theaters laid out like temples; cinema screens like distant echoes of stained glass windows; the ability of films to create a world and exert absolute power over it and its inhabitants; not to speak of the very essence of the act of filming, which is to separate light from darkness. Oh yes.

And if we accept that cinema functions like a religion, then it goes without saying that Hollywood has to be Mount Olympus. This is the dwelling place of the gods, where they live, love, tear each other apart, fight, and make up. And we mere mortals gaze up at them, identifying with one icon or another according to our dreams and aspirations and how life is treating us.

Then among these icons there are the forces of good, say James Stewart, Gary Cooper, and John Wayne, and of evil, such as James Cagney, Robert Mitchum, and Richard Widmark. Some struggle for redemption (Bogart and De Niro), others fight for freedom (Nicholson and Brando). And there are the patron saints of the misunderstood, such as James Dean and Montgomery Clift. Among the goddesses there are those who are remote and untouchable, like Greta Garbo and Ingrid Bergman; the dangerous ones like Marlene Dietrich and Veronica Lake; the sex symbols like Marilyn Monroe, Ava Gardner, and so many others; and the child-women like Louise Brooks and Shirley MacLaine.

Through their films, through the stories they have told and the characters they have played, these actors have all embodied different aspects of humanity, thereby making Hollywood a mirror of the world. Sometimes of course—then as now—the mirror anticipates an image of a world yet to be. Terrifying though it may seem, Hollywood has created, thanks to its skills and powers of seduction, a moral code, a philosophy, a way of life to which the young people of the Western world are drawn as soon as they are old enough to watch—and therefore to love—a Walt Disney film.

The fact is that for many of us who were born after World War II, our system of values; the standards of courage, honesty, and heroism we espouse; our perception of good and evil; our capacity for endurance in the face of the trials of life—for all this we owe far more to *Casablanca* (1942) and *The Searchers* (1956) than to Jonah and the whale, Noah's Ark, and the Book of Job. Hollywood has been the (unloaded) weapon of America as a superpower, a propaganda tool without precedent. It embodied the spread of American influence and also its hegemony, and it imposed—in the most pleasurable of ways—a certain idea of democracy and freedom. By a stroke of luck, the values espoused by Hollywood have been generally humanist ones; and by an even greater stroke of luck, the Hollywood machine has always relied on human beings—and on artists—to make the things on which it all rested: films. It was quite possibly the head-on collision between cynicism at its most twisted and idealism at its most convinced that transformed the neighborhood of Los Angeles into a modern Olympus. In one corner were the likes of Harry Cohn, Jack Warner, and John Kennedy Sr.; in the other, figures such as John Ford, Charlie Chaplin, Frank Borzage, and King Vidor.

On the one side was a total and absolute devotion to turning a profit, and a political will to impose on the world a form of consumerism and an economic supremacy that could serve as a tool in carrying out the Marshall Plan. This vaulting ambition required an ability to level tastes to a standardized format across the globe, and for this it needed a portfolio of narratives that could be universally applied. The type of stories that touch the innermost depths of everyone they reached, couched in a language that went beyond words, that could be understood by all.

On the other side lay the aesthetic, artistic, and sometimes political quest of screenwriters, directors, and actors who were of necessity seeking to win over as many as they could. Here again—though for different reasons—creating a universal appeal was the goal. To reach and touch the most intimate recesses of our souls, and to tell a little of the truth.

When films honor all their promises and fulfill the ambitions of all, artists and money men alike, then the machine is functioning at its most effective and magnificent best. Hollywood has always been completely clear about the way it works: success is the sine qua non, the non-negotiable condition of freedom. Stanley Kubrick was the most eloquent and positive embodiment of this principle, Michael Cimino the reductio ad absurdum of squandered talent.

In a world that functioned with a brutal intensity, that handed certain individuals the power of life and death over others' careers, there were some artists who managed to slip through the net and to produce works of such limpid clarity that they give the illusion of having been created in conditions of perfect freedom. Charlie Chaplin, Ernst Lubitsch, Billy Wilder, and Alfred Hitchcock were only some of the directors who made remarkable and original films; films that not only met the toughest economic conditions imposed by the money men of Hollywood, but were also deeply personal, punctuated with moments of inspiration, and above all guaranteed to give pleasure to tens and sometimes hundreds of millions of people across the planet. In the end, it's hugely encouraging for us all to know that this type of achievement was and is possible, and you don't need to be a director to see it as a cause for celebration.

In the early days of the silent era, the approach to filmmaking varied greatly from country to country. Germany, caught up in major new movements in painting and the visual arts such as the Bauhaus and expressionism, produced films that were highly graphic and imbued with the spirit of painting and architecture. Their characters, meanwhile, were often conceptual and allegorical, rather than rounded human personalities. Russian filmmakers explored experimental techniques extensively, especially montage, and for them cinema was a way of educating the new Soviet citizen. Preoccupied with glorifying Soviet history, and more particularly the role of the workers, these directors, too, had little interest in telling individual stories. Here once again the human and the individual were a secondary consideration. In both France and Britain, the dominant literary tradition created a cinema derived from books and plays, classic or contemporary. Adventures and incidents played a prominent part, but with a handful of exceptions, there were few characters on a truly human scale.

In the end it was Hollywood that saw the birth of the first films on social themes and told from the viewpoint of their characters, with neither the grandiloquence of Russian cinema nor the classicism of its French counterpart. In movies from *The Kid* (1921)—possibly the first of the type—to King Vidor's *The Crowd* (1928), a new sort of hero emerged: an individual living in a real social context that was familiar and recognizable, who struggled with life's problems like everyone else. A simple and direct depiction of the man in the street, with whom viewers could identify and empathize in a far more obvious fashion. In this respect, probably Murnau's best films—or at least those that have retained most appeal today—were the ones he made after he had emigrated to America, *Sunrise* (1928) and *City Girl* (1930). The narrative technique appears obvious to us today, but at the time these films were unique. And this was the approach that emerged victorious. It's the way most stories have been told ever since.

Every country that makes films has had its golden age, a time of brilliant, important, excellent films, but throughout it all Hollywood has been constantly in the forefront, imposing its flawless expertise. This sustained and enduring level of achievement has rarely been found elsewhere. The Hollywood machine was unique in that it always assimilated the fact that it needed artists in order to constantly reinvent, to maintain its excellence, and to keep in contact with the famous man in the street who—as Hollywood never forgot either—was also and perhaps most importantly a potential viewer. This ruthless economic system, in which profit was the openly declared objective, nevertheless gave expression to men and women who talked the language of their times. The Marx Brothers, Anthony Mann, Howard Hawks, Sam Peckinpah, Samuel Fuller, Blake Edwards, Mel Brooks, Francis Ford Coppola, Martin Scorsese, Terrence Malick, the Coen brothers, David Fincher, and hundreds of other artists have been essential to the fruitful functioning of the machine. And the beauty of it all is that the money men know that they can't do without them. In essence, at the very heart of the machine, Hollywood offers us a vision of the world that is fundamentally cheering. It tells us that even in a world ruled by the implacable principles of free enterprise, idealists are indispensable, and creativity is the raw material without which management is nothing. It is still possible—even vital—to retain our integrity, honesty, and consistency, even when everything seems to be pushing us in the opposite direction. The most ruthless system will always need to create positive values, and ultimately human beings will always have something to say, as long as they have the will. What is extraordinary about Hollywood is that for nearly a century—even if it almost proved fatal for some, such as Orson Welles and John Garfield— art and industry have understood that to fight against each other is a sort of fratricide, and that they have never been as good or as strong as when they work together.

It is probably this unique history, the combination of power, money, talent, and energy devoted to the art of storytelling, that accounts for the fascination that Hollywood still exerts over us today. Having made a film about Hollywood, which on my search for locations gave me the opportunity to make a pilgrimage to all these legendary places, I know that Hollywood still exerts its full power. There is something spiritual about walking through the doors of Paramount, or going into the studio where *The Gold Rush* (1925) was made, or filming part of a set from *Casablanca*. And because this film also made it possible for me to meet some of the icons of my childhood, my teenage years, and my adult life, I know, too, that I am still capable of looking as stupid as I did not so long ago in front of my poster of *The Great Escape*. And that, after all, has to be a good thing.

The Age of Innocence

From the innovations of D. W. Griffith to the genius of Charlie Chaplin, from Babylonian epics to the rapture of the close-up, silent movies lasted less than twenty years but turned the world upside down. Making movies became a compulsion. "Creativity is a drug I cannot live without,"[1] Cecil B. DeMille was to say. Hollywood's first full-length feature film was directed by him.

It was just a century ago, when these pioneers of cinema, this band of visionaries invented their own legend, and on the way revolutionized a quiet little community known as . . . Hollywood.

The Kid, dir. Charles Chaplin, 1921.

1. *The Autobiography of Cecil B. DeMille*, Donald Hayne, Prentice-Hall Inc., 1959.

To modern eyes, silent movies may look like a different world. The way the actors express themselves is different, their gestures seem either too fast or too slow, the actresses' porcelain-doll lips mouth words, but no sound emerges. Naive dialogue is written on boards, and the music races to keep up with the action.

It is a world that seems all the stranger to us for the fact that we rarely see these films projected at the speed at which they were meant to be shown. Filmed in the early days using hand-cranked cameras and sped up during projection, with a live accompanist, the films became distorted over the decades in order to be shown on television with music. The result (even if fortunately corrections can now be made) is that these films, often in sepia versions and with added soundtracks, appear frenetic in pace and subject to abrupt changes of mood. The American critic Pauline Kael was to observe that showing silent movies in these conditions was "the worst crime ever committed against our cinema heritage."[2]

Yet, despite these unpromising conditions, who has not at some point found themselves unexpectedly caught up in a scene from a silent movie? Who can resist the spectacle of Charlie Chaplin, his eyes brimming with tears, clasping little Jackie Coogan in *The Kid* (1921)? Or indeed any scene of Chaplin acting the clown? Or the breakneck stunts or deadpan humor of Buster Keaton? Or the thrill sequences of Harold Lloyd, the shy young man in horn-rimmed glasses.

Close-up on Greta Garbo's face. Mystery, eroticism—her soul seemed to be laid bare in an astonishing play of subtlety and complexity. Nothing could have been further from the image of many silent film actors, who lent their haunting movies a sensitivity, a volatility summed up in the loose, untamed tresses of Lillian Gish.

It is difficult to comprehend how an invention as dazzling as cinema could have failed to find an earlier solution to the thorny problem of sound synchronization, but it was also *because of* the lack of dialogue that the images of silent movies were so powerful. From 1910, the vocabulary of filmmaking was invented, as those in the know bandied about terms such as depth of field, ellipsis, sequence shot, flashback, and even triptych. Everything was now in place, and the combination of a cinema that at first sight appears so antique, with such cutting-edge modernity, is breathtaking in its impact.

On the subject of flashbacks, let us go back a little farther. Los Angeles, 1886. On one of those fine, hot days that had made the reputation of this new El Dorado, Mrs. Daieda Wilcox, the young wife of a Kansas real estate agent, fell in love with a magnificent 118-acre (48-hectare) stretch of woodland—mainly evergreen oaks and fig trees—on the slopes of Cahuenga Canyon. For a handful of dollars, Harvey Henderson Wilcox bought this slice of paradise for his wife, who—despite the fact that no holly grew in the vicinity—decided to call her future ranch "Hollywood."

Daieda then set about imposing her own ideas on Hollywood, clearing the oaks and planting pepper trees, and rearranging the fig trees in formal rows, à la française (she was to set up a small

FACING PAGE, TOP: *Broken Blossoms*, dir. D. W. Griffith, 1919. Lillian Gish and Richard Barthelmess.
FACING PAGE, BOTTOM: *Flesh and the Devil*, dir. Clarence Brown, 1926. Greta Garbo and John Gilbert.

---

2. In the television documentary series *The Silent Years*, dir. Gary Graver, Orson Welles, prod. Ricki Franklin, 1971.

fruit canning business), building charming churches (less "heathen" than the existing Mexican mission churches), and, in 1887, laying out a main street, Prospect Avenue. All that remained was to secure a good price for the plots of land flanking the avenue that was later to become Hollywood Boulevard.

Hollywood developed into a model Prohibition-era town, a quiet and respectable neighborhood where nothing rocked the boat, and where all unnecessary excitement was avoided. This was especially true of second-rate entertainment like that new invention that was sweeping the rest of the country and the world: the cinema.

By the turn of the century, some time had already elapsed since the French "magician" Georges Méliès, the first person to really "tell a story" on screen, had made a woman vanish from the screen; in 1896, the American inventor Thomas Edison's forty-seven-second clip *The Kiss*, the first kiss in cinema history, had caused outrage; and at the legendary first public projections organized by the aptly named Lumière brothers, audiences had already been made to jump out of their seats at the sight of a railway engine thundering directly towards them from the screen.[3] The passé effects of the magic lantern were left far behind. Now the public could marvel at images that moved *in real life*, and nothing was going to stop this new technology.

It is impossible to say who the true inventor of the cinema was, or exactly when it happened: this was a joint development, with everyone "borrowing" from everyone else's inventions. To simplify, we owe the first motion picture camera, the Kinetograph, and the Kinetoscope, a wooden box with a peephole that enabled a viewer to watch twenty-second scenes, to Thomas Edison in New York. And to the Lumière brothers in Lyon we owe the Cinematograph, the first form of projection on a big screen.

Cinema Grew Up Very Fast

As early as 1903, one of Edison's super-charged team, Edwin S. Porter, showed *The Great Train Robbery*, a twelve-minute film ending with a striking close-up of a bandit firing at the public. The Western was to become an all-American specialty. This was a whole new world, where on Sundays,

worn out by the working week, immigrants would flock to rackety and disreputable "nickelodeons," where in exchange for a nickel a multinational and often illiterate public would be brought together by the common language of the silent film, to be carried away by universal stories drawn from the Bible or fairy tales, or to gallop alongside William S. Hart, the first cowboy of the silver screen. The conquest of the "Wild West" was already a favorite subject: in the days of the Kinetoscope, audiences were jostling to see "peepshows" featuring real-life Calamity Janes or Buffalo Bill shooting at targets.

And although these movies were shot at Fort Lee, New Jersey, along the cliffs of the Hudson River, the

The Great Train Robbery, dir. Edwin S. Porter, 1903.
Justus D. Barnes.

3. *L'Arrivée d'un train à La Ciotat*, shown to the public by the Lumière brothers in January 1896 (and not during their first great public projection of ten short films at the Grand Café de Paris, on December 28, 1895).

brand-new motion picture industry that was developing on the East Coast was nonetheless a wild setting worthy of the Far West. Its sheriff was Edison, who had patented his creations and could therefore claim to be the sole inventor of the projection of moving pictures, with the right to pursue his rivals for unauthorized infringement.

In 1907, when small new motion picture companies were springing up everywhere, Thomas Edison brought together the largest companies—Biograph, Vitagraph, and French companies that had set up in America such as Pathé Brothers and Star Film—under the umbrella of the Eastman-Edison Trust, which controlled all their output. The use of Eastman Kodak film became compulsory, for instance, at the risk of having the set invaded by private detectives who would unwind and expose any unauthorized reels.

But all makers of motion pictures, whether members of the Eastman-Edison Trust or not, came up against the same obstacles: bad weather and monotonous landscapes. There was talk of shrewd operators shooting movies in Los Angeles, on the beaches of Malibu, or in fields of wild poppies. In 1900, Edison was already filming in the orange groves around Santa Barbara.

In 1909, one of the first American film studios from Chicago, the Selig Polyscope Company, set up in Los Angeles. That same year, in quest of the magical light of the West, a young prodigy of the Biograph company, David Wark (D. W.) Griffith, was sent to Southern California with a troupe of actors including Mary Pickford, Lionel Barrymore, Blanche Sweet, and Mae Marsh, to be joined a little later by the young Gish sisters. They were the first to penetrate what then appeared to them as the "hamlet" of Hollywood, which had been forced by its exploding population and lack of water to become part of the "unstoppable" city of Los Angeles.

The time now seemed far away when doughty Daieda Wilcox had named her "mirage" Hollywood after a property in Illinois that a fellow

TOP: Poster for the play from which was adapted the original version of *The Squaw Man*, dirs. Oscar Apfel and Cecil B. DeMille, 1914. The film was remade in 1931.
BOTTOM: *The Squaw Man*, dir. Cecil B. DeMille, 1931. Warner Baxter and Lupe Velez.

passenger on a train journey had told her about and that she liked the sound of (although others claim that the original Hollywood was in fact in Ohio, or even in Ireland, and was as large as 160 acres [65 hectares]). As soon as the first cine cameras appeared on its soil, Hollywood's dreams of tranquility vanished in a puff of smoke.

D. W. Griffith's *In Old California* (1910), a romance set against the backdrop of the Mexican conquest of California, was the first short film ever shot in Hollywood. And since everything has to start somewhere, the first motion picture studio to establish itself officially in Hollywood, the Nestor Motion Picture Company, was set up in 1911 on the corner of Sunset Boulevard and Gower Street.

Nestor, Vitagraph, Lubin—one after another, New York studios opened up in Hollywood. Their names are now forgotten, swallowed up by more powerful studios founded by a wave of young and visionary entrepreneurs, also from the East Coast and largely second-generation Jewish immigrants from Central or Eastern Europe. These future kings of Hollywood were men such as William Fox and Carl Laemmle (who founded Universal Studios in 1912); men of ferocious determination who had seen the future in nickelodeons and who—motivated as much by a shrewd business sense as by a desire to assimilate—invested their parents' savings in them, whether from the Warner family's vegetable stall or the fur business owned by the family of Adolph Zukor, future owner of Paramount.

Among these remarkable risk takers were Samuel Goldwyn, also known as Samuel Goldfish, and his brother-in-law Jesse L. Lasky. One day they were having lunch with a bored young actor and writer called Cecil B. DeMille, who announced his intention to go off to fight in the Mexican Revolution. Goldwyn and Lasky offered him a different kind of adventure: founding with them the Jesse L. Lasky Feature Play Company, which would later become Paramount Pictures. The deal was signed on the corner of a tablecloth.

Cecil B. DeMille and D. W. Griffith, the two giants of silent movies, had followed similar paths. Both came from religious and cultured backgrounds—especially DeMille, whose parents were playwrights. Both had been actors, and had come to motion pictures out of necessity, as they could not live from the theater. Both were confident and charismatic. D. W. Griffith was the epitome of the southern gentleman, his suit always freshly pressed as if from the finest tailor and sporting a hat to set off his chiseled features. Cecil B. DeMille, brought up in North Carolina, wore the high boots and jodhpurs of an explorer and was never seen without a tie. Both Griffith and DeMille thought motion pictures lacking in nobility; both were immediately smitten with them.

From 1908 to 1914, Griffith overtook DeMille, who was six years his junior, to make no fewer than 450 short films of all genres, many of them adapted from the novels of Charles Dickens and all of them breaking new ground in narrative techniques. If Billy Bitzer, his faithful chief cameraman, told him that a shot was impossible, Griffith would retort that that was all the more reason to do it. Convinced that audiences could watch more than two reels of film without "damaging their eyes," Griffith left Biograph to set up his own company. Feature-length films were already being made in Europe. Inspired by the historical movies of the Italian director Giovanni Pastrone, which established the rules of the epic even before Griffith and Cecil B. DeMille, and whose *Cabiria* (1914) and systematic use of travelling shots were to be a major influence on Griffith's work, in 1912 he began filming *Judith of Bethulia*.

But it was Cecil B. DeMille who was to make Hollywood's first feature-length film. In a barn that was to become the epicenter of the Hollywood film industry, he co-produced and directed the *The Squaw Man*, lasting seventy-four minutes and starring the young leading man Dustin Farnum, alongside Red Wing, a genuine Native American princess who became a silent movie actress. Filmed in 1913, the first "true" Hollywood film was released on February 15, 1914. The barn still exists. Relocated, it now houses the Hollywood Heritage Museum. From that point on, film production took off.

FACING PAGE: *The Birth of a Nation*, dir. D. W. Griffith, 1915. Lillian Gish (top).

The whole town and its outskirts became one vast set for motion picture fanatics. The Antitrust Law of 1915 put an end to the Edison diktat: now the conquest of Hollywood could really begin.

In the countryside nearby, D. W. Griffith recreated the battlefields of the Civil War. *The Birth of a Nation* (1915), adapted from Thomas Dixon Jr.'s book *The Clansman*, a pro-Confederacy drama (and apology for the Ku Klux Klan) that was part melodrama and part the epic story of two families with sons fighting on opposing sides, came as a shock. Its innovative screenplay was to influence every generation of directors (including for instance Francis Ford Coppola in *The Godfather*, which follows the same parallel editing).

A Phenomenal Success

Between them, D. W. Griffith and Cecil B. DeMille invented the box office, and sent the price of cinema tickets up. DeMille was moreover to make two equally successful remakes of *The Squaw Man* (in 1918 and 1931). He also made two versions of *The Ten Commandments*, one in 1923 and the other in 1956 with Charlton Heston: following the silent movie vogue for lavish and exotic productions where dialogue was of less importance than images, biblical epics had become his specialty.

Intolerance, dir. D. W. Griffith, 1916.

What was also shocking, unfortunately, was the segregationist stance of *The Birth of a Nation*, which became one of the most controversial films in cinema history. Griffith's response to the accusations that rained down upon him, a year later, was *Intolerance* (1916). This colossal enterprise with a cast of sixty thousand interwove four stories on the theme of intolerance: the first contemporary, the second set at the time of the Saint Bartholomew's Day Massacre, the third around the Passion of Christ, and the last around the fall of Babylon. Was it this son of a Confederate officer's way of saying that he was responsible for his art, and to understand his argument you had to be as erudite as he was? "The best pictures I did were not popular," he was to say, "The lousy ones, like *The Birth of a Nation*, only a cheap melodrama, were popular."[4]

Audiences found *Intolerance* disconcerting, and Griffith, who had financed the project, spent the rest of his life paying off his debts. By the time he built the monumental sets for *Intolerance* at the foot of the Hollywood hills, most of the American motion picture production industry was centered on Los Angeles. In the eyes of the world, Hollywood itself had become the Babylon of the cinema.

The Wedding March, dir. Erich von Stroheim, 1928. Erich von Stroheim.

4. Ezra Goodman, *The Fifty-Year Decline and Fall of Hollywood* (New York: MacFadden Books, 1962), 10.

Intolerance: A Mine of Talent

Among Griffith's assistants and editors were Tod Browning, who later directed *Freaks* (1932), and Victor Fleming, director of *The Wizard of Oz* (1939) and *Gone with the Wind* (1939). Erich von Stroheim, later to become notorious as a monocle-wearing German villain, or "the man you love to hate," was a byword for excess and intransigence behind the lens, directing and acting in extravagant dramas such as *Foolish Wives* (1922), *The Merry Widow* (1925), and *The Wedding March* (1928), all films that denounced corruption through sex and money, not only through words, but also through the beauty and texture of their images.

Another Austrian assistant director on *Intolerance* was Josef von Sternberg, an earlier immigrant to the United States than von Stroheim, who also adopted the "von" in his name (neither of these luminaries was of aristocratic birth). Von Sternberg was to be forced by producer Irving Thalberg to mutilate von Stroheim's masterpiece, *Greed*. After all, it was ten hours long!

It has to be said, the pioneers of the silent era were themselves undeniably loud mouths, who worked with film as feverishly as others labored to extract black gold from the Californian soil. "Men unhampered by a literary education had a greater facility for visual narrative than men trained all their lives to use words. . . . Silent-film directors were mostly young men, but in those barnstorming days youth did not mean inexperience. Recruited from all branches of the industry, they came from every conceivable background. Sam Wood had worked on pipelines for an oil company. . . . Clarence Brown had been an auto salesman. W. S. Van Dyke had been a lumberjack, gold miner, railroader and mercenary."[5] Indeed there was something primitive about these fiercely practical, experienced men, avid for adventure, from whose ranks there were already emerging figures of the stature of Raoul Walsh, John Ford, and King Vidor: the kings of the action movie, the Western, and films of pacifism and social critique.

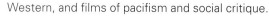

A Whirlwind of Movies

Between 1912 and 1929, no fewer than ten thousand films were made in the United States. Among this whirlwind of movies, there was also a more sophisticated current that had blown in from Europe. With Robert Wiene's *The Cabinet of Dr. Caligari* (1920) as the catalyst, Hollywood was fascinated by German expressionism, which foreshadowed film noir. F. W. Murnau, crowned with the success of *Nosferatu* (1922) and *Der letzte Mann* (*The Last Laugh*, 1924), was brought to America by Fox, to be followed by Fritz Lang, whose masterly *Metropolis* (1927) anticipated the entire genre of science fiction films to come. Hollywood also enticed Swedish masters such as Victor Sjöström (*The Wind*, 1928) and Mauritz Stiller (who agreed

London After Midnight, dir. Tod Browning, 1927.
Lon Chaney.

5. Kevin Brownlow, *The Parade's Gone By . . .* (Berkeley: University of California Press, 1976).

to work for Louis B. Mayer only on condition that he also hired Stiller's compatriot Greta Garbo).

The Hollywood silent era was also a world of romance and a greater refinement that heralded the stylish melodramas of the 1930s, such as the Austro-Hungarian Frank Borzage's *7th Heaven* (1927), itself influenced by German expressionism, or the high comedies of the German director Ernst Lubitsch, who created his own light and urbane style known as the "Lubitsch touch." Meanwhile the shadowy world of producer David O. Selznick was taking shape, who had already spotted an Englishman by the name of Alfred Hitchcock.

And the actors were equal to the challenge. While on the one hand there were Latin lovers, such as a certain Rudolph Valentino, on the other there were creatures from another planet such as Lon Chaney, the versatile tragedian capable of lyricism or horror, born to deaf parents and famous for his ability to transform himself physically, however grueling the process, as in *The Hunchback of Notre Dame* (1923) and *The Phantom of the Opera* (1925). Many of the horror films of this groundbreaking actor have been lost. Yet in the view of a contemporary star such as Johnny Depp, Lon Chaney remains an unassailable hero: "I developed my technique as an actor through the admiration I felt for silent movie actors. The expressions in their eyes, in their bodies, it's all there. . . . Buster Keaton and Lon Chaney are among my absolute heroes. Very early on, when I was just starting out as an actor, I used to love watching them. The virtuoso way they moved fascinated me, of course, but it was also the idea that they didn't have the support of dialogue to lean on."[6]

And then there were the Barrymores: John, Lionel, and Ethel, born into a long line of actors, and themselves grandfather, great uncle, and great aunt of Drew Barrymore: "When I found members of my family in old films, I took my career more seriously," she has explained on Turner Classic Movies. "Seeing my own face in the pronounced features of these exceptional actors made me aware of my responsibility. I found my grandfather John particularly touching: the most theatrical, he was also the most vulnerable. Watching him in *Dr Jekyll and Mr Hyde* (1920), this man whose career fell apart because of alcohol, moved me to tears. As for my Great Aunt Ethel, nobody realizes that she was called Hollywood's first 'It Girl'!"

The early years of cinema saw a significant number of women in the key roles of producer and director (often the same person). The first writers of screenplays worthy of the name were also women, including Frances Marion, who created the little girl persona and many other roles for Mary Pickford.

John Barrymore.

---

6. Johnny Depp, "Le cinéma muet et moi," in *Obsession, Le Nouvel Observateur* supplement (April 1, 2012).

And the first director of a narrative fiction film (*La Fée aux choux*, or *The Cabbage Fairy*, 1896) was the Frenchwoman Alice Guy, who emigrated to New York to set up her own production company, Solax. Having started out as a secretary to Léon Gaumont, Guy described the cinema as her "Prince Charming," and made some six hundred short and medium-length films in all. A sign in her studio advised her actors to "Be Natural." D. W. Griffith would have agreed with her: although he liked his actresses to be "spirited," he also schooled them from the outset to keep their body movements to a minimum in order to avoid the pitfalls of being too theatrical. An equally important and prolific female director (as well as actress and screenwriter) was Lois Weber, who in *Hypocrites* (1915) became the first to put nudity on screen. The actresses of the silent era all shared one quality: they were all captivating and endearing. But even the most apparently fragile of them, such as the Gish sisters, were in fact indefatigable, with a relentless capacity for work. Many of them deserve to be "rediscovered." Marion Davies, unjustly viewed as a bad actress because of the way she was later portrayed by Orson Welles in *Citizen Kane* (1941), was in fact a funny and talented comedienne. In the King Vidor silent comedy *Show People* (1928), she played an ingénue who wants to get into the movies; studded with cameo roles by "real" movie stars, the film paints a fascinating behind-the-scenes portrait of the Hollywood of the time.

Mary Pickford, meanwhile, was the "girl with the curls" and America's sweetheart, who played to adoring audiences in films such as *The Poor Little Rich Girl* (1917), directed by one of the French directors imported to Hollywood, Maurice Tourneur, or *The Little Princess* (1917)—even if the sight of a twenty-five-year-old actress playing a child is slightly disturbing to a modern audience. The public also worshipped the couple she was to form with the swashbuckling Douglas Fairbanks Sr. Their mansion, Pickfair, was to become the symbol of "Hollywood royalty." In 1919, in order to control the distribution of their own independent films, Mary Pickford and Douglas Fairbanks Sr. went into partnership with Charlie Chaplin and D. W. Griffith, and together the four most bankable Hollywood stars set up United Artists. Chaplin took advantage of this to build his own studios on La Brea Avenue, where they still stand.

TOP: *Ben-Hur*, dir. Fred Niblo, 1925. Ramón Navarro.
BOTTOM: *Lights of Old Broadway*, dir. Monta Bell, 1925. Marion Davies.

Charlie Chaplin

One of a kind. The greatest and most intelligent artist of his times, who combined a sublime talent for mime with a philosophy that was both funny and warmly humane. Hollywood would never have survived without humor.

Charles Spencer Chaplin was born in London in 1889; his parents were both penniless music-hall entertainers and his early life was one of grinding hardship. As as a young comedian touring America Chaplin came to the attention of Mack Sennett, who had also worked at Biograph and was the owner of the Keystone Studios. Mack Sennett was to slapstick comedy what Cecil B. DeMille was to the historical epic. Known for his saucy *Bathing Beauties*, Sennett was to cultivate

Safety Last, dirs. Fred C. Newmeyer and Sam Taylor, 1923. Harold Lloyd.

an extraordinary hothouse of comic talent, including the cowboy Tom Mix (who was to unseat William S. Hart), Harold Lloyd, Harry Langdon, and the comedy duo of Mabel Normand and Roscoe "Fatty" Arbuckle. All of them did their own dizzying stunts and knockabout routines themselves, taking the streets of Los Angeles by storm under the bemused gaze of passersby, and pinching gags from each other. Frank Capra started out as a gagman for Sennett, alongside director Leo McCarey, who recalled: "All of us tried to steal each other's gagmen. But we had no luck with Keaton, because he thought up his best gags himself and we couldn't steal *him*!"[7]

Chaplin, Keaton, and Lloyd, producers and directors of their own films, became inextricably linked with the Hollywood machine. It was in 1915, when he borrowed Fatty Arbuckle's outsize trousers that Charlie Chaplin, a disciple of the French comedian Max Linder, created the wily, touching, and indestructible persona of "The Tramp," immortalized in *The Kid*, *The Gold Rush* (1925), *The Circus* (1928), and countless other classics of silent comedy.

The career of Fatty Arbuckle—similarly multitalented, and the discoverer of Buster Keaton and Bob Hope—never recovered from the false accusation, in 1921, that he been responsible for the death of an actress. Though acquitted, he never lived down his salacious treatment in the scandal sheets of the time, which decried him as a symbol of the excess and decadence of a Hollywood that—in the popular imagination—was heaving with orgies, just like in a Cecil B. DeMille movie. Even as the flashing 45-foot letters *Holly . . . Wood . . . Land* were going up in the Hollywood Hills, a fledgling star system was already turning against its compromised stars.

A Changing World

But let us return to Drew Barrymore's description of her Great Aunt Ethel as an "It Girl," a magical combination of lightness, modishness, sex appeal, and that certain "it" that guaranteed a universal appeal. World War I was over, and Hollywood films were now a dominant influence in a changing world. By 1919 the Jazz Age was beginning, and 80 percent of the world's movies were made in Hollywood. Cause for celebration! Gone was the era of prim Victorian maidens, of Jezebels and Cinderellas, of Theda Bara and the first kohl-eyed screen incarnation of Cleopatra. These gave way to flappers, to the glossy bobs of Louise Brooks and Colleen Moore, and to the confident sexuality and exuberance of Clara Bow. In contrast to the

TOP: Poster for *The Black Pirate*, dir. Albert Parker, 1926.
BOTTOM: Poster for *The Kid*, dir. Charles Chaplin, 1921.

7. Leonard Maltin, *The Great Movie Comedians* (New York: Bell Publishing, 1978), 36.

chaste heroines of D. W. Griffith, Cecil B. DeMille offered emancipated womanhood in the form of Gloria Swanson, whom he showcased in a series of comedies of manners alongside his epics.

And then, as when Jean Dujardin as George Valentin in *The Artist* (2011) dreams that he is in a world where everyone can speak except him, the nightmare of every silent movie actor became a reality: the "talkies" had arrived at last. The rest is history. For every Swedish accent that was accepted, countless careers were cut short by the arrival of dialogue. If you have seen *Singin' in the Rain* (1952), you get the picture.

For the studios this was an opportunity to get rid of stars who were too expensive, and to offer the public new faces like Joan Crawford and Gary Cooper. Yet if *The Jazz Singer*, with its troubling

D. W. Griffith, Mary Pickford, Charlie Chaplin, and Douglas Fairbanks, c. 1920.

blackface imagery, announced in 1927, "You ain't heard nothin' yet," the silent movie was to reach its apotheosis in 1931 with Charlie Chaplin's *City Lights*. Chaplin was to defy the conventions of cinema to the end, for it was in 1936—at the height of the talkies explosion—that he created his masterpiece, *Modern Times*, using all the complexities of the silent tradition. Charlie Chaplin: a career in movies stretching from 1914 to 1967. Not many would be that fortunate.

It was only with difficulty that F. W. Murnau recovered from the commercial failure of *Sunrise* (1927), a hugely impressive drama of passion, betrayal and fidelity, with staggering expressionist-inspired scenes, for which the twenty-two-year-old Janet Gaynor was awarded the Best Actress in a Leading Role award at the first Academy Awards ceremony in 1929. Unlike Cecil B. DeMille, who was to continue to set the world of film alight into the 1950s, winning the Oscar for Best Picture in 1953 with *The Greatest Show on Earth*, the pioneering director D. W. Griffith was to die in 1948 at the age of seventy-three, a penniless and forgotten alcoholic. *Abraham Lincoln* (1930), his second response to the accusations of racism that were to weigh on this giant of the cinema throughout his life, who was in fact liberal and progressive except when it came to his blinkered views on the Old South, passed unnoticed. The Russian genius of silent cinema, Sergei Eisenstein, director of

Three Monkeys, Buster Keaton.

the immortal *Battleship Potemkin* (1925), declared that he owed his career to him.

Josef von Sternberg, for his part, benefited from the fall of his master, Erich von Stroheim. But it was when he was invited to Berlin to film *The Blue Angel* (1930) that his career took off, and he returned to Hollywood as a triumphant Pygmalion, with Marlene Dietrich on his arm.

It was in 1950, when the silent era was a bygone age, that Billy Wilder offered the most poignant portrait of that time, in *Sunset Boulevard*. While Gloria Swanson and Cecil B. DeMille played themselves, Erich von Stroheim featured as the outmoded film director Max von Mayerling, and Buster Keaton made a cameo appearance. After a period without work, Keaton continued working to the end, belatedly receiving an Honorary Oscar in 1960, six years before his death. In 1952 Chaplin gave him the role of the piano-playing clown in *Limelight*, a moving tribute to their glory days. The days when Hollywood took pride in encouraging the freedom of its best artists. The days when movies made up for their lack of dialogue with scenes of comedy and emotion that remain unsurpassed to this day. Beautiful and cruel, anguished and ambitious, naive and side-splitting, thrilling and hair-raising, through the lens of motion picture camera the silent movies reinvented life—and invented the Hollywood legend.

The Return of the Silent Film

In 2012 *The Artist*, directed by Michel Hazanavicius, became only the second silent film in cinema history to win an Oscar for Best Picture, after William Wellman's *Wings*, which triumphed at the first Academy Awards ceremony in 1929.

TOP: *The Navigator*, dirs. Donald Crisp and Buster Keaton, 1924. Buster Keaton.
BOTTOM: *Sunrise*, dir. F. W. Murnau, 1927.

Lillian Gish

It is a cavernous apartment near Sutton Place by the East River where she has lived for decades. Lillian Gish greets a visitor with a twinkle in her pale blue eyes. At ninety-four, she looks frail and is hard of hearing. But still sprightly, she does not use a cane. Tea is ready in the darkened and slightly faded rococo library-drawing room full of assorted mementos of her very long career.

She admits candidly to being astonished at finding herself in a movie again, sharing top billing with Bette Davis, 81, in Lindsay Anderson's *The Whales of August* (1987). They play bickering elderly sisters. It was to be the last film of a career that had started in 1912 when she and her younger sister Dorothy were chosen by D. W. Griffith to appear in their first feature, *An Unseen Enemy*, a short made for Biograph studios. She still refers to him as Mr. Griffith. He became a Pygmalion and she appeared in several of his masterpieces. *The Birth of a Nation* in 1915, the following year as Eternal Motherhood in *Intolerance*, at the time the most expensive film ever made, and then in *Broken Blossoms* (1919) and *Orphans of the Storm* (1921). She often played long-suffering and virginal heroines and was one of the earliest stars of the silent screen with her good friend Mary Pickford. She told it all in her 1969 memoirs, *The Movies, Mr. Griffith, and Me*. After the arrival of the talkies, she went back East and worked mostly on stage. She would return to film with impactful performances in *Duel in the Sun* (1946) and *The Night of the Hunter* (1955) with her unforgettable face-off with Robert Mitchum.

I have been working since I was five years old.

"I kind of grew up with D. W. Griffith. Mother liked working for him because he never used our names. She did not take the most money: she took the people who didn't use our names. Because no one in our family ever had anything to do with theater or film. You know in our family a lady gets her name in print only three times: when she gets born, married, and when she dies. That's it. Mother's people came here in 1634 and my father's two years earlier, or later. And we are related to our twelfth president, Zachary Taylor. So we come from quite a respectable family.

D. W. Griffith: I was around thirteen the first time we met. [In fact, she was nineteen and lied, saying she was sixteen.] Because he could not tell one of us from the other, he put a red hair ribbon on Dorothy and a blue one on me. And he called us Red and Blue. He took us upstairs to where the company was and he called out the plot and people would walk through and they ended up chasing us around the room and shooting up at the ceiling! We thought we were in a madhouse. [*Laughs.*] We would not go there anymore without Mother.

FACING PAGE: In *The White Sister*, dir. Henry King, 1923.

BELOW, LEFT: With Lionel Barrymore in *Duel in the Sun*, dir. King Vidor, 1946.

BELOW, RIGHT: With Bette Davis in *The Whales of August*, dir. Lindsay Anderson, 1987.

For *Birth of a Nation*, when that came out, he had to go to Mother and say I have to put her name on the program because you want another name and Dorothy said no. He did not like that name, Gish. Like fish, dish! And Dorothy said if that was good enough for Mother that it is good enough for us. And we didn't change it.

D. W. Griffith wrote the stories, maybe he got a little piece out of the morning papers and wrote a story around that. All the actors would stand in a room and he would call the plot until all the actors knew it and then they started to speak. He didn't tell them what to say. And at the end, when we knew what we were doing and saying, he had the man who wrote the subtitles come in and take down what you said. The only thing in writing I ever saw his name on was for my pay once a week.

Early Hollywood it was. I did not go into films until 1913. Before that I did theater. I was up at six because I put on my own makeup. I never had a makeup man, never had a man fix my hair. It was so long I could sit on it and they didn't know what to do with it—they wanted to take scissors and cut it off! Dorothy and I never had gone to the hairdresser in our lives.

For *Intolerance*, I helped with the research, for the French story and the Babylonian period. That was the biggest set ever built by anyone to this day. For one scene I remember he wanted to go up in a balloon to photograph it, but it could not work.

Mae Marsh [another Griffith discovery with whom she co-starred in *The Birth of a Nation* and *Intolerance*] is the only actress I was ever jealous of and I have never been jealous of anyone. I told her and she asked why. 'Because you get the part I think I can play,' I said, 'and when I see you on the screen you are better than I would be.' She had that quality that you loved and would die for.

When I had a choice of parts, I would always let Dorothy pick what she wanted to play and I took the other part because she had less belief in herself. And I always wanted her to be best.

I like the camera to be at eye level. The camera doesn't lie. We used to say everything with our eyes and it is the eyes that tell the story. I don't have a favorite film. You never please yourself in everything. You are never satisfied with yourself. Each time you try to do your best. The theater is so nice because you never have to see yourself. They tell you that you are wonderful and if you hear it for long enough, in the end you think you are."

Interview by Jean-Paul Chaillet at 430 East 57th Street,
New York City, April 10, 1987.

Portrait, c. 1920.

PHOTOPLAY

N.S.E.

DECEMBER
25 CENTS
30 cents in Canada

NRA CODE

The Beauty Who Sits Alone

The
First
Stars

They were creatures of flesh and blood—and yet, viewed through a camera lens, with skillful lighting and the aid of a well-honed publicity machine, and above all through their own charisma, more dazzling than a thousand movie projectors, they emerged as stars.

The term was not new: in 1896 Georges Méliès called his company Star-Film. Audiences were quick to give their favorite actors affectionate nicknames: Gilbert M. Anderson, who played three parts in *The Great Train Robbery* (1903), became "Broncho Billy," while Mary Pickford was "Little Mary." In the early years, actresses were often known by the name of the studio that employed them, becoming the "Vitagraph Girl," the "Biograph Girl," or the "Imp Girl"; and since respectable society thought making movies was rather shameful, they were perhaps grateful for the anonymity.

Greta Garbo on the cover of *Photoplay* magazine, December 1935.

In divulging the name of the delightful Imp Girl—Florence Lawrence—and increasing her salary, Carl Laemmle created the star system. At Biograph, Florence Lawrence (not to be confused with Florence Turner, the Vitagraph Girl) had played Mrs. Jones in D. W. Griffith's Jones series of comedies. Finding herself supplanted by younger actresses and plagued by injuries and ill health, she retired in 1924. She committed suicide eight years later. The world of moving pictures was a ruthless one.

But for those who passed the test and had a thick enough skin, the game was well worth the high stakes. "Two of the most successful [stars] of all time, Charles Chaplin and Mary Pickford, are classic examples. Chaplin rose from $150 a week at Keystone in 1913 to over a million dollars for eighteen months' work in 1917. Mary Pickford went from $25 a week at Biograph in 1909 to the same million dollar bracket in 1917."[1] Chaplin was also the first to exploit the idea of merchandising in the movies, with fans fighting over his "Tramp" doll in the shops.

The emergence of the stars was accompanied by new demands: gone was the time when a public that had come from the four corners of the globe would happily accept a motley crew of heroes and heroines of every variety. Pre-Raphaelite muses and gypsies from *The Thousand and One Nights* alike gave way to a more manicured glamour that reflected the new American identity.

Jazz babies and flapper girls distilled a new, carefree style, but the Wall Street crash of 1929 and the Great Depression were to usher in a more elegant, soigné generation of female stars such as Norma Shearer, who were matched by leading men of greater sophistication and maturity. Allowing oneself to be carried away by all these perfect features, glowing complexions, and flashing eyes in close-up on 50 foot-high screens became a world of forbidden delights, filled with unspoken obsessions and revealing the subconscious desires of an increasingly egalitarian society. Movie theaters were the new temples, where audiences no longer merely adored but worshipped. Magazines for movie fans such as *Photoplay* sprang up to feed an eager public with fabricated stories from the private lives of the gods and goddesses of Hollywood.

Who has not attempted to define what makes a star? For André Malraux, a star was someone who was "capable of a minimum of acting talent, whose face expresses, symbolizes, embodies a collective instinct."[2] In comparing the very first movie stars with those who made the transition into the world of talkies, we have tried in our turn to explore that mysterious quality that is the essence of these heavenly creatures of the silver screen. And what makes some of the stars in this galaxy shine so brightly. The selection that follows is of necessity selective and subjective, but all those included—attractive, witty, energetic, glamorous, or subversive—were among the greatest leading men and ladies in cinema history. Even Lillian Gish (see the previously unpublished interview on p. 28), when she allows a lock of blonde hair to escape from her cap in Victor Sjöström's *The Scarlet Letter* (1926), reminds us that she could quicken the pulse. A hint of vanity in this archetypically virginal actress brings us all the closer to her. And the ability to make us believe we can touch them, while remaining unattainable, makes all the magic of the stars.

Portrait of Florence Lawrence, pioneer of the star system.

1. Richard Lawton and Hugo Leckey, *A World of Movies* (New York: Random House Value Publishing, 1985), 10.
2. André Malraux, *Esquisse d'une psychologie du cinéma* (Paris: Gallimard, 1939).

Mary Pickford

Born into a Canadian family for whom acting was a business, the young Gladys Smith was "managed" by her mother. D. W. Griffith spotted her girlish charm, and transformed her into "America's sweetheart." Between 1909 and 1933, the huge star of the silent screen made fifty-two films, distributing them herself through United Artists, which she founded with her mentor Griffith, her husband Douglas Fairbanks, and Charlie Chaplin. Having made her fortune—and having failed to appreciate the serious implications of the arrival of the talkies—she retired to her fairytale mansion, Pickfair. In 1929 she was awarded the Academy Award for Best Actress for her part in *Coquette*, in which she sported a bob that shocked her fans. She was awarded an Honorary Oscar in 1975, four years before she returned to light up the sky.

Portrait, c. 1920.

Charlie
Chaplin

Charles Spencer Chaplin: the very definition of cinema. The British-born giant of cinema created a persona recognized the world over (which he memorably transformed into an inflatable globe to parody the lust for power in *The Great Dictator* of 1940) and left us with unforgettable images: Chaplin the boxer, Chaplin the barber, Chaplin's table ballet, Chaplin falling in love with the blind flower girl; in short, the whole gamut of emotions, gags, and lyricism. The creator of every aspect of his films (even the music), a fearless critic of injustice, he was banished by a Hollywood that has always been frightened of free thinkers and free spirits. A Hollywood that was later to ask his forgiveness. Happily—as Chaplin continued to show right up to *A King in New York*, made in 1957 but not released in America until 1972—ridicule never killed anyone.

Portrait, 1930.

Theda
Bara

And William Fox created the first vamp of the silver screen: thanks to an entirely fabricated publicity campaign, the Ohio-born actress Theodosia Goodman became the kohl-eyed Theda Bara (an anagram of "Arab death"), born on the banks of the Nile to a father who was a French artist and a mother who was an Arabian princess, endowed with occult powers and capable of driving men to suicide. For five years, she smoldered her way through films such as *Cleopatra* (1917), directed by J. Gordon Edwards (a relation of Blake Edwards), and *Salome* (1918).

Portrait in the role of Salome. *Salome,* dir. J. Gordon Edwards, 1918.

Pola
Negri

Born into a gypsy family, the young Apolonia Chaupiec studied dance and drama in Warsaw, Saint Petersburg, and Berlin, where Ernst Lubitsch took her under his wing and cast her in *Madame DuBarry* (1919) in Germany. Known in Hollywood as *Passion*, the film earned her a reputation as a passionate femme fatale, which Hollywood appropriated. Flouting morals and flaunting her conquests—even though she boasted of having become engaged to Rudolph Valentino just before his death—Negri wrapped herself in her erotic persona just as she did in her expensive capes, eventually to be overtaken in the public's affections by that other exotic femme fatale, Greta Garbo.

Portrait, 1921.

Douglas
Fairbanks Sr.

The swashbuckling hero of *The Mark of Zorro* (1920), *The Thief of Bagdad* (1924), and *Robin Hood* (1922), Fairbanks was involved in every aspect of his films. For *Robin Hood*, he had all of medieval Nottingham rebuilt at the Pickford-Fairbanks Studio, with sets by Frank Lloyd Wright. Dubbed the "King of Hollywood" (a title that was later passed on to Clark Gable), he divorced Mary Pickford in 1933 and his career went into decline. Elected first president of the Motion Picture Academy of Arts and Sciences in 1927, he presented the first Academy Awards. Not to be confused with Douglas Fairbanks Jr., his son by his first marriage.

Portrait in *The Thief of Bagdad*, dir. Raoul Walsh, 1924.

John
Gilbert

John Gilbert was known for his military bearing, as in King Vidor's *The Big Parade* (1925), trademark moustache, and piercing gaze. When the ladies' man leans his handsome profile toward Garbo in Clarence Brown's *Flesh and the Devil* (1926), she is understandably lost. This was the first of their films celebrating loves that could never be, echoed in real life when Garbo is said to have stood him up on their wedding day. Misfortune, depression, and drinking followed. The actor with the high-pitched voice mimicked by Gene Kelly in *Singin' in the Rain* (1962) was Gilbert. In truth MGM boss Louis B. Mayer had it in for him. Greta Garbo insisted that director Rouben Mamoulian cast him in *Queen Christina* (1933), but this was not enough to save a career that was already blighted.

Portrait, c. 1930.

Greta
Garbo

Marlene
Dietrich

With their iconic features and husky accents, the cult status of many of their scenes, and their universal appeal, they are inseparable from the myth and history of Hollywood. "Life is so gloriously improbable!" declares the Swedish actress from the ship's prow in *Queen Christina*. "Falling in love again. Never wanted to. What am I to do? I can't help it," sings the German femme fatale in *The Blue Angel* (1930). The two followed similar paths, losing their fathers very young and being discovered by a Pygmalion figure. Greta Lovisa Gustafsson, four years younger than Maria Magdalena Dietrich, was the first to arrive in Hollywood. It was because MGM was so successful with their Swedish actress that Paramount decided to mount a counter-attack with their own German siren. The two studios both imposed rigid diets on the plump young actresses, altering hairlines here and extracting molars there to create two svelte beauties with sensual foreheads and high cheekbones, ready to play their part in one of the century's greatest legends.

Mauritz Stiller filmed Garbo in slow motion to create a subliminal effect, before passing her on to directors who knew all the tricks of the Hollywood trade. Clarence Brown, who directed her in her first talkie, *Anna Christie* (1930), said that in the rushes you couldn't see her acting. Her restraint was intoxicating. Joseph von Sternberg, meanwhile, raised Dietrich to the ranks of the screen goddesses in increasingly torrid productions, including *Shanghai Express* (1932), *The Scarlet Empress* (1934), and *The Devil Is a Woman* (1935), declaring that each of their seven films together was the last.

Garbo was dubbed the "Divine" Garbo: hard to outdo, though Dietrich cleverly matched her "butterfly" makeup, androgynous persona, and lethally seductive looks. And she had the best legs in Hollywood. Both were illusionists of genius. Garbo, weary of being confused with her screen persona, took an early retirement that only added to her mystique. Dietrich carried on to the end, singing on tour and giving her public what they craved: dreams and glamour. Two grandes dames of the cinema.

LEFT: Portrait of Marlene Dietrich in *Dishonored*, dir. Josef von Sternberg, 1931.
RIGHT: Portrait of Greta Garbo in *The Kiss*, dir. Jacques Feyder, 1929.

Gloria
Swanson

"I decided that when I became a star, I would be a star to the tips of my fingers."[1] No, this is not Norma Desmond, but Gloria Swanson at the height of her fame. From the sophisticated, liberated comedies made by Cecil B. DeMille, who forsook his biblical epics for her, to *Queen Kelly* (1929), sabotaged by her disagreements with Erich von Stroheim, the feline and diminutive Swanson was larger than life in her excesses, her marriages (including to a French marquis), and her spirit of independence in a man's world. But during the Great Depression her feathers, furs, and jewels seemed out of place. As her character Norma Desmond famously declared in *Sunset Boulevard* (1950), "I am big. It's the pictures that got small."

Portrait, 1929.

1. Don MacPherson, *Leading Ladies* (New York: St. Martin's Press, 1986).

Rudolph
Valentino

With his god-like looks and photogenic acting style, the Italian actor was a sex symbol and star on such a scale that he has been called the first rock star. When he died of peritonitis aged just thirty-one, there were rumors of despairing female fans committing suicide, and his funeral was a huge popular and media event. Valentino was a former tango dancer at Maxim's when he was noticed by a talent spotter from Metro Pictures, and his sensual qualities exploded onto the screen in Rex Ingram's *Four Horsemen of the Apocalypse* (1921), in which his dancing of the tango elevated him to the status of *the* Latin lover, more attractive than even Ramón Navarro. *The Sheik* (1921) and *The Son of the Sheik* (1926) confirmed his triumphant place among the leading Hollywood stars.

Portrait in *Cobra*, dir. Joseph Henabery, 1925.

Louise
Brooks

With her unique "look" and vivacity, Louise Brooks became an influential figure of the Jazz Age, but it was when Georg Wilhelm Pabst, transfixed by the twenty-three-year-old American actress, invited her to Germany to star as Lulu in *Pandora's Box*, in 1929, that she became the archetypal man-eating androgynous woman, a disturbing and iconic figure of erotic cinema. Disillusioned with Hollywood, she fell into oblivion, working as a salesgirl before reinventing herself as a film critic. Of herself she wrote: "The great art of films does not consist of descriptive movement of face and body but in the movements of thought and soul transmitted in a kind of intense isolation."[1] The first modern actress.

Portrait, 1928.

---

1. Louise Brooks, *Lulu in Hollywood* (New York: Knopf, 1982).

Clara
Bow

"In a feminine mythology dominated by European stereotypes, she brought a good-natured eroticism, smelling sweetly of corn and apple pie. Louise Brooks, Joan Crawford, Jean Harlow, and Marilyn Monroe could never have existed if Clara Bow had not come before them."[1] It was the film *It* (1927), in which she played an enticing shopgirl, that earned her the famous "It Girl" sobriquet. At the age of sixteen, after a childhood of deprivation, Bow got her first break when she won a talent contest. The judges were bowled over, noting: "She has a genuine spark of divine fire." With her personality, determination, and looks, not to mention her remarkable talent, it is hardly surprising that she made no fewer than forty-nine films in eight years.

Portrait, 1927.

1. Jean-Loup Passek, *Dictionnaire du cinéma* (Paris: Larousse, 2001).

Joan
Crawford

Lucille Fay LeSueur came from a modest background in Texas, and her determination to escape from it contributed to her image of ambition and devotion to her fans. She embarked on a campaign to gain recognition as a flapper girl. Self-promotion as a dancer and actress led to parts in some twenty silent movies, and standing in for Norma Shearer. A fierce rivalry grew up between the two actresses, which was exploited by George Cukor in *The Women* (1939), the first turning point in her career. *Mildred Pierce* (1945) was to be the second. Meanwhile all her films, whether she played hard-boiled women to be reckoned with or put-upon victims, were imbued with an exhilarating cocktail of storybook romance and Hollywood glamour, luring audiences with the promise of guilty pleasure. The power of both her conviction and her features—with famously square mouth and eyes like searchlights, constantly reinvented by Max Factor—made her the photogenic star par excellence.

Portrait, c. 1939.

Jean

Harlow

The original "platinum blonde" (named after Frank Capra's 1931 vehicle for her), Harlow (born Harlean Harlow Carpenter) was "made" by MGM and after shining luminously became the embodiment of the myth of the blonde superstar who burns out tragically young. She was just twenty-six when she died, from a kidney infection that (so the disputed story goes) her Christian Scientist mother prevented from being treated properly. Born in Kansas City, Missouri and launched by Howard Hughes in *Hell's Angels* in 1930, she draped her spectacular physique in figure-hugging white satin gowns that recalled the silent era, but her suggestiveness and risqué delivery, bordering on a brassiness borrowed from Mae West, set the pace for the talkies. She wrapped James Cagney and Clark Gable round her little finger, and her films—including *Red-Headed Woman* (1932), *Red Dust* (1932), *Bombshell* (1933), *Libeled Lady* (1936), and *Saratoga* (1937, completed posthumously)—all showcased her magnetic sex appeal and screen presence. Her scandalous private life (her second husband, producer Paul Bern, shot himself) and her premature death further deepen the complexity of the blonde bombshell who perfected the persona of the dumb blonde.

Portrait, 1932.

John
Wayne

After his family moved to California from Iowa, the young Marion Morrison was irresistibly drawn to the film studios. His encounters with the cowboy star Tom Mix, and then in 1927 with John Ford, for whom he originally worked as a prop boy, led to bit parts, until he was spotted by his second mentor, Raoul Walsh, who renamed him John Wayne in 1930 and cast him in the outdoor epic *The Big Trail*. Tall and rugged, muscular and swaggering, with a spare acting style and a famously laconic delivery, meting out rough-and-ready justice according to a homespun frontier philosophy, Wayne came to embody the American myth of *How the West Was Won* (1962) and became one of the greatest Hollywood superstars.

Portrait, 1931.

Gary
Cooper

Born Frank James Cooper to English parents in Montana, he was partly educated in England, and was at home in the saddle as in a tuxedo. With his strong jaw, handsome features, and roguish twinkle, he introduced the vogue for "real" men. And real womanizers. Cooper had affairs with many of his leading ladies, including Marlene Dietrich (*Morocco*, 1930, and *Desire*, 1936), Patricia Neal (*The Fountainhead*, 1949, and *Bright Leaf*, 1950), Grace Kelly (*High Noon*, 1952), and Clara Bow, to whom he owed his first significant role in *Wings* (1927). Ernst Lubitsch and Frank Capra, meanwhile, cultivated his image as the perfect gentleman, even if he was forever to be associated with westerns. His performances in Frank Borzage's *A Farewell to Arms* (1932) and Sam Wood's *For Whom the Bell Tolls* (1943) were among his finest. He won Oscars for Best Actor in *Sergeant York* (1941) and *High Noon*, and an Honorary Oscar in 1961. He died of cancer six months later, aged sixty.

Portrait, c. 1930.

Clark
Gable

Born in Ohio, where his father was an oil-well driller, the young William Clark Gable dreamed of becoming an actor. He became involved in touring theatre, where he met the theater manager Josephine Dillon, seventeen years his senior, who was to become his mentor, coach, manager, and wife. After working as an extra on silent movies—where his prominent ears drew criticism—he honed his inimitable charms with MGM. On loan to Columbia, he displayed his comic talents in Frank Capra's *It Happened One Night* (1934), for which he won the Academy Award for Best Actor. He also made cinema history in *Mutiny on the Bounty* (dir. Frank Lloyd, 1935), and the part of Rhett Butler in *Gone with the Wind* (for which he was loaned at a high price to David O. Selznick) sealed his status as a Hollywood superstar. In 1942, following the tragic death of his third wife Carole Lombard, Gable joined the US Army Air Corps. On his return to Hollywood, where he was universally popular, he made one movie after another. John Ford's *Mogambo* (1953) and John Huston's *The Misfits* (1961), Gable's last film, were to become an indelible part of the myth of this irresistible actor, described by *Life* as "all man . . . and then some."

Portrait, 1931.

Tippi Hedren

Behind most stars, there is a Pygmalion. After Alfred Hitchcock saw Tippi Hedren in a TV commercial, he put the unknown, thirty-one-year-old model under personal contract and for the casting of his new film *The Birds* (1963), he shot some expensive screen tests in which he reproduced scenes from his classics, including *Rebecca* (1940) and *To Catch a Thief* (1955).

Watching Tippi (a nickname for Tupsa, which means "little girl" in Swedish) as Melanie, the gorgeous heiress in *The Birds*, or as a frigid bride in her second movie with her mentor, the underrated *Marnie* (1964), with her perfect walk, composure, and diction—the sophisticated Hitchcockian eroticism twisted up in her chignon—is fascinating. Along with Lauren Bacall, Tippi Hedren is the most brilliant example of a fashion model born to make Hollywood history. She is also the symbol of a screen goddess crystallized in a part—the last of the great Hitchcock heroines—that prevented her from having a career.

At eighty-three, the iconic actress, still striking, is a strong personality who runs a retirement facility in California for performing lions and tigers. For years, the "little girl" was scared to tell the truth about a Pygmalion who wanted to keep his creation to himself. Here, in Tippi Hedren's words, is the legend told from another angle.[1]

The Legend Becomes Her

"I always loved movies but could never have imagined becoming a part of the Hollywood legend. I loved the movies from the 1940s. I loved Katharine Hepburn. What an incredible actor! Those movies from the golden age of Hollywood were so attractive because they had great stories, and they had passion. They really meant something. They helped during and after the Great Depression, they kept us sane, they were a delight for people. So it was pretty amazing for me to have *The Birds* as my first film!

I never intended to become an actress. I became involved with fashion when I was in high school [a talent scout spotted her getting off a streetcar]. Before that I was doing figure skating in Minnesota and desperately wanted to be in an ice show. That didn't happen, so I started modeling. I had already done a huge number of commercials when Mr. Hitchcock noticed me. I had just divorced, and Melanie and I [her daughter is the actress Melanie Griffith] had just moved to California.

Hitchcock and his wife saw this ad [for a diet drink], which was running *a lot* on *The Today Show*, he had executives meet me for four days, and then I was sent to the agency MCA where I was told that, only after I signed the seven-year contract, we would meet Hitchcock. I did not have a bit of stage fright for the screen test. It amazed me, but I was so sure of what I was doing. Because of my experience in commercials I was very comfortable with the camera, and could concentrate on learning the craft of acting, and I loved all of it.

The Making of a Star

I am aware of being part of the legendary casting of the Hitchcock blondes: Ingrid Bergman, Kim Novak, Grace Kelly, Eva Marie Saint, Janet Leigh. The blonde look I always had. But Hitchcock was so specific. He was entirely in control of his vision and worked closely with all the departments of the studio so it would be executed exactly as he wanted. He had the best people to do it and lots of means. That was the studio system. Even at the end of the studio era, it was still in full force. Mr. Hitchcock knew precisely what he wanted the great Edith Head to create for me. She designed my entire wardrobe, even for the publicity. The costumes in the past were so exciting. The designers had those big sewing rooms for them and worked so hard. I had six green dresses for *The Birds*, pretty torn by the end of the six-month shoot so I didn't keep any mementos!

At first, it was wonderful. When I first entered the world of Hollywood I was impressed by the social scene. I was taken by Hitchcock to all those restaurants where you would meet just about *everybody*: stars, directors, screenwriters. *It was real*. There were all those social events where we'd sometimes go together, or they'd be at the Universal Pictures studios. Cary Grant came to visit on the set of *The Birds* and told me: 'I think you are the bravest woman I have ever met.' Everybody loved him. Cary Grant was handsome and elegant, but also charming, joyful, funny.

Before Hitchcock became so controlling with me, we had great times. He was not only my director, he was my drama coach. We had many interesting sessions about how an actor develops the character, breaks down a script, how you figure out the relationships of the

FACING PAGE: In *Roar*, dir. Noel Marshall, 1981.

RIGHT: With Sean Connery in *Marnie*, dir. Alfred Hitchcock, 1964.

other people in the movie. There is so much that went on that was fabulous and so useful to me for the rest of my career. But I did finish *Marnie* with great difficulty. On that film, we didn't speak to each other anymore.

Beautiful Bird in Danger

The shooting of *The Birds* became a nightmare. Hitchcock only worked from 9 to 5 and we finished each day with martinis. So I was very fortunate with those hours—until we had to shoot this scene in the room, where I opened the door and the birds attack me. When I first read the script I said, 'How will we be filming those birds when they start to attack me?' He said, 'Oh, we'll use the mechanical birds like we did with the children.'

The morning that we were to start, I was in my dressing room with my favorite raven, Buddy Raven, sitting on my dressing table and the assistant director came in and said, 'The mechanical birds don't work, we have to use real ones.' I picked my jaw up off the floor; there had been no intention of using mechanical birds. There was a cage built around the door that I come through and there were four boxes of ravens and gulls and a few pigeons thrown in and bird trainers with gauntlets up to their shoulders when they hurled birds at me for one week after the other. I had an eye cut open. I ended up in doctors' care for a week and Hitchcock said, 'She can't rest for so long. We have nobody else to film.' If you look at that movie there aren't many scenes I am not in and the doctor said, 'What are you trying to do, kill her?' I didn't hear the answer. [*Laughs.*]

Everyone admired Hitchcock's talent and so did I. But then he became obsessed with me and I wouldn't accept it. It was like being engulfed. I know it could not

have happened with Grace Kelly, who was supposed to make her comeback with *Marnie*. She would have just laughed at him. But I was nobody, and his obsession was so embarrassing that I did not say anything while my parents were alive. I do know of one another Hitchcock actress, Vera Miles, who had the same kind of problem and she did the same thing I did—get out—even if it meant he would ruin her career.

When I got out of *The Birds* and *Marnie* all the producers and directors wanted me and all he had to do—because they had to go through him to get to me— was to say, 'She isn't available.' After *Marnie* there was talk of my receiving an Academy nomination and he stopped that before it even got started.

I learned years after meeting François Truffaut at a dinner—he came from France to see Hitchcock as he had great respect for him—that he wanted me to play in *Fahrenheit 451* [1966, the part went to Julie Christie]. I learned about all those sorts of things later. Truffaut had told Alfred Hitchcock about his desire to work with me. Hitchcock told me later that he had convinced Truffaut that this was not a good idea.

I was dealing with one of the most powerful men in motion pictures. Hitchcock kept paying me my $600 a week for two years. He would eventually give the contract to Universal who asked me to do a film I didn't want to do, threatening that if I refused, I would be out of the contract. I said: 'That's a deal!'

From Hitchcock to Chaplin

I am the only female actor who worked with both Hitchcock and Chaplin, the two greatest Hollywood directors. I was asked to work in Charlie Chaplin's last film, *A Countess from Hong Kong* (1967). A great honor. But my part was actually a cameo. Chaplin thought I wouldn't have accepted if he had told me the truth from the start. Hitchcock's direction was all done off screen in a very subtle way. Chaplin was the opposite. He would arrive on the set and become the character of Sophia Loren, my character, the character of Marlon Brando. And he was so good! I loved it, but Brando didn't and wanted out. The script was too silly and it was a big failure. Maybe it would have worked in a silent film! It was too bad. Very sad.

LEFT AND FACING PAGE: In *The Birds*, dir. Alfred Hitchcock, 1963.

I spoke with Hitchcock for the last time during the filming of *A Countess from Hong Kong* in London. The studio wanted us to get together. I made a suggestion that it would be wonderful if Hitchcock and Chaplin would get together for a photograph. It would have been so powerful. He said: 'Why would I want to do that?' [*Laughs.*]

Then in 1970 I did a movie which made me discover Africa, and the lions. I made fifty films, but none of the same caliber as *The Birds* and *Marnie.* Alfred Hitchcock said he would ruin my career and he did, but he taught me so much, and he did not ruin my life. I am still an actress, but my main job is to raise money to keep my Shambala Preserve open, to rescue big cats, lions and tigers born in the United States to be sold as pets or for financial gain. Janet Leigh said she could not take a shower for years after *Psycho* [1960]. Thankfully, I did not have the same reaction to birds, but at Shambala, we serve about 500 pounds of meat every day so we also have the largest flock of ravens that live there and follow us around the whole preserve. [*Laughs.*] My life is still surrounded by big black birds!"

1. She revealed her troubles with the director to the author Donald Spoto in the book *The Dark Side of Genius: The Life of Alfred Hitchcock* (London: Collins, 1983).

Interview by Juliette Michaud at the Four Seasons Hotel, Beverly Hills, July 31, 2012, and by telephone from the Shambala Preserve, April 23, 2013.

The
Dream
Factories

Hollywood: movie mecca. Everyone—actors, directors, screenwriters, novelists—converged on this place of wonder and perdition, torn between the opposing forces of art and money, show and business. Someone had to organize this extraordinary wealth of talents, egos, and means. Enter the moguls, the people who hired and fired in Hollywood—children of immigrants, who had risen from humble beginnings to become kings of the silver screen, and who, in the first half of the twentieth century, would give the world their own version of the American dream.

Studio break. Actors and extras during the filming of *Footlight Parade*, dir. Lloyd Bacon, 1933.

The Studio System

A system, based on the vertical industrial model and encompassing contracts, production, promotion, distribution, and ticket sales. Antitrust laws, what antitrust laws? In the hands of these ruthless entrepreneurs, the fate of independent moviemaking companies was soon sealed. The movie business was too new and too lucrative—it was quoted on the stock exchange—to allow feelings to get in the way. Buyouts, mergers, start-ups: even in Washington the feisty confidence of these risk takers inspired admiration.

Visionaries or wheeler-dealers—and perhaps would-be artists—the men who ran the five "major" studios of Hollywood's golden age—Paramount, Warner Bros., Fox, MGM, and RKO—as well as those then described as "minor"—Universal and Columbia—were all bitten by the same bug: all of them were transfixed by the cinema; for all of them, this was their eureka moment. And then there was United Artists, founded by Charlie Chaplin and Mary Pickford among others: artists who wanted to protect their business affairs.

Universal

First among these moguls, and the most sympathetic of them, was the German immigrant Carl Laemmle, known as "Uncle Carl" by his employees, who included eighty members of his own family. In 1912 he bought Nestor (the first Hollywood studio) in order to set up Universal. The acquisition of a vast stretch of land in the San Fernando Valley and the adoption of the logo of a proud terrestrial globe at the beginning of each movie did the rest. Universal was the first of the legendary Hollywood studios. Like Columbia and United Artists, it was not immediately considered one of the "big five" because it did not possess its own movie theaters to guarantee ticket sales for its films.

Paramount

Adolph Zukor was a Hungarian orphan who arrived in America with forty dollars. He made his fortune through distributing a French feature film starring Sarah Bernhardt. His Famous Players film company went into partnership with Jesse L. Lasky, Samuel Goldwyn, and Cecil B. DeMille, before merging in 1916 with their distributors, Paramount. The Paramount Famous Lasky Corporation would not become Paramount Pictures until 1933, before becoming a subsidiary of Gulf and

FACING PAGE: Posing for the traditional photograph, MGM, 1943.
ABOVE: The HOLLYWOOD sign dominating Cahuenga Peak in Santa Monica.

Western. The Paramount logo was a mountain in Utah ringed by stars representing its artists, including Gloria Swanson, who contributed to the studio's success. Zukor also had the brainwave of going into partnership with his friend Marcus Loew, the movie theater owner who founded Loew's Theatres in 1910.

MGM and RKO

In 1920 Loew bought Metro Picture Corporation, and in 1924 he acquired two more companies, the Goldwyn Picture Corporation (Samuel Goldwyn was everywhere) and the Louis B. Mayer production company. Metro-Goldwyn-Mayer was born. Dedicated to dreams and to sumptuous family entertainment, with the famous roaring lion as its logo, it was to be run by Louis B. Mayer. Small and determined, this son of a Russian-Jewish immigrant who had set up a scrap metal business in Canada was a charming despot practiced at turning the most unlikely materials into dollars. On the way, MGM had swallowed up Cosmopolitan Productions, with stars of the stature of Marion Davies, protégée of the conservative newspaper magnate William Randolph Hearst, who was a considerable asset.

In parallel, under the moguls' aegis, a group of producers emerged who aspired to becoming independent, and who learned their trade as they moved between studios. In the 1920s, MGM appropriated for itself the "Boy Wonder" Irving Thalberg. Until 1925, a director had the right to ask a producer to leave his set or movie theater if he so wished. Irving Thalberg, with his motto "Movies aren't made, they are remade," was to reassert the power of the producer. He married the studio star Norma Shearer. MGM also poached David O. Selznick, the son of a silent film distributor, who had proved himself by his running of Radio-Keuth-Orpheum (RKO), one of the five major studios of the golden age, with its radio tower logo known as the "Transmitter." RKO, the archetypal example of the merging of financial interests at the beginning of the talkie era, was in a way the brainchild of Joseph P. Kennedy, father of the future American president. Kennedy was a major investor in the movies, and had a relationship with Gloria Swanson. At RKO, Selznick discovered George Cukor and Katharine Hepburn. Not a bad start. RKO was also the megalomaniac millionaire Howard Hughes (and his actresses), who was

Logos of the big studios:
ABOVE: 20th Century Fox and Paramount.

to sink a studio that had created the great partner-ship of Fred Astaire and Ginger Rogers, as well as two films of seminal importance, *King Kong* (1933) and *Citizen Kane* (1941).

David O. Selznick

David O. Selznick (he added the "O" on a whim), who married the daughter of Louis B. Mayer, symbolized the artistic and innovative ambition of Hollywood. In founding Selznick International Pictures, which was to produce *Gone with the Wind* (1939) and Hitchcock's *Rebecca* (1940), he established himself as one of Hollywood's most legendary moguls. It was to him that MGM owed its glamour. Leo the lion, by contrast (who was to be succeeded by several others over the decades) was the idea of Howard Dietz, perhaps inspired by the lions of the New York Public Library on Fifth Avenue, which Sam Goldwyn could see from his office windows. The MGM motto was *Ars gratia artis* ("Art for art's sake").

Each studio cultivated its own style, encap-sulated in its logo. While Paramount was all stars and suave urbanity, Universal, soon to be run by the twenty-one-year-old Carl Laemmle Jr., offered horror films such as *Bride of Frankenstein* (1935), *Dracula* (1931) and later *Psycho* (1960), *The Birds* (1963), and *Jaws* (1975).

Warner Bros.

Warner Bros., founded in 1913 by the Polish-Jewish brothers Harry, Albert, Sam, and Jack (whose name was actually Wonskolaser), who for their first screening borrowed chairs from the undertakers next door, remained faithful to its modest beginnings with realistic gangster films starring leading men such as Humphrey Bogart and James Cagney, who specialized in depicting tough underdogs. The Warner Bros. shield logo was more restrained than the rest (even if today it is cleverly "hijacked" visually at the beginning of each film in order to draw the viewer into the

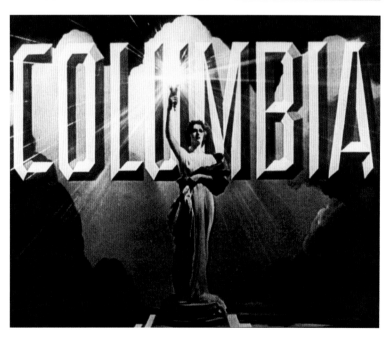

FROM TOP TO BOTTOM: Metro Goldwyn Mayer, Warner Bros. Pictures, and Columbia.

atmosphere). The Warner Bros. stable was home to Rin Tin Tin (who received the most votes for Best Actor at the first Academy Awards in 1929, although the Academy decided that giving it to a dog might damage the award's reputation), *The Jazz Singer* (1927), and producer Darryl F. Zanuck.

20th Century Fox

In 1933, Zanuck left Warner Bros to found 20th Century Fox when William Fox, who had founded the Fox Film Corporation in 1915 and was the toughest of all the moguls, suffered the dual blow of the consequences of the Wall Street crash and a serious car accident. Exit the shrewd businessman, with a talent for poaching the best talents in the movies—not just to nurture them, but also, and principally, to deprive other countries of them. Everyone knows the fanfare composed by Arnold Newman for the Fox logo with its spotlights. Fox produced films with fine sentiments. In business it was ruthless. The studio turned its back on Marilyn Monroe in order to leave the field free for Elizabeth Taylor, and lived to regret it: *Cleopatra*, made in 1963 and still one of the most expensive films in history, nearly sank Fox.

Columbia

As for Columbia Pictures, founded by Jack and Harry Cohn in 1918, it was not until the arrival of Frank Capra and then Rita Hayworth, who may have been one of the models for the famous goddess-like figure holding aloft the studio torch, that it gained respect. And, believe it or not, Disney, founded in 1923, was then a modest independent company (the Disney Brothers Cartoon Studio) that started out as quiet as a mouse.

Each studio was like a large village, friendly and convivial, as conceived by Carl Laemmle, who was the first to have the idea of allowing tourists to visit his studios sets. If only he could visit the

LEFT: Portrait of David Selznick, 1950s.
RIGHT: Mary Pickford flanked by Samuel Goldwyn and Jesse L. Lasky, 1930s.

Universal Studios "adventure theme park" today! At MGM the sets were real: the little houses with white picket fences, the church, the school where Mickey Rooney and Judy Garland fooled around on the benches—all these existed in real life as well as for the purposes of filming.

Their most impressive feature was the production departments, from wardrobe to weapons, from paint to makeup, and from research libraries to carpentry shops, with the smell of sawdust that still strikes tourists who visit Warner Bros.—reminders of the craftsmanship as well as the industry that helped create the Hollywood legend, which relied for its creative genius on the patient, painstaking work of skilled craftspeople. It is not difficult, in the labyrinth of sets and offices—the lot—that one now has to drive through in golf buggies, to imagine Bette Davis sitting in the sun, knitting between takes. Or Robert Taylor screwing up his deep blue eyes as he lights another cigarette. In the cafeteria at lunchtime you would find yourself eating between Henry Fonda and Maureen O'Hara. That was normal.

From 1920 to the start of the 1950s, the studio system was, to borrow Charles Dickens's famous phrase, the best of times and the worst of times. Watching any of the wealth of box-fresh, polished movies it produced is enough to be reminded of the best of them. Several directors, working within the same studio, with the finest technical teams and actors and every means at their disposal, were able to produce bodies of work of dazzling consistency. The careers of William Wyler, John Ford, Alfred Hitchcock, Joseph L. Mankiewicz, and of the galaxy of directors who had fled Nazi persecution, including Fritz Lang, Douglas Sirk, William Dieterle, Curtis Bernhardt, Robert Siodmak, Anatole Litvak, and Billy Wilder, are testimony to the studio system at the peak of its powers and achievement. Forever grateful though these maestros were, it was nevertheless a gilded cage. As Vincente Minnelli observed in his autobiography, "The only real freedom was to turn a project down."[1]

LEFT: Portrait of Darryl F. Zanuck.
RIGHT: Portrait of Jack Warner.

1. Hector Arce and Vincente Minnelli, *I Remember It Well* (New York: Doubleday, 1974).

For the history of Hollywood was littered with broken careers and abused talents, abandoned in the wake of the studio system. Olivia de Havilland was the first to file a lawsuit against Warner Bros. in protest at the draconian contractual conditions imposed by the studios and Orson Welles, frustrated by the restrictions he faced in Hollywood, went into exile in Europe. And then there was the Motion Picture Production Code, known as the Hays Code, a censorship code adopted voluntarily by the studios in 1930 in an attempt to preempt government intervention from Washington—a subject to which we shall return. Other Hollywood masterpieces reveal the dark side of this movie mecca: Vincente Minnelli's *The Bad and the Beautiful* (1953) has Kirk Douglas playing a producer based on Selznick, while Nicholas Ray's *In a Lonely Place* (1950) stars Humphrey Bogart as a repressed screenwriter. Self-portraits such as these revealed a far more complex Hollywood hidden beneath the glamorous surface; but this was also a Hollywood brimming with talents poised to bypass a system that was about to be brought down by its own stars.

In the 1940s, eight big independent producers, including United Artists, now a prolific production company, filed a lawsuit against Paramount Pictures, challenging the studio's monopoly over the movie theaters that showed its films, thereby closing all opportunities to independent producers. In 1948 the momentous case of the United States versus Paramount Pictures was settled by the Supreme Court, with Paramount on the losing side. The new antitrust law meant that Paramount lost its monopoly, and brought down the other major Hollywood players with it. The studio system was broken up. The final nail in its coffin was the explosion of the television industry.

Nowadays everything has changed, yet everything is the same. Columbia may have bought up everything and been renamed Sony. Soulless corporations may now oversee a system that churns out television series on a conveyor-belt system. But all the great studios, with the exception of RKO, are still in existence. Despite all the revolutions that have taken place in Hollywood, the attitudes created by the moguls and the clash between independent and studio films still survive, showing how the biorhythms of this great dream machine, this perpetual movement between art and money that constantly eludes individual controls, continue to ensure the functioning of the well-oiled machine. Now let us go to the heart of this formidable machine, which in the 1930s controlled a production system that was quite simply staggering.

ABOVE: Entrance to Paramount Studios.
FACING PAGE, TOP: Entrance to Universal Studios.
FACING PAGE, BOTTOM: The Warner Bros. building.

TOP: Gary Cooper sitting on his new Chrysler during a break at Paramount Studios, 1937.

BOTTOM: Recording the famous roar of the MGM lion, 1928.

FACING PAGE, TOP: Filming at RKO Studios, c. 1950.

FACING PAGE, BOTTOM LEFT: Cary Grant and Howard Hughes during the filming of *Wings in the Dark*, dir. James Flood, 1934.

FACING PAGE, BOTTOM RIGHT: Henry Fonda preparing to film a scene in *Fort Apache*, dir. John Ford, 1948.

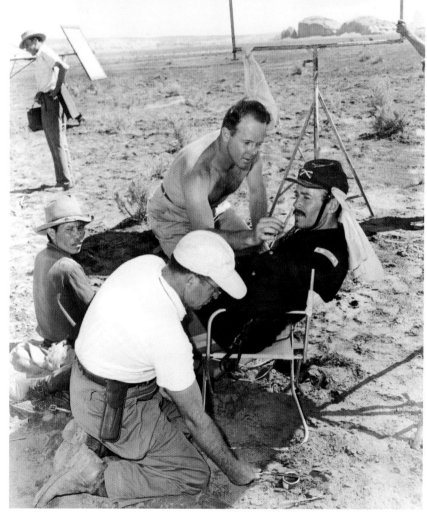

ABOVE: Ernst Lubitsch on set, 1929.

FACING PAGE, TOP LEFT: Audrey Hepburn having her makeup touched up during the filming
of *How to Steal a Million*, dir. William Wyler, 1965.

FACING PAGE, TOP RIGHT: Alfred Hitchcock during the filming of *Marnie*, 1964.

FACING PAGE, BOTTOM LEFT: Buster Keaton preparing for a scene in *Speak Easily*,
dir. Edward Sedgwick, 1932.

FACING PAGE, BOTTOM RIGHT: Marlene Dietrich's hair being done during the filming of *Kismet*,
dir. William Dieterle, 1944.

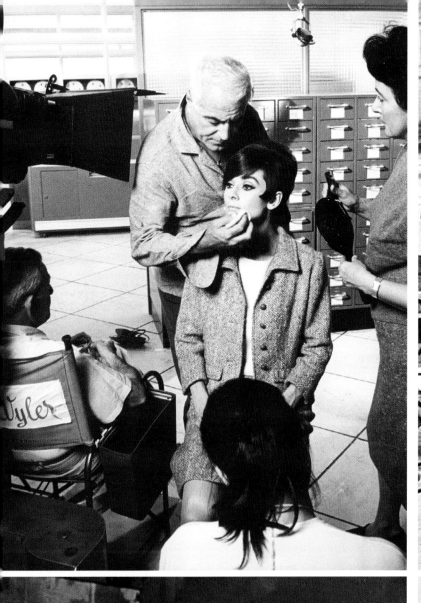

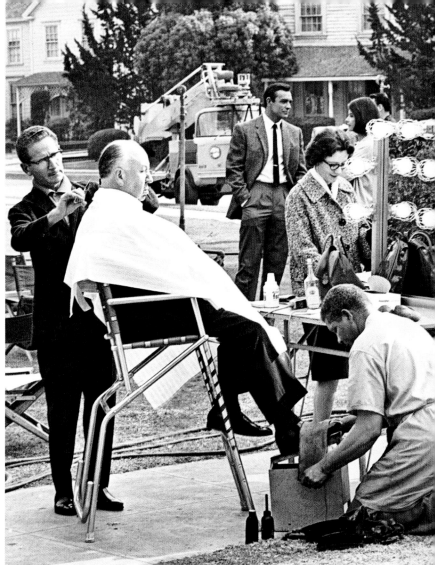

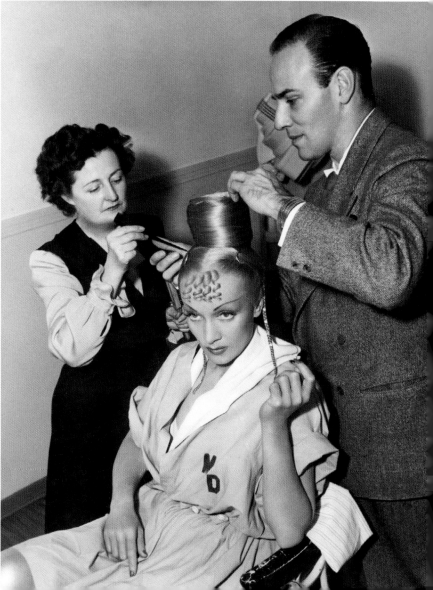

Shirley MacLaine

On this sunny Friday the 13th, Shirley MacLaine has agreed to this interview at her Malibu beach apartment to talk about her legendary career. Born April 24th, 1934, Warren Beatty's big sister, this legend and icon of American cinema has never stopped working since she began her acting career in 1955. She has been directed by Alfred Hitchcock, Vincente Minnelli, Billy Wilder, Herbert Ross, John Schlesinger, Bob Fosse, Mike Nichols, and many more. The candid and petulant muse of Frank Sinatra and Dean Martin. The girl with a golden heart who Jack Lemmon was smitten with. The explosive widow who stood up to Jack Nicholson, getting an Academy Award for her performance.

And now that unmistakable face, with the pretty freckles of an eternal gamine, is welcoming us into her home. Totally relaxed and unpretentious, she is taller than one might suspect. Her eyes are remarkably clear, in turn laughing or intimidating. These days she spends most of time at her New Mexico ranch but when in California Shirley MacLaine lives in the eight-unit complex she bought just after arriving in Hollywood. The one she kept for herself, apart from its breathtaking view of the Pacific, is a surprisingly simple sanctuary. There are no objects of great value in plain sight; there's only one picture of her on the wall: taken the night she received her Oscar, alongside Jack Nicholson. And some family pictures, mostly of her daughter Sachi (whose father was the producer Steve Parker). The doormat at the entrance says, "Welcome to the UFOs and to their team!"

At the end of the conversation, she looks at some of the movie stills presented to her, commenting on them with great humor. She asks about Brigitte Bardot, looks tenderly at one of Judy Garland, remembers when Ursula Andress had the dressing room next to hers. She stares a bit longer at a photo of Robert Mitchum with whom she had a long and complicated love affair. And, for the first time, we sense a flicker of nostalgia.

Is being called a "legend" flattering or annoying?

I don't know what it means. They say that because you're still alive [*Laughs*].

Did you dream of becoming an actress as a little girl?

I was a movie fan. My brother and I went to the movies quite often. But my dream was classical dance. I started ballet when I was two. When they said I was too tall for ballet, I went to Broadway, not thinking at all, then, about cinema.

You were nineteen when the powerful producer Hal Wallis, known as a "star maker," noticed you on Broadway in *The Pajama Game*.

And only because I was replacing, on Bob Fosse's advice, the lead who had twisted her ankle! Hal Wallis put me under contract with Paramount, but he had no idea what to do with me, until he learned that Alfred Hitchcock was looking for a young girl who was a bit cuckoo for *The Trouble with Harry* [1955].

How do you remember your first encounter with Alfred Hitchcock?

It took place in a hotel room in New York. I remember Hitch playing with his legs, short and heavy: he played at crossing and uncrossing them very quickly in the air, to show me what a fat man was able to do!

FACING PAGE: Portrait, 1977.
RIGHT: With Jack Lemmon in *The Apartment*, dir. Billy Wilder, 1960.

Then we did a first reading with John Forsythe, Edmund Gwenn, and Mildred Natwick. I had never seen a script in my life. I read in a way that I thought was the funniest and the most believable. When we finished, Hitch told me, "You have the guts of a bank robber!" [*Laughs.*]

After that did you take acting lessons?

Never. My trump card was spontaneity. Not to be beautiful has also been a gift in my career. It allowed me to express myself more freely. And my mother had been an acting teacher and an actress. Acting ran in the family.

You arrived in Hollywood in 1955 when the "myth" was at its height: the movie stars from the 1930s were meeting the

new generation of actors; the majors were living their last hours of glory. What was your first impression of Hollywood?

The glamour of that era is not a myth. It was a golden age that we will never know again. The studios were not run by men who only thought in terms of box office, but by tycoons who were obsessed by the magic of the movies. All those men, Louis B. Mayer, Harry Cohn, the Warners, even Hal Wallis who I did not hold in high esteem: all of those emotional pirates, they knew what they wanted to make. They were so insistent on their own vision being correct that nobody could talk them out of it. Mike Todd, the producer of *Around the World in Eighty Days*, was like that, too. That's why Billy Wilder, William

With Audrey Hepburn in *The Children's Hour*, dir. William Wyler, 1961.

Wyler, Alfred Hitchcock, Bob Fosse, Mike Nichols, all of those men I worked with, had this sense of trust when you were working with them, that they were at the same time the directors and the dictator on the set. You did what they wanted because you knew that their vision was the only one. But it was more than that: Hollywood was "grandiose," because there was a social life, a sense of community which made it easier to put projects together. Actors were performing in nightclubs, we had dinners and cocktails at each other's places; the artistic stimulation was fabulous. Maurice Chevalier, with whom I made *Can-Can* [dir. Walter Lang, 1960, also with Louis Jourdan and Frank Sinatra], was really one of the centers of this Hollywood social life. God, what a charming man! A true showman. I always knew Hollywood and Las Vegas were a bit "fake," but I immediately loved those places where I could create my own reality, a reality of success or failure. Today, the success lasts

only the time of a weekend box office, then we go home. The business is run by agents and the marketing department. The magic is gone. Then, of course, it was not all ideal.

Contracts, for instance.
You bet! I am the one who ended that: I sued Hal Wallis who hired me for eight years as if he owned me. I accused him of white slavery. Then, the star system dissolved.

After *The Trouble with Harry*, you made a movie with Jerry Lewis and Dean Martin, *Artists and Models* (dir. Frank Tashlin, 1955).
When I was a kid I was a big fan of their duo. So I jumped at the opportunity. But it turned out to be the movie before their last one together. There was a lot of tension on the set.

Three years later you became inseparable from the Rat Pack: Frank Sinatra, Dean

Martin, Sammy Davis Jr., Peter Lawford, and Joey Bishop. Was it Dean Martin who introduced you to Sinatra?
No, after seeing me in a show on TV, Frank called Vincente Minnelli to ask him to hire me for *Some Came Running*. Frank also suggested that my character should die at the end: he knew it would get me an Academy Award nomination—and it did! I like that film a lot. Vincente Minnelli really knew what he was doing.

Were you fascinated by the Rat Pack?
I was only twenty. It was the first time that I met such attractive, over the top, funny men who drank and behaved just like in movies. And those Don Juans were my mentors and my buddies. With me, the guys from "the Clan", as they called themselves, were very correct. They saw me as their mascot.

There is a photo taken on the set of *The Children's Hour* [dir. William Wyler, 1961], with you and Audrey Hepburn surrounded by Dean Martin and Frank Sinatra. They used to visit you on the set of your films?
Always! And I also went to bug them on their movies. They always wanted to include me in a scene. That's how I got a cameo in *Ocean's Eleven* [dir. Lewis Milestone, 1960]. In exchange, they gave me the car that you see in my scene. The shooting of *Ocean's Eleven* was insane! They had a show at night, went to bed at 4 a.m., slept two

hours, and went back on set. They were caught in the vortex of their own energy.

In your autobiography, *My Lucky Stars: A Hollywood Memoir*, you evoked the connection between Frank Sinatra and the Mafia. Were you aware of it from the start?

No, the first five years I did not know. Then it became a big dilemma for me. I want to say, to the defense of Frank and of Dean, that this affiliation happened despite themselves: they sang in clubs owned by mafiosi, which forced them to know them. Having said that, there was always the Hollywood-Washington-Chicago triangle.

You were also close to the Kennedy family.

The Clan was close to them before the Kennedys cut off their relationship with Frank because of his connections with the Mafia.

Did you know Marilyn Monroe?

Yes. [*Pause*] Marilyn possessed a deep, fascinating, and interesting intelligence, which did not show. Billy Wilder invited her to a screening of *The Apartment*. She was wearing a fur coat with something very messy under it, as if she has grabbed the first thing she could find in her closet before going out. No makeup at all. At first I did not recognize her! She immediately *got* the film, when most of the people didn't understand if it was a drama or a comedy. Marilyn, she understood.

Is it true that you almost sang for the infamous President Kennedy birthday?

I was also supposed to replace Marilyn for her last film, the one she did not finish [*Something's Got to Give*, dir. George Cukor, 1962]. She was sick; she had a bad case of sinusitis, and did not show up on the set. I was on standby to take on the part. It was not a good idea and I really hoped she would come back. At the time of the Kennedy birthday, Marilyn was going through a very rough time. The night of the party, we were waiting for her, waiting, and she was still not there. I even put on an appropriate evening gown to go sing on stage, when she finally arrived. Strange common karma that we both had, without really knowing each other.

How do you see her destiny?

Marilyn was really an orphan. She had nobody to take care of her. She had sex appeal, but she probably didn't like sex, she had the beauty, but she thought she was not pretty. At the same time it is because of those paradoxes that she was so human, and people identify with her. That's the reason why she was, and will remain a legend.

Who, besides the Rat Pack, were you friends with in Hollywood?

My old time friends are Goldie Hawn, Barbra Streisand, Debbie Reynolds. And of course there was Liz Taylor. I also really like Lauren Bacall, a fascinating woman. Lots of humor.

Did you become friends with Audrey Hepburn on the set of *The Children's Hour?*

I adored her! We made a pact: she taught me how to dress, I taught her how to curse! Our parts were difficult [they play two teachers accused of being lesbians], and we helped each other. Alas, we did not stay close. As wonderful as the life of an actor is—to travel, to meet new people—it does not help to establish life-long relationships. I have known a lot of actresses, but I could not say we were friends.

Grace Kelly?

Sure, I knew her. I am not surprised that she became a princess. She had a gift with people. She understood them without judging them.

Irma La Douce, dir. Billy Wilder, 1963.

With John Forsythe in *The Trouble with Harry*, dir. Alfred Hitchcock, 1955.

With Frank Sinatra in *Some Came Running*, dir. Vincente Minnelli, 1958.

Were you impressed at first by Robert Mitchum on *Two for the Seesaw* [dir. Robert Wise, 1962]?

Mitchum, along with Alan Ladd, was my idol when I was a teenager. He is one of the people who really counted in my life. He had the most intelligent, poetic, and incandescent spirit. I was always attracted by men for their spirit, for their character.

You had so many legendary male partners on screen that we cannot mention them all, but perhaps it was with Jack Lemmon [*The Apartment*, dir. Billy Wilder, 1960] and Jack Nicholson

[*Terms of Endearment*, dir. James L. Brooks, 1983] that you formed your most memorable on-screen couples.

Nicholson has a dangerous side, you never know what he is going to do from one minute to the next and I adore that. With Lemmon we were more like sister and brother, which worked very well on screen. People could identify with us. But even If I adore those two Jacks, I was never really friends with them. I made a good "movie couple" with Frank and Dean, too. But the movies that we made together are not as great as *The Apartment*, which is a true classic, isn't it?

The Apartment is such a perfect film, Billy Wilder at his bittersweet best.

And we started with only twenty-nine pages of script. Billy didn't know how he would end the story. They knew that I was hanging out every weekend with Dean and Frank learning how to play gin rummy so they included the gin rummy scene. We were making up the story as we went along without complaining. We were working hard, that's all. Billy said that he was not an author, but he was the only one in Hollywood who could spell that word [*Chuckles*].

***Irma La Douce* [1963], Billy Wilder and Jack Lemmon again, got you another Oscar**

nomination, but you had to wait for *Terms of Endearment* to receive the Oscar for best actress. Is that why, on stage, you claimed, "I deserved it!"
[*Laughs.*] I like late blooming.

Any regrets on films you passed on?
Alice Doesn't Live Here Any More because I did not know who Martin Scorsese was and he didn't seem to know either. And *Breakfast at Tiffany's.* Everybody is entitled to make a mistake.

What is your definition of a star?
I'll give you Julia [Roberts] as an example. From her first day on *Steel Magnolias*, I knew that she was a star.

What makes an actor a star?
When Julia is on screen you don't want to stop looking for fear of missing some of the show. But there's the je ne sais quoi that makes a star, and I don't know how to define it. I just know how to recognize it because very few people have it. The actors really standing out are usually the ones that crave love the most. All actors are like that more or less: needy children. And you often find sad or sordid family stories behind this devouring lack of love.

Were you and your brother Warren like that: hungry for love and fame when you first arrived in Hollywood?
If Warren and I have been such perfectionists, so determined, it was to compensate for the frustrations of our parents. My

Portrait, 1970.

mother stopped acting to raise her children. My father was a musician who dreamed about being in a circus. He was a drinker, and there were fights at home. If I started dancing so young, it was to escape the tensions at home, which, later, probably, helped me to become an actress. As for Warren, he would have been a star with or without me. Our destinies as actors are not linked.

How do you see yourself?
I don't see myself as a great artist. I am not obsessed enough with my own personality for that. I see myself as somebody who had had a lot of human experiences. To me, I am a bohemian.

Interview by Juliette Michaud at Shirley MacLaine's apartment in Malibu, California, October 13, 2000.

The
Golden Age
of the
Studios

While America was starving and Europe was swept by rumors of war, Hollywood's output became as sparkling and effervescent as champagne. This was the age in which every genre flourished: Dracula and Frankenstein, Tarzan and Robin Hood, Laurel and Hardy and the Marx Brothers. Studios in full possession of every means unleashed their power and their imagination. Gangster movies and comedies rattled out at dazzling speed. Katharine Hepburn, Cary Grant, Bette Davis, Humphrey Bogart, Spencer Tracy, and James Stewart exploded on to the screen. Frank Capra, Ernst Lubitsch, George Cukor, and Howard Hawks directed films crackling with talent and creativity, rebellion and escape, boldness and daring, lavish splendor and glamour. Until finally it was all gone with the wind.

Marlene Dietrich and Gary Cooper in *Desire*, dir. Frank Borzage, 1936.

"They told me I was going to have the tallest, darkest leading man in Hollywood."[1] This, according to Fay Wray, was how RKO introduced her to the notion of playing opposite a giant gorilla. It was 1932. With its central idea of dramatizing a creature created wholly through special effects, *King Kong*, directed by the documentary filmmakers Merian C. Cooper and Ernest B. Schoedsack, was a crazy gamble. On the set, the model of the Empire State Building was a mere ten inches tall. On the film's release, crowds thronged to see this modern take on Beauty and the Beast, the great allegory of nature and civilization as revisited by the grown-up children of Hollywood.

It was the height of the Great Depression; the triumph of the talkies was on the wane. Between 1930 and 1933, production in Hollywood slowed down considerably. Budgets were tightened, bank-ruptcies multiplied. From the production companies' point of view, the success of the talkies was dazzling, but the costs of equipment were so high that many movie theaters were being put out of business. Plunged abruptly into poverty, America was in the grip of a profound malaise. For the studios, this was yet another reason to focus on the light at the end of the tunnel. The public was anxious to forget its troubles and Hollywood was there to help.

The system by which the studios functioned in isolation was being set up. The sound engineers were ready to go, the screenwriters were tapping away on their typewriters, the most photogenic actors on Broadway were imported at great expense, and James Cagney, Bette Davis, Spencer Tracy, Clark Gable, Humphrey Bogart, and Katharine Hepburn, among others, had been tempted by enviable offers. "Bogie," as Spencer Tracy was soon calling him, would not appear until the end of the decade, dragging his air of bruised cynicism from one third-rate Warner Bros. movie to the next. But for the moment, everyone wanted (and needed) to work to protest against the vagaries of a machine that employed all its talents and ingenuity to make audiences thrill and dream, laugh and love. In the 1930s, Hollywood was to intensify its curiosity and eclecticism, to take risks, to shower the public with a vitality that was to ensure the growing influence of the cinema for twenty years to come.

Yet the transition to the talkies was long and difficult. There was too much dialogue or not enough, and everything seemed up in the air. Murnau's last film (he died soon after), *Tabu*, made in 1931 with the father of documentary films Robert Flaherty, was a reminder that the 1920s had created the quintessence of cinema almost ahead of its time. The fantasy and imagination of RKO, with its great gentle ape and its wonderful musical routines was needed to rediscover the panache of the silent era. It also needed men such as the veteran King Vidor, the Hollywood filmmaker concerned with the individual, as in *The Crowd* (1928), to direct *Hallelujah!* (1929), the first great talking—or rather singing—film. Filmed far from the studio, in Tennessee and Arkansas, this portrait of a black rural community did not completely escape the all-pervasive paternalism of the time, but it did at least set out to understand African-American life in a non-stereotyped manner. In the view of King Vidor, moreover, who had invested his own money in the project, the film was more a progressive comedy drama than a musical. And if Hollywood was to spend the first half of the century carefully avoiding giving offence to white, puritan America, contrary to the common perception, propaganda through dreams did not take off immediately.

Carole Lombard surrounded by Cary Grant, Clark Gable, and Ricardo Cortez, c. 1930.

---

1. Fay Wray, *On the Other Hand: A Life Story* (New York: St. Martin's Press, 1989).

Following a series of scandals that had besmirched the image of Hollywood (including the death of an actress and the mysterious murder of a bisexual director during a party on William Randolph Hearst's yacht), and in reaction to the increasingly "adult" content of films, leagues of decency were formed. Among the do-gooders, the former drama critic and Hollywood trade journal publisher Martin J. Quigley, the Jesuit priest Daniel A. Lord, and the President of the Motion Picture Producers and Distributors of America, Will H. Hays. Together, with the help of the Episcopalian believer in a "natural moral law," Cecil B. DeMille, they laid the groundwork for the ten commandments of Hollywood: the Hays Code. As early as 1929 a code of practice was drawn up, and Hollywood was asked to respect it. Relieved to have avoided federal government intervention, the studio owners, who were still struggling to find acceptance in "good" Los Angeles society, signed up to anything they were asked to, while quietly saying to themselves that it committed them to nothing, and that they would carry on doing whatever they wanted. Which was exactly what they did.

A Freedom of Tone

The films of the pre-Code period, which lasted from 1929 to 1934, were distinguished by an astonishing freedom of tone. Punchy scenes, (very) skimpily clad girls, some of whom might be pregnant out of wedlock, heroines involved in clandestine activities and taking advantage of men who were scarcely any better—and the worst of it was, they were all so appealing. In these films, familiar stars appeared in unfamiliar guises. In Alfred E. Green's *Baby Face* (1933), whose tagline was "She had *it* and she made *it* pay," the young Barbara Stanwyck played a young girl who unashamedly slept her way to the top. James Cagney, better known until then as a tap-dancing juvenile lead, displayed

King Kong, dirs. Ernest B. Schoedsack and Merian C. Cooper, 1933.

an amoral quality that was electrifying; and even Clark Gable was capable of shaking up bourgeois values. The results were viewed as provocative and sometimes willfully sensational.

But the Hollywood machine was no longer content with merely making the cash registers ring. It was developing a conscience. At Warner Bros., for instance, films reflecting the problems of an America in crisis were encouraged. *I Am a Fugitive from a Chain Gang* (dir. Mervyn LeRoy, 1932), with Paul Muni, helped improve prison conditions. *Wild Boys of the Road*, directed by William Wellman (1933) explored the ravages of unemployment on young people. And in *Heroes for Sale*, also made in 1933 by the indefatigable Wellman, a World War I veteran becomes addicted to morphine and is condemned to a life of poverty.

Antihero

In launching a vogue for gangster films, Warner Bros. also created a new type of leading man, the antihero. *Little Caesar* (dir. Mervyn LeRoy, 1931) and *The Public Enemy* (dir. William Wellman, 1931) starred Edward G. Robinson and James Cagney respectively as criminals who were victims of their tough, deprived social backgrounds. Certainly it was ungentlemanly of Cagney to smash a half grapefruit into Mae Clarke's face in *The Public Enemy*, but she had it coming and audiences sympathized. Projected into an ultraviolent milieu, the public was riveted.

In *Scarface* (1932), the millionaire Howard Hughes spared no expense in adapting a novel about Al Capone (who had been in prison for a year but was present in everyone's minds) with Paul Muni in the leading role. With his handsome, drawn, and very modern features, the Yiddish Theater of New York actor made a perfect Tony Camonte (aka Capone). Howard Hawks, at home in all genres, co-directed; the film was the beginning of a twenty-year collaboration with Hollywood's finest screenwriter, the hugely gifted former journalist Ben Hecht. Together they wrote *Scarface* in eleven days, filming took six months, and release was delayed by the censor for a year. A good screenwriter was worth his weight in gold. Many came from journalism, which gave them an ideal grounding for films about social problems and gangsters. And they had the chutzpah, combined with a penchant for drinking, that made them perfect for the screwball comedy (to which we shall return). In screenwriting departments, where hacks and pen pushers were cheerfully treated like cattle, movie greenhorns were flabbergasted to find themselves handing out instructions to giants of literature such as William Faulkner and F. Scott Fitzgerald, who had come to Hollywood to cash in on their talents.

TOP: *Hallelujah!*, dir. King Vidor, 1929.
BOTTOM: *The Divorcee*, dir. Robert Z. Leonard, 1930. Chester Morris and Norma Shearer.

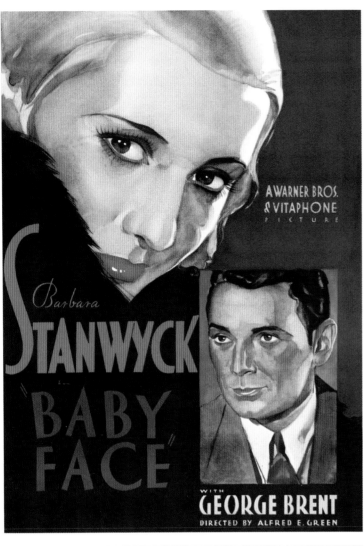

Hollywood Uncensored

The public went wild for all this "slumming it." Even Norma Shearer, MGM's *Marie Antoinette* (1938), was emancipated in Robert Z. Leonard's *The Divorcee* (1930). Lubitsch also joined in, offering a defense of a ménage à trois in *Design for Living* (1933). And we may imagine that Irving Thalberg could himself hardly get over having produced the astonishingly avant-garde *Freaks* (dir. Tod Browning, 1932), a cruel story featuring a cast of sideshow performers with a startling range of deformities.

For the censor, who regretted having allowed King Kong's desire for an angelic blonde (although Fay Wray was in fact very dark and wore a blonde wig throughout the filming), this was the last straw. From 1934, the code was rigorously applied. "Decency" had won. The studio owners took advantage of this development to become increasingly autocratic. Jack Warner decreed that he would produce no more gangster films (and with the end of Prohibition, audiences had had enough). The studio fell back on less ambitious detective films; Fox branched out into adventure films aimed at a wide public; and MGM opted for sentimental movies.

But if the moguls thought they were safe from scandal, they were forgetting to take into account the talented teams that they had themselves employed. Censorship gave birth to the art of double-entendre and suggestive remarks that paradoxically inspired the frenetic brio of Hollywood's golden age. The new game now lay in sidestepping the traps laid by the censor. Plots had to have the inevitable happy ending (Griffith was the first to develop this technique), but Hollywood was now in a state of perpetual re-examination. Add to this the public's tremendous appetite for entertainment, and you had the makings of an intoxicating whirlwind of creativity that billowed from the chimneys of the dream machine, rapturous, delirious, baroque, and affecting every genre.

Yet another ingredient was added by the talkies, which, although they initially spelt the demise of some genres (including the western, which was to have a renaissance in this decade with Raoul Walsh, John Ford, and John Wayne, and to which we shall return in chapter 10), also created new genres. To begin with, there was the horror genre, in which Universal scored a double triumph with *Dracula*, starring Bela Lugosi, and *Frankenstein*, starring Boris Karloff. In *Tarzan the Ape Man* (1932), the eponymous hero was played to perfection by the former champion swimmer Johnny Weissmuller, who with Maureen O'Sullivan

TOP: *Little Caesar*, dir. Mervyn LeRoy, 1931. Edward G. Robinson and Douglas Fairbanks Jr.
CENTER: *The Public Enemy*, dir. William Wellman, 1931. James Cagney.
BOTTOM: *Scarface*, dirs. Howard Hawks and Richard Rosson, 1932. Paul Muni
FACING PAGE, CLOCKWISE FROM TOP LEFT:
Baby Face, dir. Alfred E. Green, 1933. Barbara Stanwyck.
I Am a Fugitive from a Chain Gang, dir. Mervyn LeRoy, 1932. Paul Muni.
Poster for *I Am a Fugitive from a Chain Gang*.
Barbara Stanwyck and Henry Kolker.
Barbara Stanwyck.

(Mia Farrow's mother) formed a legendary couple and founded an enduring and well-loved franchise. *The Adventures of Robin Hood* (1938), directed by the Warner Bros. veteran Michael Curtiz, meanwhile set the standard for adventures set in a picturesque version of the Middle Ages. This Technicolor gem starred Errol Flynn in a typically swashbuckling role (originally intended for James Cagney), with the gentle and feminine Olivia de Havilland as Maid Marion, as ever making a demure foil to his irresistible rakishness (however much it got on her nerves).

Color now exploded on to the screen. *Becky Sharp*, made by Rouben Mamoulian in 1935 with Miriam Hopkins and adapted from William Thackeray's *Vanity Fair*, was the first feature-length film to be shot entirely using the three-strip Technicolor process. The British director Michael Powell, to

TOP, LEFT: *Freaks*, dir. Tod Browning, 1932. Harry Earles (center) and Olga Baclanova.

TOP, RIGHT: *Frankenstein*, dir. James Whale, 1931. Boris Karloff.

BOTTOM, LEFT: *Tarzan the Ape Man*, dir. W. S. Van Dyke, 1932. Maureen O'Sullivan and Johnny Weissmuller.

BOTTOM, RIGHT: *Dracula*, dir. Tod Browning, 1931. Bela Lugosi.

whom we owe one of the finest color films in cinema history, *The Red Shoes* (1948), always claimed to have been inspired by the glowing palette of *Becky Sharp*.

The Foundations of the Walt Disney Empire

In 1937, when Popeye was still more popular than Mickey Mouse, who already had a comic strip devoted to him, Walt Disney released his first feature-length color animated film, *Snow White and the Seven Dwarfs*. The whole galaxy of Hollywood stars attended the premiere for which its dogged creator had fought relentlessly, at a cost of 1.5 million dollars at the time. For greater realism, Disney the perfectionist had used real actors as models, and added a touch of rouge to Snow White's cheeks on each frame of the film. Walt Disney had started to build his empire.

Comedy Gathers Pace

In 1931 audiences discovered four stowaways on board a ship, Groucho the pessimist, Harpo the sex-obsessed mime, Chico the master of disguise, and Zeppo who would soon leave the act. *Monkey Business*, directed by Norman McLeod, was the Marx Brothers' first feature-length film. After Zeppo's departure, the three remaining brothers developed their unique form of witty buffoonery and slapstick, inventing the existentialist humor that they raised to sublime heights in *Duck Soup* (1933), *A Night at*

Snow White and the Seven Dwarfs, dir. David Hand, 1937.

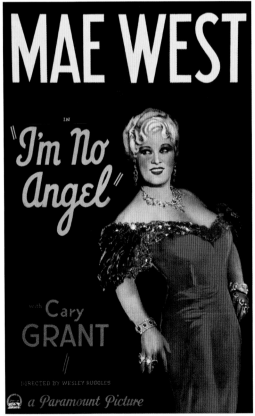

the *Opera* (1935), *A Day at the Races* (1937), and *A Night in Casablanca* (1946), and that was later to become Woody Allen's stock in trade.

In the face of this frenetic activity, Laurel and Hardy laughed their way into the talkies and continued to keep their audiences doubled up, countering the general hysteria with a touching and genial stoicism and few words; *Pardon Us* (dir. James Parrott, 1931) was their first feature-length film. Stan Laurel and Oliver Hardy—the skinny Englishman and the rotund American—were to become the most celebrated comedy duo on the planet.

Everybody loved W. C. Fields, W. C. Fields detested everybody—especially children, women, and animals. The unique comedy actor cultivated a misogynistic, hard-drinking persona that attracted a cult following. He displayed another, equally piquant side to his talents as the replacement for Charles Laughton as Mr. Micawber, in George Cukor's excellent version of *David Copperfield* (1935). Mae West could almost be seen as a female version of W. C. Fields, though with added sex appeal. Her hand-on-hip attitude and bawdy one-liners accelerated the imposition of censorship

ABOVE: *Pack Up Your Troubles*, dirs. George Marshall and Raymond McCarey, 1932. Stan Laurel and Oliver Hardy.
LEFT: Poster for *I'm No Angel*, dir. Wesley Ruggles, 1933.

in Hollywood. Mae West was already creating mayhem on Broadway. She loved men, lots of them; she wasn't really beautiful but every blonde inch of her exhaled sinfulness. She was priceless, incomparable. "When I'm good I'm very good. But when I'm bad, I'm better," she purred in *I'm No Angel* (1933). Was it because the young Cary Grant was her leading man in that film that he always kept that little half-smile above the dimple in his chin?

From Burlesque to Romantic Comedy

At the same time, American comedy was establishing its pedigree by refining the burlesque. The former gagmen for Mack Sennett and Hal Roach, Frank Capra and Leo McCarey (director of *Duck Soup*) found their own style and created a new one, the screwball comedy, when a male and female lead exchange quick-fire repartee, fight like cat and dog for an hour and a half while becoming increasingly infatuated with one another, and finally fall into each others' arms.

Emboldened by the success of *Lady for a Day* (1933) a few months earlier, in 1934 Frank Capra directed the ancestor of the road movie, *It Happened One Night*. In this

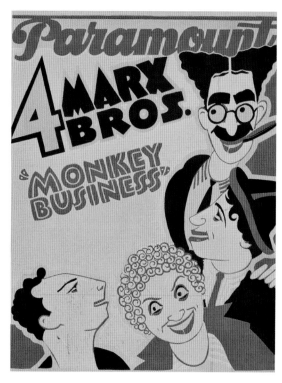

charming screenplay, a spoiled heiress and a scandal-sheet reporter, finding themselves together on a night bus, fight as they steadily fall in love. All of the stars who were offered the parts, from Constance Bennett to Robert Montgomery, turned them down. MGM finally agreed to lend Columbia Pictures, then a struggling minor studio, the new screen idol Clark Gable, who was not to the taste of the leading actress, Claudette Colbert. Colbert agreed to play opposite him only if her fee was doubled. Capra rose to the challenge, and the film was so successful that it paid off Columbia's debts. *It Happened One Night* won five Oscars: Best Picture, Best Director, Best Leading Actor, Best Leading Actress, and Best Writing, Adaptation for Capra's long-suffering collaborator Robert Riskin. The paradigm for the American romantic comedy was in place.

The Marx Brothers.
TOP: Chico, Harpo, Groucho, and Sam Wood (Samo), 1935.
CENTER: *A Night at the Opera*, dir. Sam Wood, 1935.
Harpo, Chico, and Groucho.
BOTTOM: Poster for *Monkey Business*,
dir. Norman Z. McLeod, 1931.

The Italian-American Frank Capra was the epitome of optimism and heartwarming social liberalism. He found a resounding heroine for his screwball comedies in Jean Arthur, who formerly acted in Westerns, and whom he cast opposite the ever more perfectly pitched and attractive Gary Cooper in *Mr. Deeds Goes to Town* (1936). In this parable, Cooper played the idealistic Longfellow Deeds, who inherits a fortune and decides to spend it on helping the poor. Capra also found his new favorite actor, James Stewart, whose benevolent persona complemented Jean Arthur's role so well in *You Can't Take It with You* (1938).

The masters of sophisticated comedy explored romantic jealousy in all its manifestations, constantly coming up with new ideas. Leo McCarey was to breathe satirical new life into the genre with *The Awful Truth* (1937), with the highly dignified Irene Dunne and Cary Grant, with whom he was to work again twenty years later in his heyday on *An Affair to Remember* (1957). In the kingdom of directors who loved to solve the romantic problems of good-looking young men and women in tuxedos and evening gowns by means of French champagne were also—naturally—George Cukor and Ernst Lubitsch.

Ernst Lubitsch and George Cukor

Ernst Lubitsch. The doyen. "At least twice a day the most dignified human being is ridiculous,"[2] was Lubitsch's basic tenet. A bon viveur with a bittersweet take on life, witty, joyful and unabashed, romantic and melancholy, the German director who had imported with him an incisive flair for capturing the repartee to be heard in the cafés of central Europe, was able to transcend the most foolish of vaudeville comedies. Producer, screenwriter, director, co-director (he secured the credit as director of *One Hour with You* [1932] after firing George Cukor), and studio owner, he enjoyed such sparkling success with *The Merry Widow* (1943), starring Jeanette MacDonald and Maurice Chevalier, that in that same year he was appointed production director of Paramount Pictures, which had gone bankrupt two years earlier. One of the most influential Hollywood directors, whose light-as-a-soufflé "Lubitsch touch" is forever associated with films that are sparkling and cultured, nuanced and subtly cadenced, capable of revealing viewers to themselves while at the same time offering them a glimpse of what paradise must be like.

George Cukor, meanwhile, was the protégé of David O. Selznick, whom he persuaded to cast the dramatic revelation that was Katharine Hepburn in *A Bill of Divorcement* (1932), to the detriment of Peg Entwistle, the twenty-four-year-old British actress who had been intended for the part (who a few months later would throw herself off the Hollywood sign). Through one dazzling film after another, Cukor became a master of elegance. His fluid direction and the attention he devoted to finding good screenplays ensured that he was to keep working until 1981.

Katharine Hepburn and Bette Davis

Two nonconformists who lived to act. Two beauties, but certainly not in the Hollywood mold. Hepburn with her angular face, high cheekbones, freckles, inimitable toothy smile, and windswept

David Copperfield, dir. George Cukor, 1935. Freddie Bartholomew and W. C. Fields.

2. Herman G. Weinberg, *The Lubitsch Touch: A Critical Study* (New York: Dutton, 1968).

hair, later caught back in a simple chignon. Davis with her sultry, outrageous expression, happy to play parts that made her look less than beautiful, always with a cigarette to hand and ever ready to slam a door at the end of a scene.

Success came quickly to both actresses, who were to become among the greatest of all time. Hepburn received the Oscar for Best Actress in 1933 for her role as the ambitious young actress in Lowell Sherman's *Morning Glory*. Bette Davis was awarded Best Actress in 1935 for her role as an alcoholic failed actress in Alfred E. Green's *Dangerous*. Each of them had her mentor and lifelong friend in George Cukor and William Wyler respectively. Both of them, despite the success of Cukor's *Little Women* (1933) for Hepburn and Wyler's *Jezebel* (1938) for Davis, briefly fell from favor, as if the public were frightened off by their talent, with its elitist, snobbish edge, and their outspoken feminism.

In the late 1930s, Hepburn (like Joan Crawford after her) was labeled "box office poison." Even her comedies with Cary Grant, such as *Bringing Up Baby* (1938) and *Holiday* (1938) couldn't save her, and the androgynous *Sylvia Scarlett* (1935) was an undeserved flop. But, of course, the 1940s were to vindicate the two actresses who were to become "national treasures."

The 1930s: A Decade for Women

To return to Claudette Colbert—French by birth but naturalized American, Emilie Claudette Chauchouin was another actress who was not strictly speaking a classic beauty. But like Rosalind Russell, she knew how to be playful, she was piquant and spirited, and was expert at juggling with layers of double and triple meanings that

TOP: *Morning Glory*, dir. Lowell Sherman, 1933. Adolphe Menjou, Katharine Hepburn, and Douglas Fairbanks Jr.

BOTTOM: *Trouble in Paradise*, dir. Ernst Lubitsch, 1932.

It Happened One Night, dir. Frank Capra, 1934. Clark Gable and Claudette Colbert. A still from the film (top) and the poster (right).

RIGHT: *Mr. Deeds Goes to Town*,
dir. Frank Capra, 1936. Gary Cooper.

BELOW: *You Can't Take It with You*,
dir. Frank Capra, 1938. James Stewart.

always managed to outsmart the censor. The muse of both Capra and Lubitsch, she also had an erotic allure thanks to the risqué costumes that Cecil B. DeMille made her wear in *Cleopatra* (1934). In short, she was enchanting.

And enchantment was needed in order to forget the death from a cerebral edema of Jean Harlow at the age of just twenty-six, while she was making *Saratoga* (1937), her fifth film with Clark Gable. Despite the missing scenes, the film's premiere was a triumph. The sudden loss of the young woman who had been transformed into a sex symbol by Hollywood, and had become the bête noire of the censor, paved the way for Carole Lombard. Spotted by Howard Hawks, who liked his heroines intelligent and sexy (like Lauren Bacall later), Lombard was a true beauty. Hawks's *Twentieth Century* (1934) propelled her to fame, with her platinum blonde hair, blue eyes, and heart-shaped face, her machine-gun repartee with the likes of Ben Hecht and Charles MacArthur, and her perfect figure swathed in clinging silver lamé. In *My Man Godfrey* (1936), she played a wealthy and cosseted young girl who fell in love with a homeless man she rescued and who became the family butler, played by William Powell—from whom the wisecracking actress was divorced. Later (in 1936) she married Clark Gable to form one of Hollywood's most celebrated couples.

William Powell was a gentleman who had survived the transition from silent films to talkies in elegant fashion, as had Myrna Loy: together they played a married couple who were detectives in the very popular series of *Thin Man* films, in which they slept in twin beds separated by a bedside table, as decreed by the Hays Code. Audiences also loved the antics of their little dog, Asta.

Bringing Up Baby, dir. Howard Hawks, 1938. Cary Grant and Katharine Hepburn.

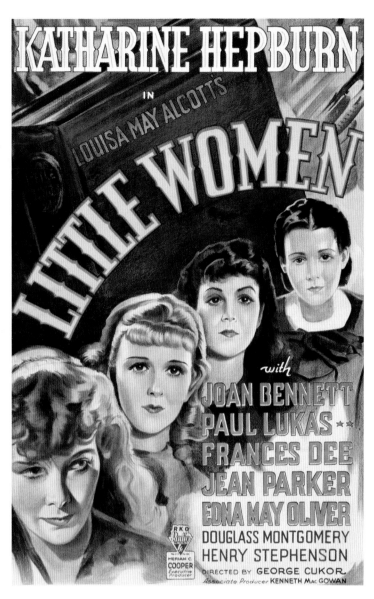

Playing opposite these fiery heroines who were constantly poised for a reconciliation and who lent the cinema a spirited pace, were leading men who now overtook them with astounding ease and assurance. The actors of the 1930s were handsome, feline, and roguish. Clark Gable, Gary Cooper, James Stewart, William Powell, and Fredric March were gods, soon to be joined by more fashion plates in the form of, Henry Fonda, Robert Taylor, and the very British Cary Grant. Nor should we forget—in this parade of manly grace—those two great drinking buddies Spencer Tracy and Humphrey Bogart. Bogart finally showed his tremendous screen presence—alongside Bette Davis, with whom he had a brief affair, and the very subtle Leslie Howard—in *The Petrified Forest* (dir. Archie Mayo, 1936). At the age of thirty-seven, Bogart had discovered his poetic gangster persona. The legend was born.

While in Hollywood the toing and froing of all these unique stars lent by one studio to another for the time it took to make a film—how many extraordinary casting combinations would never have seen the light of day had it not been for this "swapping" system between the studios—fascinated the public, in Europe the cinema newsreels were becoming ever more chilling.

In Berlin, Fritz Lang's masterpiece *M* (1931) was the portrait of a psychopath (played by Peter Lorre) in the tradition of the *Dr. Mabuse* films, which was to have a huge influence on the American detective novel. It was banned by the Nazis, who thought it was aimed at them. Summoned by Goebbels to work for Hitler, Lang fled Germany the same day for Hollywood, where he became a

LEFT: Poster for *Little Women*, dir. George Cukor, 1933.
RIGHT: Portrait of Katharine Hepburn, c. 1935.

great American director. He began with *Fury* (1936), a dark tale of lynching worthy of Spencer Tracy, the most conscientious and revered of Hollywood actors. His thing: you never caught him acting. In 1937 Tracy was to win an Oscar for *Captains Courageous*, adapted from the novel by Rudyard Kipling and directed by Victor Fleming. The following year he received another Oscar for *Boys Town*, directed by Norman Taurog. He had not yet declared his love for Katharine Hepburn.

Yet despite superb social parables such as *Our Daily Bread* (dir. King Vidor, 1934) and above all the remarkable *Modern* Times (1936)—perhaps inspired by René Clair's *A nous la liberté* (1931) and featuring the first big role of one of Charlie Chaplin's muses, the unabashed Ziegfeld girl Paulette Goddard—for the moment Hollywood kept its head buried firmly in the sand. The bruised and battered audiences in the movie theaters could count on a diet of luxury, splendor, flamboyance, and the very quintessence of glamour. As in *Grand Hotel*, directed by Edmund Goulding in 1932, with its

constellation of stars of the art deco era: Greta Garbo, John and Lionel Barrymore, Joan Crawford, and Wallace Beery. This was the film in which Joan Crawford defined her style, with glistening lips and lashings of mascara. There was nothing the male leads opposite whom she played, such as Clark Gable, could teach this leading lady.

Greta Garbo found her voice: a deep, husky voice that—in Clarence Brown's *Anna Christie* (1930)—caused a sensation, particularly with the unforgettable line when the streetwalker Anna drawled, "Gimme a whisky." The advertising campaign for this film consisted of two words: "Garbo Talks!"

Garbo and Dietrich. In a class of their own. Queens, empresses, symbols of intoxicating romance. Garbo became increasingly mesmerizing as she herself became ever more disenchanted with the cinema. Dietrich caused a scandal by wearing a tuxedo in the restaurants on Hollywood Boulevard. Nothing was too daring for Garbo and Dietrich. As the androgynous *Queen Christina* (1933), as playful and far-sighted as her benefactor Rouben Mamoulian, Garbo reigned supreme. In *Camille* (1937), more divine as the lady of the camellias than any of George Cukor's other actresses, she was radiant. In the increasingly outrageous productions of Josef von Sternberg (the blonde "afro" wig she donned to sing "Hot Voodoo" in *Blonde Venus* (1932) was particularly amazing) and in *Desire* (1936) by Frank Borzage (the great specialist in loves that could never be), in which she drove Gary Cooper crazy, Dietrich created an erotic persona that was to prove immortal. The exotic foreign female was to haunt the American imagination.

In Hollywood she had to be white, however. All the more reason, therefore, to mention Dietrich's fellow actress in *Shanghai Express* [1932], Anna May Wong, a star born in the Chinatown neighborhood of Los Angeles. Her character as an Oriental seductress was a studio invention, but with her magnetic screen presence she managed to avoid any danger

TOP: Poster for *Saratoga*, dir. Jack Conway, 1937.
BOTTOM: *The Adventures of Robin Hood*, dirs. Michael Curtiz and William Keighley, 1938.

of caricature. In 1935 she suffered the most severe disappointment of her career after being passed over for the part of O-Lan in *The Good Earth* in favor of a Caucasian actress, which all but signaled the end of her life in film.

In 1938, a young French actress, Danielle Darrieux, enjoyed a brief success in Hollywood, delighting the public with her spontaneity in Henry Koster's *The Rage of Paris* (1938), in which she played opposite Douglas Fairbanks Jr. But like her fellow Parisiennes Micheline Presle and Michèle Morgan, whom Hollywood also wanted to lure away from their native city, Darrieux chose to return to Paris.

The studio system did not suit everyone. Bravo to Olivia de Havilland, who won her lawsuit against Warner Bros., which had trapped her in one bland role after another. Her courageous victory was to encourage her fellow actors to rebel against their draconian contracts. Following her example, Bette Davis also succeeded in securing screenplays worthy of her immense talents. The rules of Hollywood were simple: stars were luxury commodities whose every detail, from their smile to their general comportment, was carefully studied. That said, although not all of them were happy with the projects they were obliged to honor, few complained of the salaries they received and there was no shortage of work.

With the country recovering painfully from the Great Depression, thanks to the New Deal and the new President Roosevelt, the arrange-

ment was not unsatisfactory. Evidently everything could be bought—including people's souls—by an industry that was more prolific than ever. In some years readers at the studios ploughed their way through nearly 80,000 literary texts. As the world teetered ever closer towards the brink of a dark reality, the dream factory carried on busily turning life into romantic novel. The rare pearl was within reach. Samuel Goldwyn, now an independent producer, was creating a lavish production of *Wuthering Heights*. On February 24, 1938, MGM bought the rights to L. Frank Baum's children's novel *The Wonderful Wizard of Oz*.

On August 25, David O. Selznick, who for his part had bought the rights to a bestseller by Margaret Mitchell, signed a contract with MGM, in which—in exchange for the distribution rights and 50 percent of the profits—the major studio that he had recently left agreed to lend him Clark Gable for *Gone with the Wind*.

Cleopatra, dir. Cecil B. DeMille, 1934. Claudette Colbert.

Greta Garbo in:

TOP, LEFT: *Anna Christie*, dir. Clarence Brown, 1930.

ABOVE: *Camille*, dir. George Cukor, 1937. With the director during filming.

BOTTOM, LEFT: *Queen Christina*, dir. Rouben Mamoulian, 1933.

ABOVE: *Possessed*, dir. Clarence Brown, 1931.
Joan Crawford and Clark Gable.

TOP, RIGHT: *Captains Courageous*,
dir. Victor Fleming, 1937. Spencer Tracy and
Freddie Bartholomew.

BOTTOM, RIGHT: *The Petrified Forest*, dir. Archie
Mayo, 1936. Bette Davis, Humphrey Bogart, and
Leslie Howard.

Oscar

In 1927, in order to unite and regulate the five main branches of the film industry (actors, directors, producers, screenwriters, and technicians), the future head of MGM, Louis B. Mayer, created the Academy of Motion Picture Arts and Sciences. Its first president and one of its founding members was Douglas Fairbanks Sr. who in 1929 hosted the First Academy Awards ceremony, presenting the famous Oscar statuettes to award-winners voted for by fellow members of their professional discipline. For their seventh anniversary on February 25, 1935, the Academy Awards were also called the "Oscars." There are several possible explanations. Some say that when the Academy Executive Secretary Margaret Herrick first saw the statuette designed by MGM art director Cedric Gibbons, she exclaimed that it looked just like her "Uncle Oscar." Others say that Bette Davis thought it looked like her husband, Harmon Oscar Nelson, or that a film critic thought up the name. At this ceremony, the six-year-old Shirley Temple was awarded a Juvenile Oscar and miniature statuette for her "special contribution" to cinema.

The Motion Picture Production Code

In order to avoid government interference in its artistic freedom, Hollywood adopted its own production code, enforced from 1934 and generally known as the "Hays Code," after Will H. Hays, first president of the Motion Picture Producers and Distributors of America, arch conservative and Presbyterian elder. Consisting of "don'ts" and "be carefuls," the code covered a wide range of moral issues deemed controversial. "Don'ts" included profanity and white slavery, miscegenation (interracial relationships), and scenes of childbirth; "be carefuls" encompassed "use of the flag," "sympathy for criminals," and so much more. The makers of Betty Boop had to lengthen her skirt and the "daring" films of the pre-Code era were forbidden. The code remained in force until 1967.

Modern Times, dir. Charlie Chaplin, 1936. Charlie Chaplin.

Filming *City Lights*, dir. Charlie Chaplin, 1931.

Mickey Rooney

Born Joseph Yule Jr. in Brooklyn in 1920 to parents who were vaudeville artists, he got his very first part in Hollywood at age six. From 1927 to 1933, he acted in hundreds of short films and in 1932, inspired by the name of his character Mickey McGuire, changed his own to Mickey Rooney.

In 1935 he was a magical and energetic Puck in *A Midsummer Night's Dream* (co-directed by William Dieterle and Max Reinhardt). Under contract with MGM at the end of the 1930s, he became a superstar with the Andy Hardy series and several Busby Berkeley musicals with Judy Garland, such as *Babes in Arms* (1939), *Strike Up the Band* (1940), and *Babes on Broadway* (1941). In 1939, as the titular character in *The Adventures of Huckleberry Finn* (Richard Thorpe), he became a world-famous symbol of youth. He had less success after the war but nevertheless had an eclectic and busy career. *The Bridges at Toko-Ri* (1954), *Baby Face Nelson* (1957), *Breakfast at Tiffany's* (1961), *Requiem for a Heavyweight* (1962), and *The Black Stallion* (1979) are some of his most memorable postwar films.

Married eight times (first to Ava Gardner in 1942 as she was also under contract at MGM), he showed no sign of slowing down well into his early nineties. He often took part in paid appearances where he talks about his career.

I am the one who gave Marilyn Monroe her name.

"I made more films than anybody in Hollywood. Two hundred and fifty. Maybe more. I started on stage at two, my parents were very poor. They were performing in burlesque, which was the entertainment before vaudeville. There were already pictures made in Europe, but they arrived later in America. For a nickel, people would go see a short film. There were just shown in tents. They had a fellow on the outside who used to be called a barker. There weren't even chairs.

The very first film I did was *Orchids and Ermine* in 1927 with Colleen Moore. I did a silent movie with Tom Mix, the cowboy. I worked for Universal and helped build the studio. When I arrived at MGM, the Tiffany of movie studios, I was seventeen and there was a lot I already experienced. My relationship with Louis B. Mayer, the head of MGM, was not a father-and-son relationship, as it was often written, but he considered everybody at MGM as a member of his family. He was not this tyrant people said he was. If I did something wrong, I was told about it, but he wasn't a tyrant. He was a gentleman that can never be replaced. He had a steam room adjacent to his office that they'd go in for a rub and a steam and this and that and where he could relax. He said 'Would you like to take a steam with me?' I said, 'Gee,

FACING PAGE: Portrait, 1988.

BELOW: *Thoroughbreds Don't Cry,* dir. Alfred E. Green, 1937.

wonderful.' And you know: Clark Gable was in there, Spencer Tracy was there. It was a special group that was invited to do that. We didn't do it every day, but we knew that it was available and he was a considerate man.

They said then that MGM was 'the studio that had more stars than there were in heaven.' Spencer Tracy, Greer Garson, Clark Gable, Walter Pidgeon, Esther Williams. My friend Elizabeth Taylor with whom I did *National Velvet* [1944]. A movie that is classically delightful. And Ava Gardner, my first wife [he married her in 1942]. She was a nice lady but unfortunately unhappy all her life. I was terribly in love with her when we got married. I was twenty-two. We were married for a year and three months. She left before I went into the army and my heart was broken. We were married too young, I was stupid to think that I could make something out of nothing. And Judy Garland, they worked her too hard. At the premiere of *The Wizard of Oz* [1939], she cried because the film was then too long, she thought it would be a bad movie. I told her they would fix it, they had to edit it again. Of course, the film made her a star. After the war, I came back to MGM and there was nobody left. I never did a bad movie during my years at MGM. But after I left, I did some movies that were so bad that they would go straight to video!

One day, Charlie Chaplin, a very dear friend, invited me to his house for advice on something he had just written. He sat down at the piano and played me 'Smile.'

I am the one who gave Marilyn Monroe her name. In 1950 we did a film together, *The Fireball*, directed by Tay Garnett. She was still Norma Jean Baker when I first met her. I told her she should be Marilyn because she made me think of Marilyn Miller, who used to be well-known way back when. One day we were talking and the phone rang. It was my writer friend Monroe Manning. She asked who it was. And I said, 'I was talking to your last name.' Later I introduced her to Johnny Hyde, who became her agent.

So many memories. When I did *Night at the Museum* [2006] with Ben Stiller, I took a walk on the 20th Century Fox lot. I remember when I did a movie there, when Fox borrowed me from Metro Goldwyn Mayer to do a picture called *Slave Ship* with Wallace Berry [dir. Tay Garnett, 1937]. I recognized a street Gene Kelly used to shoot *Hello, Dolly!* [1969] with Barbra Streisand, otherwise it had changed like all the other changes. I accepted this film only to work with my old friend Dick Van Dyke who had also agreed to do it. Today a lot of people I've known, all my friends are gone. Esther Williams, Janet Leigh, Spencer Tracy, Busby Berkeley, Frank Sinatra are gone. Hollywood is a memory. It's just a sign on top of a mountain."

Interview by Jean-Paul Chaillet and Juliette Michaud
at the Four Seasons Hotel, Beverly Hills, November 11, 2006.

With Ava Gardner, 1942.

1939, a Golden Year

A yellow brick road somewhere over the rainbow and a Shakespearian Heathcliff; a Southern belle played by a delicate English rose and an English queen embodied by an American star; Greta Garbo roaring with laughter and James Stewart mounting an assault on Washington; a stagecoach menaced by Geronimo and an all-female cast in a film all about men. Throw in lavish amounts of ambition, quality, variety, liberalism, and profitability, and you have an idea of the exceptional year that was 1939 in Hollywood. While the storm clouds of war were gathering in Europe, that was already a *Dark Victory*.

Gone with the Wind, dir. Victor Fleming, 1939. Clark Gable and Vivien Leigh.

Hollywood Excellence

Bette Davis played a hedonistic heroine whose headaches were diagnosed by Dr. Frederick Steele (played by George Brent) as a brain tumor. Dr. Steele operated to remove the tumor and fell in love with his patient—who he discovered only had a year to live. According to Turner Classic Movies, *Dark Victory* was "a great melodrama with Bette Davis in her favorite role."[1] Lying on the cusp between America's emergence from the Great Depression and its entry into the war, 1939 represents Hollywood excellence at its very peak, a simultaneous eruption of everything that made the movies such a joy to so many—provided, that is, they were not fans of *cinema vérité*. For in the Land of Oz that was Hollywood, truth was the product of the most magical of all fictions: the art of creating a world of make-believe that was so meticulously fashioned, so brilliant and engrossing, so haunting and fascinating that nothing could have seemed less false.

The year 1939 was to see the consecration of the independent producers who wanted to take the place of the moguls, obsessed with the quality of their films, guided by their artistic vision, drawing the entire industry into an extraordinary quadrille, a complex choreography in which projects, stars, and directors were incessantly swapping partners. The most impressive example of a dancer who arrived breathless but triumphant at the end of the glittering waltz of 1939 was Victor Fleming, who almost reluctantly found himself directing two of the last great successes of that year: *Gone with the Wind* and *The Wizard of Oz*.

Working simultaneously on two different films was not uncommon in Hollywood's dream factory. The sixteen-year-old Judy Garland bounded out of filming for *Babes in Arms* and into *The Wizard of Oz*, while Mickey Rooney, three years her senior, leapt from Richard Thorpe's *The Adventures of Huckleberry Finn* to yet another movie in the *Andy Hardy* series. Both were to be awarded special Juvenile Oscars that year, with Rooney receiving special recognition for his embodiment of the spirit of youth on the cinema screen.

Cedric Gibbons, star set decorator at MGM, struck set after set in that memorable year, including those for *The Wizard of Oz*, *Ninotchka*, *Babes in Arms*, and *The Women*. And then there were the unexpected working partnerships. Ten screenwriters, at a conservative estimate, worked on *The Wizard of Oz*; and F. Scott Fitzgerald found himself simultaneously polishing the scripts of *Gone with the Wind* and *The Women*. Fortunately, he was to make enough notes during his Hollywood years to allow the posthumous publication, in 1941, of *The Last Tycoon*, inspired by Irving Thalberg, the fiercely ambitious independent producer who had died of pneumonia three years earlier, aged just thirty-seven.

Dark Victory, dir. Edmund Goulding, 1939. Bette Davis.

---

1. *1939: Hollywood's Greatest Year*, Turner Classic Movies documentary, 2009.

To get back to *Dark Victory*, directed by the Englishman Edmund Goulding, the male actors—the very dignified George Brent, the newcomer Ronald Reagan, and Bette Davis's old friend Humphrey Bogart—took a relaxed approach, fully aware that this was a vehicle for Davis, who deployed her full range, from emotional crises and ironic repartee to grand gestures in a high-society setting.

That same year she appeared with shaven eyebrows, ageing and unglamorous, and buttoned into a stiff Tudor bodice and ruff in *The Private Lives of Elizabeth and Essex*. The lavish costume drama, directed by Michael Curtiz, told the story of the romance between Elizabeth I and the Earl of Essex, played at the insistence of Warner Bros. by Errol Flynn, whom Bette Davis held in regal contempt. Olivia de Havilland, forced by the studio to follow dutifully wherever Flynn led, looked on in the role of Lady Penelope Gray. Davis later wrote in her memoirs that in every scene she longed for Laurence Olivier to appear instead of Flynn.

But the brilliant scion of the British theater was busy playing Heathcliff, a role which did not thrill him either. His previous experience in Hollywood had been a disappointment—after two days of filming on *Queen Christina* (1933), as Greta Garbo's leading man, he was replaced by John Gilbert—and his lover Vivien Leigh had been turned down for the part of Cathy (as had Bette Davis, much to her indignation). Sylvia Sidney and the "French lover" Charles Boyer were originally supposed to play Cathy and Heathcliff, but they themselves thought they were unsuitable for the parts. But audiences were delighted by Hollywood's take on Emily Brontë's tumultuous Victorian romanticism. With *Wuthering Heights*, William Wyler, at the height of his career when he worked with Samuel Goldwyn (with whom he made eight films), emerged as one of Hollywood's finest craftsmen.

Vivien Leigh did not need to worry that she had wasted her talents in the heather of the desert landscape of the San Fernando Valley, where *Wuthering Heights* was filmed. Within a few months she had been cast in the most coveted role on the planet, Scarlett O'Hara. In 1936 a young journalist who had been forced to give up work and stay at home because of an ankle injury was encouraged by her husband to write a book. The writer was Margaret Mitchell, and the thrilling saga of love and war that she penned was *Gone with the Wind*. David O. Selznick's assistant, who had read it before it was published, pestered her boss until he gave in and bought the film rights for $50,000. Having grown up in the ruthless world of the movies, Selznick knew what he was doing: he called one of the two great Hollywood gossip columnists, Louella Parsons, who swelled the rumor that he had struck gold. The book's success a few months later and the American public's love affair with Rhett and Scarlett confirmed that he'd won the jackpot.

The extraordinary story behind the making of *Gone with the Wind* is now part of cinema history, but it bears repeating. Selznick launched a national poll to ask the American public whom they would like to play Scarlett and Rhett. The result? Bette Davis and Clark Gable. Warner Bros. agreed to loan Olivia de Havilland to play the gentle Melanie, but refused to release Bette Davis (who after her second Oscar-winning performance in *Jezebel* [1938] felt perfectly at home in the old South)

The Little Princess, dir. Walter Lang, 1939. Shirley Temple.

unless the part of Rhett Butler went to Errol Flynn. Clark Gable, accustomed as he was to playing roles that were an extension of his own personality, didn't give a damn for a part which he thought was far too complex. MGM loaned him to Selznick in a lucrative deal, while promising the actor that in exchange they would facilitate his marriage to the lovely Carole Lombard. Leslie Howard was no keener to play the part of the weak Ashley, and also had to have his arm gently twisted. An army of screenwriters was employed on Selznick's orders, meanwhile, to distil the thousand or more pages of Margaret Mitchell's essentially realist southern saga into a passionate romance between a spoilt miss and a renegade. And then there was George Cukor, designated director. All the pretty girls in America trooped through Selznick's office as part of a nationwide casting call, and all the actresses then in vogue auditioned for the part. But with filming due to start in a few days, he had still not found his Scarlett O'Hara.

While Judy Garland had been the obvious choice to play Dorothy in *The Wizard of Oz* (although Shirley Temple had been first choice), the part of Scarlett seemed to present an insoluble headache.

Yet there was hardly an actress who hadn't auditioned for it: Katharine Hepburn had been turned down, to her fury; Norma Shearer knew she wasn't right; at the age of thirty-six, the outspoken and flamboyant Tallulah Bankhead, though Selznick's favorite, was judged too old to play Scarlett at sixteen. Miriam Hopkins, Lana Turner, Joan Bennett, and Jean Arthur had all been in the running. In the end, it was Paulette Goddard, the most petulant of them all, who led the field. But Charlie Chaplin wasn't keen, and the puritan ladies' leagues were no keener on the debauchee's wife being signed. With reference to Goddard, Vivien Leigh was later to say, "When I put on Scarlett's dress for the barbecue scene, the first that I played, it was still warm from another actress."[2]

David O. Selznick first saw Vivien Leigh, on the MGM lot, on the arm of his brother Myron. Filming had already begun there, on December 10, 1938, for one of the film's major set pieces, the burning of Atlanta. The flames were fed by the Great Wall and Temple of Jerusalem sets used in *King Kong* (1933), with an empty cart driven past by a stuntman. Rhett, Scarlett, Melanie, Prissy, and the baby in their flight from Atlanta were superimposed later. With her delicate shoulders and dark hair shot with auburn highlights, Leigh was prettier than the character in the novel, but Myron Selznick knew what he was doing: Leigh *was* Scarlett. The British actress had come to Hollywood to visit the attractive Laurence Olivier. As they were both already married, their relationship

The Private Lives of Elizabeth and Essex, dir. Michael Curtiz, 1939. Bette Davis.

2. *Gone with the Wind* press kit, December 1939, *Studio magazine*, November 1991.

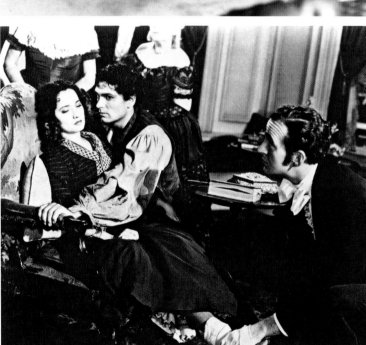

Wuthering Heights, dir. William Wyler, 1939. Laurence Olivier, Merle Oberon, David Niven, Geraldine Fitzgerald, and Leo G. Carroll.

caused a scandal. Leigh got the part, but only after making a deal with the British producer Alexander Korda, and a great deal of hype, that Olivier would not be allowed on the set. (Leslie Howard, meanwhile, was forced to maintain the fiction that his fiancée was his secretary.)

Leigh made a public declaration of her surprise at being chosen at the last moment for so coveted a role. Others would later maintain that this apparently delicate flower, famed for swearing like a trooper in real life, had been preparing for the part for three years. It is not hard to imagine how on first reading the book she might have known that she was born to play Scarlett O'Hara—and how right she was.

David O. Selznick could boast of having introduced not only Vivien Leigh to the American public in 1939, but also Ingrid Bergman, whom he had brought to Hollywood from Sweden to film a remake of the Swedish movie *Intermezzo* with Leslie Howard.

1939, a Vintage Year

But before all this enchantment could work its magic, there was real work to be done. Shooting a film is never a restful business. But the films of 1939 were exhausting. In *Stagecoach*, John Ford set the western back in the saddle by sending John Wayne and the eponymous stagecoach off into the Arizona landscapes that were to make his films famous, under a hail of arrows fired by "Indians" under the legendary Geronimo. In the Capitol building, meanwhile (or at least Columbia Pictures' version of it), James Stewart played a young and idealistic senator who fought political corruption through an exhaustive reiteration of American ideals—literally so, as the character who could have been the brother of Mr. Deeds filibustered in front of his cynical fellow senators until he dropped from exhaustion. By the time he had finished filming *Mr. Smith Goes to Washington*, James Stewart really had lost his voice. *Studio magazine*

Gone with the Wind, dir. Victor Fleming, 1939.
Clark Gable and Vivien Leigh.

described it as "A flag-waving movie, a true defense of American democracy, summing up all the wonderful 'naive idealism' of Capra's work."[3] Stewart's energies were restored later that year in the arms of Marlene Dietrich on the set of *Destry Rides Again*, directed by George Marshall, a baroque blend of glamour, comedy, and western.

The Making of *Gone with the Wind*

Gone with the Wind, from the start of shooting, broke all records and ratcheted levels of nervous strain up to a previously unprecedented high. For his first ball scene, George Cukor—known as a "woman's director" and immediately adored by Vivien Leigh, but given the cold shoulder by Clark Gable who felt neglected on set—had conceived the ill-fated notion of asking Olivia de Havilland to do a long improvisation. The following morning he received an incendiary memo from David O. Selznick, who had practically given up sleeping and was doped up to the eyeballs with amphetamines. He wanted to make one thing clear: *Gone with the Wind* was *his* movie, and no changes were to be made without his permission. Cukor was fired.

Humiliated but used to the whims of the dictatorial Selznick, Cukor consoled himself by making *The Women*, a witty all-female production based on the play by Anita Loos, which was originally to be directed by Ernst Lubitsch. Lubitsch decided to take on the ultimate challenge: making the glacial Greta Garbo laugh in *Ninotchka*. He succeeded, as evidenced by the immortal tag line, "Garbo laughs." It was therefore a more serene Cukor who cast several actresses who had been turned down for the

TOP: French poster for *Gone with the Wind*.
BOTTOM: Portrait of Olivia de Havilland.
FACING PAGE: Vivien Leigh as Scarlett O'Hara.

3. Thierry Klifa et al., "Le Film du siècle," *Studio magazine. Cent ans de cinéma*, March 1995.

ABOVE: *Love Affair*, dir. Leo McCarey, 1939. Irene Dunne and Charles Boyer.

LEFT: *The Hunchback of Notre Dame*, dir. William Dieterle, 1939. Maureen O'Hara and Charles Laughton.

FACING PAGE, TOP: *The Roaring Twenties*, dir. Raoul Walsh, 1939. James Cagney and Humphrey Bogart.

FACING PAGE, BOTTOM: Myrna Loy, William Powell, and their famous little dog Asta made six films in the *Thin Man* series, including W. S. Van Dyke's *Another Thin Man* in 1939. (This photograph shows them in *The Thin Man Goes Home*, dir. Richard Thorpe, 1945.)

part of Scarlett, including Norma Shearer and Paulette Goddard, in *The Women*. He exploited the old rivalry between Shearer and Joan Crawford to wonderful effect, and on the advice of Olivia de Havilland gave a break to Joan Fontaine, who had appeared in George Stevens's adventure film *Gunga Din*. Filmed in black and white, with a magical fashion parade in color in the middle, *The Women* is a gloriously glamorous and feminine delight.

The new director on *Gone with the Wind* was Victor Fleming, torn from the very end of filming for *The Wizard of Oz*. The missing scenes, including Judy Garland singing "Over the Rainbow," were directed by King Vidor, who for his part had refused to continue working on *Gone with the Wind* after clashing with David O. Selznick. With the robust Victor Fleming in charge, Clark Gable rediscovered both an old friend and his own magnificent form. Vivien Leigh, meanwhile, continued privately to go to George Cukor for coaching in the evenings.

The rushes were dazzling. The aerial shots of the Confederate casualties near the train station in Atlanta, for which a special crane had to be built, drew gasps of admiration from the film's bankers and investors, who promptly lined up the million dollars that Selznick needed to complete the movie. Promises of success to come helped to stave off the fatigue that weighed down the cast and crew after five months of filming. Since Olivier's return to the London stage, Vivien Leigh, who had formed

Mr. Smith Goes to Washington, dir. Frank Capra, 1939. James Stewart.

a friendship with Olivia de Havilland, had been living on her nerves. In an interview in the press kit published on the release of *Gone with the Wind* in December 1939, she recalled the pressures under which they had all worked: "You recall that one night Rhett Butler climbs a grand staircase carrying Scarlett in his arms. We were ready to film this scene in the late afternoon, after a particularly difficult day. As often happens, a few things went wrong, and poor Clark had to carry me to the top of the stairs nearly a dozen times before the take was satisfactory. Even the strapping Gable was beginning to feel tired, as the set designer had not skimped on the height of the staircase. 'Let's try once more, Clark,' said the director. Clark pulled a face, but he picked me up and climbed the stairs. 'Thanks, Clark,' said Fleming, 'I didn't really need that take, I'd just made a bet that you were in no state to carry on.' Clark laughed at the joke. I'm not sure I would have reacted the same way if I'd been in his place."[4]

Fiddle-dee-dee, indeed. The strain was made even harder to bear by the increasingly menacing news from Europe. The storm clouds were gathering. Victor Fleming, a bluff, cheerful individual who in fact suffered from depression, had a breakdown and was replaced for some scenes by Sam Wood, who had just finished filming the quintessentially British *Goodbye, Mr. Chips*, another key film of 1939; contrary to all expectations, the Academy Award for Best Actor that year went to Robert Donat in the title role. To speed up the filming process, Selznick divided the film crew into three units.

After five months of filming and 250,000 feet of film, the first cut of *Gone with the Wind* was five hours long. Edited down to three hours and forty minutes, it was a major triumph at its lavish Atlanta premiere and throughout the world. From the wind-blown title sequence—a revolutionary innovation at a time when titles were dashed off in standard fashion—and the proud announcement "Selznick International in association with Metro-Goldwyn-Mayer has the honor to present its Technicolor production . . ." against a glorious southern sky, from Max Steiner's soaring "Tara's Theme" and the first of Walter Plunkett's breathtaking costumes, the audience knew that Hollywood was about to sweep them away on a swelling tide of magnificence.

"David O. Selznick's romantic, glossy style of moviemaking has kept *Gone with the Wind* the standard by which Hollywood and the American film industry measure their efforts. Its particular combinations of excellence still attract and satisfy audiences on a scale that cannot be matched by many

Michael Curtiz, 1939.

4. *Gone with the Wind* press kit, December 1939, *Studio magazine*, November 1991.

GRETA GARBO

NINOTCHKA
le film lancé par le slogan "GARBO RIT"
une comédie de ERNST LUBITSCH
d'après un scénario de BILLY WILDER
avec MELVIN DOUGLAS_BELA LUGOSI_INA CLAIRE_

(V.O.)

contemporary films, let alone any other that is almost half a century old. The legendary status of *Gone with the Wind* was created for eternity, and erected a monument to the genius of David O. Selznick."[5]

But one actress in this monumental Hollywood blockbuster, one of the most lucrative and well-loved films of all time, was completely unknown to the public at large. Hattie McDaniel, who played Mammy, became the first black actress to win an Academy Award—a major step forward, even if a black actor was not to receive the same recognition until Sidney Poitier won the Oscar for Best Actor in 1963. There was a large body of opinion, moreover, that held that rewarding a black artist for playing a maid was merely reinforcing the stereotype. McDaniel and the other African-American actors of the film were unable to attend the Atlanta premiere due to the segregation in the South. Clark Gable even threatened to boycott the premiere in their support. But the moving acceptance speech of the forty-four-year-old actress, who had already had a consistent career in Hollywood (including *Show Boat* [1936] and *Nothing Sacred* [1937]) remains an unforgettable moment in the history of *Gone with the Wind*.

ABOVE: *Ninotchka*, dir. Ernst Lubitsch, 1939. Greta Garbo and Melvyn Douglas.
FACING PAGE: *The Women*, dir. George Cukor, 1939. Norma Shearer, Joan Crawford, and Rosalind Russell.

5. Ronald Haver, *David O. Selznick's Gone with the Wind* (New York: Wings Books, 1986).

David O. Selznick, who had worried about producing a new *Birth of a Nation* (and although the part of the scatterbrained maid Prissy, played by the excellent Butterfly McQueen, was designed to play to the gallery, he had prudently erased numerous pro-Confederacy allusions that might have offended), emerged triumphant. At the age of thirty-four, he was the king of Hollywood.

Out of thirteen nominations, *Gone with the Wind* won eight Academy Awards (1939 was the last year when the winners were announced to the press in advance). Without such a champion, the choice would have been difficult. Of the 460 films that came out in 1939, 39 are considered masterpieces or of major importance. They ranged from *The Hound of the Baskervilles* with Basil Rathbone to William Dieterle's *The Hunchback of Notre Dame* with Charles Laughton and Maureen O'Hara, also including the original version of *Love Affair*, directed by Leo McCarey, with Irene Dunne and Charles Boyer (to be remade by McCarey practically frame for frame with Cary Grant and Deborah Kerr); William A. Wellman's *Beau Geste* with Gary Cooper in the French Foreign Legion; *Confessions of a Nazi Spy* by Anatole Litvak, the first anti-Nazi film, a semi-documentary with Edward G. Robinson produced by Warner Bros; and *Each Dawn I Die*, directed by William Keighley with James Cagney.

Behind the lens, technical wizards also helped create pictures as ravishing as great paintings. Gregg Toland's work on the black-and-white photography of *Wuthering Heights* won him an Academy Award. It was Toland who was to lend *Citizen Kane* (1941) its particular texture two years later. William Cameron Menzies, meanwhile, won an Academy Honorary Award "for outstanding achievement in the use of color for the enhancement of dramatic mood in the production of *Gone with the Wind*."

Gone with the Wind and *The Wizard of Oz*: one an ode to romance and passion, the other to childhood and joy, to the good and bad fairies that punctuate our lives. When Dorothy-Judy Garland left monochrome behind to enter the full-color Land of Oz, the whole of America emerged from the Depression. Hollywood had every reason to be jubilant. But although the American film industry had ignored the storm clouds of war as far as it was able—while accepting the shameful clauses dictated by the regimes of Mussolini and Hitler in order to carry on exporting films to Italy and Germany, by which they agreed, for instance, to refrain from depicting any negative images of fascism, a fact that remains little known to this day—make-believe was about to be overtaken by reality.

In the same month that *The Wizard of Oz* was released, France and the Netherlands mobilized their armies. While the Old South lost a war again on the silver screen, Germany invaded Poland. On December 7, 1941, Japan attacked Pearl Harbor. Judy Garland might tell Toto as often as she liked that "there's no place like home," but soon the winds of war would carry off everything in their path. At the peak of their beauty, fame, and talent, the stars of Hollywood would now have to play their part in a real war.

The Hound of the Baskervilles, dir. Sidney Lanfield, 1939.
Basil Rathbone and Ida Lupino.

The Wizard of Oz, dir. Victor Fleming, 1939. Judy Garland.

The Twelfth Academy Awards,

honoring the best in film for 1939, held in the Coconut Grove at the Ambassador Hotel in Los Angeles, hosted by Bob Hope

OUTSTANDING PICTURE: *Gone with the Wind*
Nominees: *Dark Victory, Goodbye, Mr. Chips, Love Affair, Mr. Smith Goes to Washington, Ninotchka, Of Mice and Men, Stagecoach, The Wizard of Oz, Wuthering Heights*

BEST ACTOR: Robert Donat in *Goodbye, Mr. Chips*
Nominees: Clark Gable (*Gone with the Wind*), Laurence Olivier (*Wuthering Heights*), Mickey Rooney (*Babes in Arms*), James Stewart (*Mr. Smith Goes to Washington*)

BEST ACTRESS: Vivien Leigh in *Gone with the Wind*
Nominees: Bette Davis (*Dark Victory*), Greta Garbo (*Ninotchka*), Greer Garson (*Goodbye, Mr. Chips*), Irene Dunne (*Love Affair*)

BEST SUPPORTING ACTRESS: Hattie McDaniel in *Gone with the Wind*
Nominees: Olivia de Havilland (*Gone with the Wind*), Edna May Oliver (*Drums along the Mohawk*), Maria Ouspenskaya (*Love Affair*), Geraldine Fitzgerald (*Wuthering Heights*)

BEST SUPPORTING ACTOR: Thomas Mitchell in *Stagecoach*
Nominees: Claude Rains (*Mr. Smith Goes to Washington*), Harry Carey (*Mr. Smith Goes to Washington*), Brian Aherne (*Juarez*), Brian Donlevy (*Beau Geste*)

BEST DIRECTOR: Victor Fleming for *Gone with the Wind*
Nominees: John Ford (*Stagecoach*), Frank Capra (*Mr. Smith Goes to Washington*), Sam Wood (*Goodbye, Mr. Chips*), William Wyler (*Wuthering Heights*)

OTHER ACADEMY AWARDS:
Best Score: *Stagecoach*
Best Original Score and Best Song: *The Wizard of Oz*
Best Screenplay, Best Art Direction, Best Cinematography (Color), and Best Film Editing: *Gone with the Wind*
Irving G. Thalberg Memorial Award: David O. Selznick

FACING PAGE, TOP: *Gone with the Wind*, dir. Victor Fleming, 1939. Vivien Leigh and Hattie McDaniel.
FACING PAGE, BOTTOM LEFT: David O. Selznick and Vivien Leigh at the Oscars.
FACING PAGE, BOTTOM RIGHT: Jean Hersholt and Hattie McDaniel.

Paths
of
Glory

War! When the American film industry mobilized, it did so on all fronts. Charlie Chaplin launched a direct attack on Hitler, the stars joined the armed forces, Bette Davis and John Garfield set up the Hollywood Canteen, Marlene Dietrich kept up the troops' morale, directors pointed their cameras towards darker subjects, and even run-of-the-mill popular films made their contribution to the war effort. In any event, nothing was ever going to be the same again: while the film directors of Europe emigrated en masse to Hollywood, a young genius of twenty-six by the name of Orson Welles was overturning every convention, both of cinema and of the American dream. Victory through filmmaking.

The Great Dictator, dir. Charlie Chaplin, 1940.

"Play It, Sam."

She was back. She was asking the pianist to play their song, one more time:

"You must remember this

A kiss is just a kiss, a sigh is just a sigh.

The fundamental things apply

As time goes by."

Ilsa and Rick had known each other in Paris. She was married. He thought he'd never see her again. But in this white-hot setting, anything was possible. *Casablanca* (1942). The title on its own is enough to evoke all the romanticism of Hollywood, and all that is so perennially appealing about this ultimate classic: a distant setting, an exotic world filled with light and shadows, the inimitable night club and champagne ambience, perfect casting, charm, emotion, humor, and a nostalgia that is both subtle and yet powerfully present for the tortured protagonists. The story of an American neutral (Humphrey Bogart) who must choose between his love for a woman (Ingrid Bergman) and helping her husband, the Resistance hero Victor Laszlo (Paul Heinreid), to get out of a town infested with French collaborationists, sums up the American position at the beginning of World War II. Initially isolationist, America was to become a brave combatant, thereby beginning good relations with the rest of the world, which until the late 1960s would retain a formidable image of the United States as a triumphant, liberating force.

The moral dilemma around the issue of serving one's country was a recurrent theme at this time, explored notably in Howard Hawk's *Sergeant York*, the highest-grossing film of 1941 with Gary Cooper playing Alvin York, a pacifist hillbilly who was forced to go and fight on the Western Front and who would become the most decorated US serviceman of World War I.

With *Casablanca*, a cocktail of romance, film noir, and patriotic suspense thriller, Michael Curtiz left the other ranks of Warner Bros. behind him to become a four-star general of American cinema, as he was to demonstrate again in 1945 with the exhilarating film noir *Mildred Pierce* (1945). Despite— or perhaps because of—its notoriously confused screenplay adapted by four screenwriters (including initially the twins Julius J. and Philip G. Epstein) from a play called *Everybody Comes to Rick's*, *Casablanca* was, and always will be a gem.

At the age of forty-one, Humphrey Bogart had just become a star, thanks to John Huston's *The Maltese Falcon* (1941), the first great classic of film noir, the genre so indissolubly linked with the 1940s. Ingrid Bergman, for her part, had with dignity managed to preserve her natural quality, imported from Sweden. The actress who three years later would win the Oscar for Best Actress for *Gaslight* (1944), directed by George Cukor, was to become one of the grandes dames of the war years. She also played another fine romantic role against the background of the Spanish Civil War, this time in Technicolor and with short hair, in Sam Wood's *For Whom the Bell Tolls* (1943).

Bergman was not yet to know that an Italian director called Roberto Rossellini would change both the mood of cinema at the end of the war, with *Roma città aperta* (*Rome, Open City*, 1945) and *Germania anno zero* (*Germany, Year Zero*, 1948), and her own life, as Hollywood condemned her for her "scandalous" love affair with the high priest of neorealism.

Casablanca, dir. Michael Curtiz, 1942. Ingrid Bergman and Humphrey Bogart.

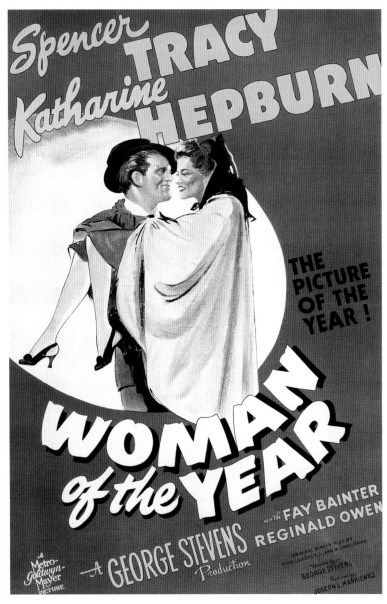

Legendary Couples

While Ingrid Bergman and Humphrey Bogart were perfectly matched on screen in *Casablanca*, the most legendary couples of the war years were equally so off screen. In 1944, Bogart and Lauren Bacall fell for each other in *To Have and Have Not*, directed by Howard Hawks. Bogart had first met Bacall when he was filming *Passage to Marseille* (1944) with Michèle Morgan. They were married in 1945. In 1942, Spencer Tracy and Katharine Hepburn filmed the first of nine comedies together, *Woman of the Year*, directed by George Stevens. Tracy's Irish Catholic upbringing meant that he would never divorce his wife, but the strength of his relationship with Hepburn was such that puritan America forgave them for living out their romance on the margins of convention.

The early 1940s also saw glamorous marriages, such as those of Vivien Leigh and Laurence Olivier, and Rita Hayworth and Orson Welles. On June 16, 1943, Charlie Chaplin married Oona O'Neill, daughter of the playwright Eugene O'Neill. He had just divorced Paulette Goddard, and this

FACING PAGE, TOP AND BOTTOM LEFT: *To Have and Have Not*, dir. Howard Hawks, 1944. Poster and still from the film with Lauren Bacall and Hoagy Carmichael.

FACING PAGE, TOP AND BOTTOM RIGHT: *Woman of the Year*, dir. George Stevens, 1942. Poster and still from the film with Katharine Hepburn and Spencer Tracy.

ABOVE, LEFT: Humphrey Bogart in *To Have and Have Not*, dir. Howard Hawks, 1944.

ABOVE, RIGHT: *For Whom the Bell Tolls*, dir. Sam Wood, 1943. Akim Tamiroff, Ingrid Bergman, and Gary Cooper.

was his fourth marriage. Oona was eighteen, Chaplin fifty-four. He was still setting tongues wagging. Lashings of romance and dynamism electrified the atmosphere in America on the brink of war, at a time when the record earnings of *Gone with the Wind* (1939) had provided Hollywood with enough ammunition to withstand a siege, and the film industry had gone to war even before the country's official entry into the global conflict.

The Perils of Nazism

From 1939, Hollywood had tried to raise public awareness of the perils of Nazism. The Venice Film Festival had already become a Fascist propaganda tool under Mussolini (it was at this time, to counter the perverted Mostra, that the Cannes Film Festival was conceived, with the first festival taking place in 1947). John Ford was one of the first to lobby the studio bosses to boycott Nazi Germany. The director of *The Grapes of Wrath* (winner of the Oscar for Best Picture in 1940), adapted from the novel by John Steinbeck, with a performance from Henry Fonda touched by grace, was involved from the outset in the special wartime units that formed within the major studios. Ford was at Pearl Harbor with his film crew on the day of the Japanese aerial attack; the result was *December 7th*

The Grapes of Wrath, dir. John Ford, 1940. Henry Fonda, Jane Darwell, and Dorris Bowdon.

(1943), with Dana Andrews and Walter Huston. But it asked too many questions and was too sympathetic to the Japanese people living in Honolulu, and so was cut to make a short, while the full-length film was to remain under censorship until the 1990s. Undeterred by this experience, Ford was to be present in every theatre of military operations, including the D-Day landings. From February to June 1945, he filmed the Battle of the Philippines, *They Were Expendable*, with John Wayne and Robert Montgomery. On the way, he picked up the third of his four Oscars (a record number for a director) for *How Green was My Valley* (1941) with Maureen O'Hara.

In 1942, when President Roosevelt set up the Office of War Information (OWI) and asked Hollywood for its support in selling war bonds and supporting the troops, a galaxy of stars responded, from James Stewart and Robert Taylor to Henry Fonda and William Holden, and from Van Johnson and Gene Kelly to the handsome Tyrone Power and the "singing cowboy" Gene Autry. Everyone found a role in the armed forces: even those who quailed at the thought of standing up in front of crowds of GIs because they couldn't sing like Frank Sinatra or Bing Crosby, or dance like Fred Astaire or James Cagney; even tough guys of few words like Spencer Tracy, John Wayne, and Humphrey Bogart were tireless in visiting hospitals and bringing comfort to the wounded.

Mobilization

From 1943, a lean year in Hollywood, a quarter of the film industry's personnel were mobilized. A quarter of its production was devoted to propaganda, vetted and corrected by the Hays Code, ever on the alert for any defeatist views of the war. Of the long list of directors who worked on propaganda films, mention should be made above all of Frank Capra and his *Why We Fight* series.

For American movie stars, this was the start of a long tradition of entertaining the troops on many different fronts. Marlene Dietrich was one of the most tireless in her efforts. She was also in

ABOVE, LEFT: Mickey Rooney entertaining American troops in Germany, April 1945.

ABOVE, RIGHT: Rita Hayworth and General Benjamin O. Davis cutting a cake at the Hollywood Canteen, 1943. A veteran receives the first piece.

ABOVE: The first anniversary of the Hollywood Canteen, with Marlene Dietrich and Bette Davis (co-founder with John Garfield) leading the festivities, October 1943.

LEFT: Marlene Dietrich visiting American troops, 1943.

FACING PAGE: *The Philadelphia Story*, dir. George Cukor, 1940. With (from right to left) Cary Grant, Katharine Hepburn, John Howard, Ruth Hussey, and James Stewart.

love, admittedly (having met Jean Gabin in Paris). Bob Hope and Mickey Rooney also caused riots wherever they appeared. Rooney was indefatigable. After joining up in 1944, he won numerous decorations including the Bronze Star Medal and universal admiration for his entertainment of the troops in numerous combat zones. The wartime pinups Betty Grable and Rita Hayworth, meanwhile, threw themselves into concert tours, hospital visits, and danced with GIs at the Hollywood Canteen. Betty Grable was the Marilyn Monroe of her era. Rita Hayworth was the poster girl for Raoul Walsh's *The Strawberry Blonde* (1941), with James Cagney and Olivia de Havilland.

The Hollywood Canteen

A club at the heart of Hollywood, at the corner of Cahuenga Boulevard and Sunset Boulevard, offering free admission and entertainment to all Allied servicemen and women in uniform, the Hollywood Canteen was set up in 1942 by Bette Davis and John Garfield, who can be seen in Howard Hawks's *Air Force* (1943). Donations and volunteers: soldiers were astounded to find themselves being served sandwiches by the beautiful Czechoslovakian star Hedy Lamarr, the sensual Linda Darnell, and Ann Sheridan, or the president of the Canteen in person, Bette Davis, who had brought a tear to the eye of the nation in *Now, Voyager* (1942). When she came to the Hollywood Canteen, the pregnant Gene Tierney caught German measles when she shook the hand of a fan who had escaped from quarantine to see her. As a result of this sad episode, her daughter was born premature and disabled. Later, doctors would attribute Gene Tierney's own bipolar disorder

to this tragedy. On screen she was a riveting femme fatale in *The Shanghai Gesture* (1941), Josef von Sternberg's first film without Marlene Dietrich.

Hollywood Canteen (1944), directed by Delmer Daves, attempted to reproduce some of the joie de vivre of this club for stars and soldiers, which by the time it closed its doors had entertained some 3 million men and women of the armed forces.

Among the flood of foreign intellectuals and directors who arrived in Hollywood during the war were two Frenchmen, René Clair and Jean Renoir. Getting their bearings wasn't easy at first. In 1944, by contrast, began the reign of the German directors whom the *Cahiers du cinema* dubbed the "disciples of Lubitsch": Billy Wilder, Otto Preminger, and Max Ophüls.

Hitchcock: Attack on Two Fronts

Alfred Hitchcock, who had come to Hollywood at the invitation of David O. Selznick and had already been dubbed the "master of suspense," was meanwhile concerned for his countrymen and women.

Rebecca, dir. Alfred Hitchcock, 1940. Joan Fontaine and Judith Anderson.

Many British stars, from Charles Laughton to Laurence Olivier, pledged to serve their country at a meeting in Hollywood. A committee headed by Dame May Whitty and Boris Karloff arranged for the evacuation of sixty London children at the height of the Blitz. Cary Grant donated virtually all of his fee from *The Philadelphia Story* (dir. George Cukor, 1940) to support this operation.

Hitchcock attacked on two fronts: his first Hollywood film, *Rebecca* (1940), from the book by Daphne de Maurier, was a masterpiece—winning the director his only Oscar for Best Picture—that made Joan Fontaine, exquisitely tortured by Hitchcock, a star at the age of twenty-two. Nominated for an Oscar, she lost out to Ginger Rogers for *Kitty Foyle*, though she was successful the following year with Hitchcock's *Suspicion*, in which she played opposite Cary Grant with an artful gaucheness that bordered on sex appeal. Now every actress wanted to be directed by Hitchcock. Meanwhile he had made *Foreign Correspondent* (1940), a tribute to his native land through the story of an American reporter (Joel McCrea) and his attempts, in a terrifying world of murder and espionage, to expose enemy spies in Britain. He had also supervised the editing of American versions of two British documentaries about the war.

Alfred Hitchcock, Cary Grant, and Ingrid Bergman deep in discussion, c. 1945.

Hitchcock continued his hunting down of the Nazis in 1946 with the glorious *Notorious*, in which Cary Grant and Ingrid Bergman, who was to be one of his muses, surrendered to "the longest kiss in the history of cinema," lasting two and a half minutes (with a break every three seconds to discuss what they're having for supper, among other matters, in order to foil the censor). Films were Hollywood's most potent weapon.

It was after learning that his own had been banned in Germany that Charlie Chaplin—leading the charge—attacked Hitler right between the eyes in *The Great Dictator*, which came out in 1940. In it he played the dual role of a little Jewish barber and his doppelganger, the dictator Adenoid Hynkel, who invites the Italian dictator Benzini Napaloni (played by Jack Oakie) to visit him in his palace. Paulette Goddard plays a young Jewish woman. Anyone who has never seen the scene in which Chaplin-Hitler plays with his inflatable globe, or who has never heard his incomprehensible and interminable speech in "Tomainian" should lose no time in seeking out this film.

In this, his first real "talkie," Chaplin once again used the weapons of humor, mockery, passion, and recklessness in the eternal battle against human stupidity—and won. Were these distant echoes of combat what made screwball comedies such battlegrounds?

In this genre that was developed even further in the films of the 1940s, the quick-fire repartee was delivered at an ever more rattling speed. In *His Girl Friday* (dir. Howard Hawks, 1940), Cary Grant and Rosalind Russell exchange bursts of machine-gun fire. And in *The Philadelphia Story*, Grant exchanges verbal fireworks again, this time with Katharine Hepburn—who thereby regained her popularity with audiences—and James Stewart, in which the American male is pilloried for our pleasure (and for theirs). Strictly one for champagne lovers. Also in 1940, Ernst Lubitsch made his finest comedy, *The Shop Around the Corner*, with Margaret Sullavan, James Stewart, and Frank Morgan. A lift for the spirits. In 1941, it was Joel McCrea and Veronica Lake who were bickering in *Sullivan's Travels*, directed by Preston Sturges, an atypical master of American comedy, who worked in a more acid, off-beat mode that is sometimes compared with the whacky cartoons of Tex Avery.

TOP: *Mrs. Miniver*, dir. William Wyler, 1942.

CENTER: *National Velvet*, dir. Clarence Brown, 1944. Mickey Rooney, Elizabeth Taylor, and Anne Revere.

BOTTOM: *Lassie Come Home*, dir. Fred Wilcox, 1943. Lassie and Roddy McDowall.

To Be or Not to Be (1942)

In the vein of anti-Hitler ideological comedies, this splendid satire intercutting the rehearsals of an acting troupe with the German invasion of Poland was sadly to leave a bitter taste. Its heroine, Carole Lombard, was killed (with her mother) in an accident involving the airplane that was bringing her back to Clark Gable from a war bond rally. Inconsolable, Gable went to ask President Roosevelt personally to allow him to enroll in the armed forces in any capacity. He embarked on intensive air force training, and also took part in making war films under the supervision of Colonel Darryl F. Zanuck.

For consolation, the American public flocked to see the MGM hit *Mrs. Miniver* (dir. William Wyler, 1942), with the beautiful redhead Greer Garson bearing the hardships of German bombardment in rural England with admirable dignity. The film was to become an inspiration to the British spirit of wartime resistance and fortitude.

In a more masculine register, war was largely depicted on screen by the partnership of Spencer Tracy and Van Johnson in *Thirty Seconds over Tokyo* (dir. Mervyn LeRoy, 1944) and *A Guy Named Joe* (dir. Victor Fleming, 1943). Well before *The Longest Day* (dir. Ken Annakin, 1962), John Wayne, for his part, played the hero in more or less memorable patriotic films such as *Flying Tigers* (dir. David Miller, 1942), *The Fighting Seabees* (dir. Edward Ludwig, 1944, with Susan Hayward), and many others. The Australian Errol Flynn fought at his side in *Edge of Darkness* (dir. Lewis Milestone, 1943) and *Objective, Burma!* (dir. Raoul Walsh, 1945).

The list is a long one: on cargo vessels, space was reserved for film reels alongside supplies and munitions. Hollywood had to produce in order to keep hope alive. There was a lot of escapism, too, naturally, with a flood of musicals. All the same, audiences were offered a greater level of realism than during the Great Depression, and thrillers conveyed the general atmosphere of anxiety. Even run-of-the-mill films took on underlying meanings.

To vary the program a little, Henry King directed *The Song of Bernadette* (1942), inspired by the life of Bernadette Soubirous, which won an Oscar for Selznick's new protégée Phyllis Flora Isley, renamed Jennifer Jones, whom he was to marry. Jacques Tourneur's

TOP: *To Be or Not to Be*, dir. Ernst Lubitsch, 1942.
Carole Lombard and Stanley Ridges.

BOTTOM: *The Song of Bernadette*, dir. Henry King, 1942.
Jennifer Jones.

Cat People (1942), with the pretty French actress Simone Simon, was to inspire an extraordinary cult following—because it showed nothing. Young audiences, meanwhile, were treated to superb classics that were less mawkish than in the past, as in the *Lassie* series, *National Velvet* (1944), with the young Elizabeth Taylor, and *The Mark of Zorro* (1940) with Tyrone Power.

In 1940, Disney, the weaver of magic spells, who had just expanded his studios in Burbank, offered two gems one after the other: *Pinocchio* and *Fantasia*. Yet it was a complete unknown who was to be the most influential figure of the 1940s, and of the decades that followed.

In New York on May 1, 1941, in company of his fellow actors from the Mercury Theater (including Joseph Cotten), the madcap actor and director who had terrorized America with his brilliant radio version of *The War of the Worlds*, making people believe that an invasion by extraterrestrials was about to take place, presented his first film, entitled *Citizen Kane*—Orson Welles was 26. The film can be summed up in a single word: innovation. With his liberal use of short focal distance to accentuate the depth of field, high angle shots, and camera angles that seem to see through walls and windows as if they weren't there, Orson Welles, a fierce admirer of D. W. Griffith and John Ford, digested the whole history of cinema to offer a new vocabulary in every frame. A wind of freedom was blowing through cinema, and it was to inspire thousands of film directors to come.

The plot of *Citizen Kane*? It was unofficially inspired by the tale of the newspaper tycoon William Randolph Hearst, who filed lawsuit after lawsuit to prevent it from being released. Pitted against him, however, was another tycoon, Howard Hughes, boss of RKO. For the moment, Orson Welles, for whose services he had paid a king's ransom, was his protégé. That same year, Wells began filming *The Magnificent Ambersons*, which received a lukewarm reception (and which merits another viewing). But the youthful prodigy had already experienced his first great disappointment in Hollywood: in 1942 he won an Oscar for the screenplay of *Citizen Kane*, but not for his revolutionary work as director.

So what was the verdict on Hollywood's war record by the end of hostilities? Triumphant. This communal war effort even led, in 1946, to new records for cinema audiences. And when film directors who had been mobilized told of their experiences in their work, the results were gems. Such as the highly moving *The Best Years of Our Lives* (dir. William Wyler, 1946), with Frederic March,

Dana Andrews, Myrna Loy, and Teresa Wright. The film was to earn two Oscars for Harold Russell, who had lost his hands on active service: one for Best Supporting Actor, and the other an honorary award for "bringing hope and courage to his fellow veterans."

Dare we, now that the atrocities are over, include Greta Garbo among the victims of the war? After the flop of *Two-Faced Woman* (dir. George Cukor, 1941), which she had herself predicted, the divine Garbo retired from cinema, so becoming even more mysterious and sphinx-like. In so doing she left the way open for a whole wave of new actresses, but the fascination she exerted would never be replaced.

ABOVE AND FACING PAGE: *Citizen Kane*, dir. Orson Welles, 1941. Orson Welles.

Farley Granger

He greets you at the door himself, his 6'3" frame quite imposing, and invites you in, his voice still firm and unmistakably suave. He has lived in this spacious apartment on the twenty-fifth floor for thirty years with his longtime companion, theater and TV producer Robert Calhoun.

He turned 81 this year and even with a cane, stands straight. Nothing in this airy living room to remind him of his past and the time he was for a brief period, a star. No photos, no mementos of the Hollywood career, which began in 1943, he recalls in rich detail in his recently published autobiography, *Include Me Out*.

He was only seventeen when mogul Sam Goldwyn offered him a seven-year contract at 100 dollars a week. With his chiseled good looks, he instantly became one of the most sought after and promising young actors. He worked with Nicholas Ray, twice with Alfred Hitchcock but soon seemed stuck with less rewarding parts. In 1953 Luchino Visconti picked him to replace Marlon Brando as the doomed lieutenant in *Senso* opposite Alida Valli. Back in Hollywood, he was never able to find roles really suited to his talent. He became disenchanted and turned to the theater, which he still insists was his true love. After a brief stint in Italy in the 1970s, he made himself rarer on the silver screen, touring the country with various plays, and appearing occasionally as a guest stars in a number of TV shows. He made his last film in 2001 and died of natural causes ten years later.

What comes to your mind when you hear the world Hollywood now?

[*Sighs.*] Oh, just that I lived there at one time and that I was unhappy. I wasn't doing what I wanted to do. Goldwyn in a sense gave me the same part to do all the time. Over and over. Typecasting me usually as the nice son or nephew from a good family. Nice, serious, and slightly innocent. Nothing exciting or adventurous as there was with Hitchcock, who chose me for *Rope* [1948] and then for *Strangers on a Train* [1951], which is my favorite movie really.

In which you play Guy Haynes opposite a creepy Robert Walker. Was Hitchcock very specific directing you?

No, not really. We had done a movie before, as you know, so he really left me alone. He was a wonderful director because he plotted out his scripts so everything was there before he even started to shoot and had everything very meticulously planned. Next to the camera on set, there was a seat and a table across it and that's where a man sat with all the storyboards of the film. Hitch would go to him and ask: "What's next" and would glance at a drawing and say, "Oh, yes." Sometimes I would ask him, "What's the matter Hitch?" and he would answer [*imitating Hitchcock's famous voice*]: "Oh, I am bored." And I think he

really sort of was. Because he would add, "I've done it all."

How different was the experience from *Rope* three years earlier?

Oh yes, very different. He was very nervous on *Rope* because of the technical challenges of ten minute-long takes. Going from one set to the other as stage hands were pulling walls out and prop people coming in with a chair and so forth. With each glitch you had to reset and do it all over again so it took a very long time and the process was made very tedious. The camera was an enormous thing and the lighting was a pain.

Did you discuss the psychology of your character in depth with him?

No. We never talked about the homosexuality of any of the characters if that is what you mean. It would have been unthinkable at the time.

When did you see him for the last time?

Around the end of 1961 or early 1962. I was touring with a play in San Francisco and he invited me to see him in his hotel room for drinks to talk about his next project, which happened to be *The Birds*. He wanted me to play Tippi Hedren's love interest. I couldn't as I was under contract and it was impossible to get out of it. He was mad at me. Anyway I didn't like the movie and it would have been better with me!

Let's go back to your film debut in 1945. Samuel Goldwyn wanted to groom you and make you a star?

Yes. He wanted to put me under contract and my parents had to come in because I was still a minor. They didn't like my name and they wanted to change it. But I like my name, so I just kept saying no to all the new names they were throwing at me.

FACING PAGE: In *They Live by Night*, dir. Nicholas Ray, 1948.
RIGHT: With Robert Walker in *Strangers on a Train*, dir. Alfred Hitchcock, 1951.

With Joan Chandler and John Dall in *Rope*, dir. Alfred Hitchcock, 1948.

Soon after signing your contract, the studio publicity department sent you to see Hedda Hopper and Louella Parsons, the powerful reigning queens of gossip in Hollywood.

Two old titties! I went to Louella's around Christmas time and there were tons of presents everywhere and a tree. She was nice and she must have been tippling a bit! As for Hedda, she took off her blouse because she said it was too hot. She interviewed me with only her brassiere on. I did not know where to look!

As you were filming your first movie, The North Star [1943], you had to finish school at 20th Century Fox where your classmates were Roddy MacDowall, Elizabeth Taylor, and Linda Darnell.

It was just a classroom where we were maybe four or five at the most at a time and where you would go when you had time off from the set. I remember Linda who at the time was playing some part in

a costume drama [*Summer Storm*, dir. Douglas Sirk, 1944] so she would come in this enormous skirt and stroll into class. She was very well developed for her age and all the boys were very impressed. [*Chuckles.*]

In 1947, Nicholas Ray chose you to star in his very first film, *They Live by Night*.

I first met him at a party in Hollywood. I didn't know who he was. He would come in and drink, sitting by himself in a corner. I found him staring at me all the time across the room and finally I asked the hostess after that happened several times, "What's with him?" And she said, "I think he wants you for his movie." And soon after I was asked to come in for a screen test with him. He was a complicated man. For someone who was so inarticulate in real life, he was the opposite on the set. Very personal and precise. He would put his arm around my shoulder and walk me over to a corner to talk to me privately about the character. He never did

it in front of the others actors. He never yelled things at people. He was terrific. Just a terrific director. I did love working with him. But at the end, the producer Darryl F. Zanuck left the studio and Howard Hughes took over. And he was only concerned with Jane Russell. He didn't like the movie at all and shelved it! For many years, it could not be seen in public. I was very disappointed because it was my first movie after serving three years in the Navy during the war. But thanks to what I called the Bel Air circuit, it was shown at the private screenings of the residences of many influential producers of the time. So they were aware of who I was. Two years later it was released in England and got smashing reviews and finally it came out in America.

What did you think of some of your contemporaries like Gregory Peck, Kirk Douglas, and Burt Lancaster?

I knew Gregory Peck, a very kind and sweet nice man, but I didn't think he was a particularly good actor. Those particular stars from the late 1950s and early 1960s were all very stiff actors. You could see them acting so hard. [*Clinches his jaw.*] I think each was lucky enough and maneuvered the system to their advantage. They all had big houses with the pool and the tennis court and threw exclusive A-list parties and invited the producers. That's the game. The first one I was invited to was at Gary Cooper's who was a master at that game. Nobody could beat them in that field!

Did you ever regret not having been more willing to play the Hollywood game that would have helped you become a star like them?

No. I never cared about fame or money.

With the 1950s a new generation of actors like James Dean arrived. Were you impressed by him?

More so by Montgomery Clift. We lived on the same block in New York for a while but I never met him. Just once at a party. I liked him better than Brando, whom I saw on stage in *A Streetcar Named Desire*. I thought he was interesting, but I liked Ethel Merman better! [*Laughs.*]

Senso represented a turning point in your career. Had you heard of Luchino Visconti?

No, never. Charlie Feldman, my agent at the time, told me he was a famous European director, that I would replace Brando who could had dropped out playing the lead, Lieutenant Franz Mahler, and that he had gotten me a very substantial three-month deal. I was going to do a play in New York but I was broke and that was a good opportunity to make money. Luchino didn't rehearse much. He never showed

With Alida Valli in *Senso*, dir. Luchino Visconti, 1954.

me the dailies and instead screened *Ossessione* [1943, Visconti's first film] especially for me. He liked to take his time. He was in no hurry to do anything. He was very precise in terms of physical poses at certain moments. He was difficult at times and a tyrant. But marvelous, too. He knew precisely what he wanted and he was the boss.

Did you keep any mementos from your films? Guy Haynes's tennis racket, the white cape worn by Franz Mahler in Senso [1954]?

No, nothing, except some of my scripts.

Do you watch your films?

No, never.

Interview by Jean-Paul Chaillet at 15 West 72nd Street, New York, June 2, 2007.

Femmes
Fatales

There were some actresses who played them to perfection: Barbara Stanwyck, Lauren Bacall, Gene Tierney. And there were others who were *born* femmes fatales: Rita Hayworth, Ava Gardner, Lana Turner, not to mention Veronica Lake, Gloria Grahame, Ida Lupino. These are women who would never let you sleep in peace.

There have always been seductresses. Femmes fatales were born in Hollywood. In the 1940s, just when men—poor things—thought the war was over.

Gilda, dir. Charles Vidor, 1946. Rita Hayworth.

"Gilda, Are You Decent?"

She tosses back a glorious mane of hair to frame a bare shoulder. A smoldering look, the heat turned up by an artful air of surprise, lips made to be kissed, perfect teeth, imperceptibly forward—perfection, in short. "Me?" asks Gilda, arch as always. Femmes fatales never messed up an entrance. Hayworth's was unforgettable, as were all her electrically charged scenes in the jewel of a film noir that is *Gilda* (1946), with Glenn Ford. The director Charles Vidor, who had already directed Hayworth in the polished musical comedy *Cover Girl* (1944), wanted to unveil the goddess that was slumbering within. He had no idea just what a bombshell was about to detonate before his eyes.

Barbara Stanwyck's entrance in Billy Wilder's *Double Indemnity* (1944) was also worth its weight in gold . . . gold as cheap as the tawdry bracelet that first catches Fred MacMurray's eye on her shapely ankle. "I wish you'd tell me what's engraved on that anklet" is the opening ploy of this shady insurance salesman, his senses awakened by the bored housewife with her all-too-obvious charms. He knows that he's met his match. She will let this sucker put all the pieces of her scheme in place. He is the puppet, and she will pull the strings.

"I'm poison, Swede, to myself and everyone around me." Under contract to MGM, Ava Gardner was bored. It was her appearance in *The Killers* (1946), directed by Robert Siodmark, who saw her for the exceptionally beautiful and glamorous panther she was, that revealed her as Rita Hayworth's rival in the man-eating stakes. In life, Ava Gardner and Burt Lancaster were friends. You would never know it, to see her twisting him round her little finger as Kitty Collins, the ruthless double-crossing part written by Hemingway, for which she was dressed in virtually the same black satin gown as Rita-Gilda wore in her famous "striptease" scene. Their lines were languid, provocative. These sirens had all the time in the world. Ava Gardner delivered hers like Humphrey Bogart or Robert Mitchum (and filmed with both of them).

Exit the quivering, big-hearted sex symbols of the 1930s. Enter the poisonous blooms and dangerous curves of the 1940s. They wore lamé like nobody else, and looked a million dollars in tweed. It was all in their walk, they way they held themselves, their impassive features, their laconic delivery. Weary of knowing all the answers, they yearned for action. And whenever they were about to light a cigarette, there was always a man's lighter to hand, or a box of matches waiting to be tossed to them.

Double Indemnity, dir. Billy Wilder, 1944. Barbara Stanwyck and Fred MacMurray.

A Strange Mixture

While feel-good comedies, high-class romances, and heroic action films flourished, Hollywood, less and less in control of its machine, allowed a note of disillusioned disenchantment to creep in, the product of a strange mixture. That of the thrillers picked up by directors who had emerged from expressionism and German fatalism, such as Robert Siodmak, Billy Wilder, and Otto Preminger, to show the Americans that the end of the war was not the solution to everything. These were troubled times, when relationships between men and women got lost on bare sets and dead-end streets. No longer would a Cora Smith (Lana Turner in Tay Garnett's *The Postman Always Rings Twice*, 1946) put up with a bad marriage without protesting. A drifter (John Garfield) only has to start working at the diner she runs with her husband and there she is, Lana Turner at her most provocative in her white shorts, dropping her lipstick at the feet of a man who already acts like her lover. The rest is history.

The giants of the roman noir, such as James M. Cain, who wrote *The Postman Always Rings Twice* and *Mildred Pierce*, and the hard-boiled, soft-centered Raymond Chandler (author of *The Big Sleep* and *The Lady in the Lake*), collaborated on the screenplays of their novels. They sold their talent and despair in order to outwit not only the censorship code but also the schemes of their own heroines. After all, what do they want in the end, these venomous creatures in stilettos?

People frequently maintain, and rightly so, that the appearance of femmes fatales reflected male ambivalence in the face of women liberated by the war. As their men went off to fight, women took over on the home front. They worked, had sex, were bad mothers. Not all of them, admittedly, but most were heading that way. In the munitions factories, now operated by an exclusively female workforce, the government was obliged to ask workers to cut the peek-a-boo lock of hair so many of them had falling over one eye. For how could you work properly if you thought you were Veronica Lake, the petite blonde vamp who made sparks fly as she rubbed up against Alan Ladd in *The Glass Key* (1942), based on the novel by Dashiell Hammett, and *The Blue Dahlia* (1946), written by Raymond Chandler?

In Hollywood, too, there was a dearth of men. As a result, women rose to high levels in the studios: screenwriters, producers, or both: *Gilda* owed its oomph to Virginia Van Upp, the most successful female producer of the war years. On the screen, the traditional role of women was smashed to smithereens. Educated or not, they all had a master's degree in sex appeal. Intelligent and strong, grasping and ambitious, they were there to give you a headache.

"Once I'd seen her, I was not in my right mind for quite some time. . . . That's how I found her, and from that moment on, I did not use my head very much, except to be thinking of her." Existentialism in the mist, the film noir voice-over has been mocked many times. Not so the femme fatale. In *The Lady from Shanghai* (1947), it was Orson Welles who admitted that he had failed to understand his estranged wife. He didn't want the worst of Rita? Then he didn't deserve the best of her, and yet she gave it to him, and even agreed to do away with her auburn mane in order to take on the cold and calculating starring role. She gets her own back by dying in a magic mirror maze, her reflection multiplied to infinity in a landmark scene. Welles wasn't over her yet.

One of the few female directors to carve out a place for herself in Hollywood in the 1940s was also one of the most highly strung and feverish of all the film noir leading ladies. In 1950 Ida Lupino directed a film that was very much ahead of its time, *Outrage*. In it, she dared to address the subject of rape and its consequences. She had made it clear in her performance in *They Drive by Night* (dir. Raoul Walsh, 1940), making her entrance with her gown trailing in the dust to stir things up between

The Postman Always Rings Twice, dir. Tay Garnett, 1946.
John Garfield and Lana Turner.

Humphrey Bogart and George Raft, that she was not just a pretty little airhead with wavy bangs. A pretty face with a slightly crestfallen expression, as if she already knew how tough the fight was going to be. They were all crestfallen, disappointed. They wanted to be loved. But madly, or not at all.

Lauren Bacall: "The Look"

Lauren Bacall was unapologetically something else. The former model with a hint of androgyny introduced by Howard Hawks in *To Have and Have Not* (1944) and *The Big Sleep* (1946) presented all the classic features of a femme fatale—the hound's-tooth check suits and the double entendres— but she was warmer. She wasn't there to kill, unless with a sideways glance. All the same, to "get rid" of a "doll" like her, the cynical Bogart had to marry her. In *Out of the Past* (1947), directed by Jacques Tourneur (son of the French director Maurice Tourneur who had moved to Hollywood), Robert Mitchum remembered a fatal love affair in Acapulco: "I never saw her in the daytime. We seemed to live by night. What was left of the day went away like a pack of cigarettes you smoked." The lady of the night was Jane Greer, a brunette: farewell, my lovely. These dark ladies knew full well how to handle a faux hard man like Mitchum. Playing opposite him in *Angel Face* by Otto Preminger (1952), Jean Simmons went to the opposite extreme. Jane Russell swayed her hips in *Macao* (1952), but was too much of a good girl. The femme fatale in this film co-directed by Nicholas Ray was Gloria Grahame. She was married to Nicholas Ray. But what she loved best of all were bad boys.

Like Rita Hayworth, who was so vulnerable, and Ava Gardner, who was convinced she couldn't act, Gloria Grahame had a complex about her appearance. It has to be said that Lee Marvin's character didn't help when he threw a pot of scalding coffee in her face (off screen) in Fritz Lang's *The Big Heat* (1953). Whatever the role played by the actress, who always appeared to be coming out of a trance, she invariably turned it into a femme fatale. She couldn't stop herself. And therein lay the problem. It was in their nature. The proof: when Henry Hathaway wanted Marilyn Monroe to play a femme fatale in *Niagara* (1953), it didn't gel. Monroe the child-woman was there to comfort men. In the era of film noir, they certainly needed it. Dana Andrews, Robert Ryan: strapping, sexy hunks, but worn out by their penchant for femmes fatales. Even the brutal villains played by Richard Widmark got caught out.

We get it. You only need to watch Gene Tierney in *Leave Her to Heaven* (1945), directed by John M. Stahl. In negligee and sunglasses, she allows the disabled younger brother of her husband (played by Cornel Wilde) to drown without lifting a finger. When her husband becomes aware of the truth, the audience is also guilty: it sides with the poisonous plant ravaged by jealousy. Gene Tierney was never as fascinating as when she was a femme fatale. In Otto Preminger's *Laura* (1944), she played a different variation on the type, one who might be dead—or who might be very much alive.

Between 1946 and 1950, femmes fatales were thus to haunt cinema screens, hell-bent on destruction in their many different ways. We should also mention Yvonne De Carlo and Lizabeth Scott, who has been compared to Lauren Bacall; all are worth watching. Even—perhaps especially—in B movies turning on charm and vitriol. Femmes fatales crystallized all the perfectionism of Hollywood: every gesture was studied, and the lighting, dialogue, and black-and-white photography were all wholly at their feet. It is tempting to link them to another type of seductress, also carefully created down to the last detail: the chic Hitchcock heroines.

At the point when espionage and paranoia were getting the upper hand, Alfred Hitchcock, under the pretext of his fascination for volcanic heat beneath an ice-cool exterior, gave life to his own fantasy in the form of neoclassical heroines, languid and elegant, with immaculate diction and

The Big Sleep, dir. Howard Hawks, 1946. Humphrey Bogart and Lauren Bacall.

comportment. Hitchcock was too clever to allow himself to be dominated by a femme fatale. And when he did film one, Marlene Dietrich, in *Stage Fright* (1950), he did not give her the starring role.

But Hitchcock's women were no less dangerous for that, and it is easy to imagine his coolly controlled blondes wanting to let down their hair and rip off their pearls. It is not difficult to picture Kim Novak in *Vertigo* (1958), Grace Kelly in *To Catch a Thief* (1955), and Eva Marie Saint in *North by Northwest* (1959) in strapless dresses and framed to their shoulders as though they were naked, slowly pulling off a single glove and starting to sing the seismic "Put the Blame on Mame," as immortalized in *Gilda*.

ABOVE: Veronica Lake, 1945.

FACING PAGE: *They Drive by Night*, dir. Raoul Walsh, 1940. Ida Lupino.

Vertigo, dir. Alfred Hitchcock, 1958. Kim Novak.

North by Northwest, dir. Alfred Hitchcock, 1959. Eva Marie Saint and Cary Grant.

The Lady from Shanghai, dir. Orson Welles, 1948. Rita Hayworth and Orson Welles.

In a Lonely Place, dir. Nicholas Ray, 1950. Gloria Grahame and Humphrey Bogart.

ABOVE: Gene Tierney, portraits, late 1940s.

FACING PAGE: *Pandora and the Flying Dutchman*, dir. Albert Lewin, 1951.
Ava Gardner and James Mason.

The
Quintessence
of
Hollywood

The studio system is dead? Long live the studio system! In order to compete with TV, Hollywood exploded into wide-screen Technicolor blockbusters, bubbly feel-good comedies, or intense adult dramas. Never had the great stars been so dazzling. The new female stars, Grace Kelly and Audrey Hepburn, introduced a note of European chic. Male roles started to become more complex and vulnerable. As a new wave of directors specialized in harsh realism, so the giants of neoclassicism—Hitchcock, Wilder, Mankiewicz, Minnelli—attained new heights. But the spirit of renewal came from a few of rebellious talents: Marlon Brando, James Dean, Elia Kazan, and Montgomery Clift. The legend was just beginning. The proof lay in one name: Marilyn Monroe.

Rear Window, dir. Alfred Hitchcock, 1954. Grace Kelly and James Stewart.

It's a Wonderful Life

In the postwar years, life was wonderful, and not just in Frank Capra's 1946 fable. *The Big Sleep*, directed by Howard Hawks in the same year, was the finest of the Bogart-Bacall films. *Letter from an Unknown Woman* (1948), with Joan Fontaine and Louis Jourdan, was the best American film by the German-born French director Max Ophüls. Delights such as *The Ghost and Mrs. Muir* (dir. Joseph L. Mankiewicz, 1947) with Gene Tierney and Rex Harrison, or *The Bishop's Wife* (dir. Henry Koster, 1947) with Loretta Young and Cary Grant, raised romantic fantasy to new heights. Charlie Chaplin disconcerted his public with the black comedy *Monsieur Verdoux* (1947). But it was to his credit that he made the film inspired by the French serial killer Henri Désiré Landru, an idea that he was so anxious to direct himself that he bought it from Orson Welles for five thousand dollars. And Welles wisely retained an influence over the direction of Carol Reed's *The Third Man* (1949), with its haunting music by Anton Karas: from his exile in Europe, Hollywood's enfant terrible experienced success once more.

When the downfall of the studios began to come into view, the stars were not yet under threat. It was in the second half of the 1940s that Joan Crawford perfected her style in the hands of the great Adrian, who designed the outfits with massively padded shoulders that were to become her hallmark and to launch a fashion. Joan Crawford was the star par excellence. In *Humoresque* (dir. Jean Negulesco, 1947), she benefited from the full gamut of Hollywood skills: the expressionistic lighting of the fatalistic films that suited her so well, the contrasts that left part of the screen in darkness, and the sumptuous sets and wardrobe. Crawford showed a more highly strung side to her persona, tougher and more fragile, as she was supposed to have been in real life. In a word, modern—and the young directors took note.

All the stars ready to take a step back from their personas, or to take risks or be adaptable, were rewarded with tremendous success. Thus one of the finest pairs of lovebirds of the decade was played by Katharine Hepburn and Humphrey Bogart in *The African Queen* (1951). By casting the "old maid" opposite the adventurer from *The Treasure of the Sierra Madre* (1948) on location in Africa, John Huston (son of Walter Huston) consolidated one of the most successful and impulsive careers in Hollywood.

With two Academy Awards already under her belt, Bette Davis found her greatest role in Joseph L. Mankiewicz's masterpiece *All About Eve* (1950), in which she played an aging Broadway star whose preeminence is threatened by an ingénue upstart (Anne Baxter). So powerfully symbolic was this tale of the forced handing down of talent from one generation to the next that it entered popular folklore. At the Academy Awards ceremony on March 29, 1951, the film won six Oscars out of fourteen nominations (a record matched only by James Cameron's *Titanic*). Even the host, Fred Astaire, appeared surprised when the two favorites for Best Actress, Bette Davis in *All About Eve* and Gloria Swanson in *Sunset Boulevard*, were beaten to the award by Judy Holliday's comical performance in *Born Yesterday*, directed by George Cukor. Nothing was certain any more.

FACING PAGE, TOP LEFT: *Humoresque*, dir. Jean Negulesco, 1947. Joan Crawford.

FACING PAGE, TOP RIGHT: *All About Eve*, dir. Joseph L. Mankiewicz, 1950. Bette Davis.

FACING PAGE, BOTTOM LEFT: *Sunset Boulevard*, dir. Billy Wilder, 1950. Gloria Swanson. Portrait.

FACING PAGE, BOTTOM RIGHT: *Sunset Boulevard*, dir. Billy Wilder, 1950. Billy Wilder.

But until the early 1950s, classic Hollywood style allied with great writing still prevailed, notably in the work of the scholarly Mankiewicz, who offered a charming display of disdain for consumer society in *A Letter to Three Wives* (1949).

A New Realism

At the same time, more realistic, hard-hitting films appeared that denounced intolerance and shone the spotlight on society's outcasts and souls in torment. These included *Kiss of Death* (dir. Henry Hathaway, 1947), which revealed a diabolical side to Richard Widmark, *The Boy with Green Hair* (dir. Joseph Losey, 1948), *They Live by Night* (dir. Nicholas Ray, 1949), *The Naked City* (dir. Jules Dassin, 1948), *Night and the City* with Richard Widmark and Gene Tierney (dir. Jules Dassin, 1950), and *Pickup on South Street* (dir. Samuel Fuller, 1953). The style and tone were harsh, and the slightly grubby images recalled the documentary style of the Italian film *Ladri di biciclette* (*The Bicycle Thieves*, 1948), directed by Vittorio De Sica. In 1955 Stanley Kubrick made *Killer's Kiss*, which had a fairly standard theme (the flight of a boxer) that nevertheless attracted notice. In 1956 *The Killing* once again confirmed his technical prowess. Still in the realm of film noir, John Huston showed he was a master of the genre in *The Asphalt Jungle* (1950): Sterling Hayden stuck to his guns; Marilyn Monroe entered the scene.

The names of the directors of Hollywood neorealism are as succinct as their films: Fuller, Ray, Dassin, Mann, Aldrich. Under the supervision of the producer-director Stanley Kramer, Hollywood also turned its attention to films with a message (which were to find their best messengers among the ranks of classical actors such as Spencer Tracy and Gregory Peck).

Directors now took the reins. Showing Frank Sinatra shooting heroin? Impossible. And yet, in 1955 Otto Preminger tackled a taboo subject head-on in *The Man with the Golden Arm*. (But it was for *From Here to Eternity* [1953] that Sinatra was to win an Oscar.) Stars set up their own production houses, capitalizing on their prestige and benefiting financially. Those who left to go back to their stage roots were to return to become all-powerful in front of the lenses of the new golden boys who had come from television. Like Henry Fonda, more pugnacious than ever in Sidney Lumet's *Twelve Angry Men* (1957). Hollywood was too preoccupied to interfere. Now the bubblegum energy of the postwar period, with its nylons and jazz, was smothered by the Cold War, the Korean War (which mobilized Hollywood to a lesser degree), paranoia about nuclear attack, and state intervention in the film industry. For Senator Joseph McCarthy, the danger came from the "reds". For science fiction, it came from Mars. And then there was that American fascination with psychiatry and psychoanalysis—heralded a few years earlier by Alfred Hitchcock in *Spellbound* (1945)—that impelled creative artists towards an examination of the unconscious and

Night and the City, dir. Jules Dassin, 1950. Richard Widmark and Gene Tierney.

its impulses, which disoriented foreign audiences and markets who were supposed to lap up anything to do with the American way of life.

In 1948 the breakup of the major studios' monopoly on distribution precipitated a crisis that couldn't have come at a worse time. For the true danger for Hollywood came neither from Russia nor from space, even if it did come with an aerial and a cathode ray tube: the real enemy was television.

In 1951 Louis B. Mayer, criticized for not having rushed to make films with a message, was fired from MGM. He died a broken man six years later. MGM was now left in the hands of faceless interests in the worlds of real estate and banking, and millionaires who knew nothing about show business (like the tycoon caricatured by Joseph L. Mankiewicz in *The Barefoot Contessa* [1954]) who soon got bored with their new acquisition.

In 1954, six years after buying out RKO, the millionaire Howard Hughes sold his new toy to an industrial trust. RKO gave up the ghost. Hollywood had opened its gates and let the enemy in.

The African Queen, dir. John Huston, 1951. Katharine Hepburn and Humphrey Bogart.

CinemaScope: An Explosion of Color

Facing up to television meant thinking big. The spread of color and the new techniques that came with it were dazzling in their effects: CinemaScope ushered in ever wider screens for projecting panoramic images in magnificent movie theaters, and Cinerama and 3D gave rise to superbly acted adventure films in lavish color. These included *Scaramouche* (dir. George Sidney, 1952) with Janet Leigh and Stewart Granger, *Ivanhoe* (dir. Richard Thorpe, 1952) with Robert Taylor and Elizabeth Taylor (who were not related except by their dark beauty and gem-like eyes), and *All the Brothers were Valiant* (dir. Richard Thorpe, 1953), which reunited Robert Taylor and Stewart Granger.

In 1953 the cinema-going public discovered the first film to be released in CinemaScope: *The Robe*, directed by Henry Koster, with the statuesque Victor Mature. There was a return to the historical epic that had been so much in vogue in the 1920s. In *Samson and Delilah* (1949), the quasi-godlike voice of Cecil B. DeMille rises over the start of the film. In 1955 it was the turn of *Land of the Pharaohs*, directed by Howard Hawks, with Joan Collins. Even the new leading man, Paul Newman, was to don a toga in *The Silver Chalice* (1954). And then there were remakes of two successes of the silent era, *The Ten Commandments* (1956) and *Ben-Hur* (1959). Charlton Heston, spotted working in the theater, made a great impression in Cecil B. DeMille's *The Greatest Show on Earth* (1952), crowned Best Picture at the Academy Awards ceremony. DeMille had an inspiration when he asked the actor to part the Red Sea with him in his new version of *The Ten Commandments*. Their faith was triumphant. In 1959, William Wyler, more dynamic and prolific than ever at the age of fifty-seven, also made use of the power of Charlton Heston for the remake of Fred Niblo's *Ben-Hur* (1925), giving form to an extraordinarily ambitious 15-million-dollar project that required 400,000 extras and three months of work for the chariot scene alone, which lasted half an hour on screen. The rewards: eleven Oscars (out of twelve nominations), including Best Picture, Best Director, and Best Actor for Charlton Heston.

Never had cinema transported so many so far, never had it been so magical. The slightest drama or comedy now took on a pyrotechnic appeal. For those who were fans of neither westerns nor swords-and-sandals epics, there was *The Bridge on the River Kwai* (1957), a war film that was supposed to have been directed by Fred Zinneman, John Ford, Orson Welles, William Wyler, or Howard Hawks. In the end it was the British director David Lean who took over, making a star of his fellow Englishman Alec Guinness and ensuring a prominent place in cinema for William Holden for a decade to come.

So many unforgettable spectacles, which in the end made little profit because they needed such great investments. Ways of making films were changing. *Quo Vadis* (dir. Mervyn LeRoy, 1951, with Robert Taylor again) was not made in Hollywood but at Cinecittà. It was on this Roman epic that one of the screen bombshells of the century, Sophia Loren, appeared as an extra. For in the age of the atomic bomb, it was a bevy of bombshells that dominated the cinema screen. Sophia Loren, Gina Lollobrigida, and Alida Valli were the new foreign beauties. Following in their wake, the "pinup girls" of the 1950s flaunted their voluptuous curves.

Ben-Hur, dir. William Wyler, 1959. Charlton Heston.

Marilyn and Audrey

But the embodiment of talent, beauty, and the determination to become a star was blonde. After several minor roles in films such as *Love Happy* (1949) with the Marx Brothers, *The Asphalt Jungle*, and *All About Eve*, Marilyn Monroe had finally come into being. Like many other starlets, she had been taken under the wing of Howard Hughes. At RKO, she was to be given a part in Fritz Lang's *Clash by Night* (1952), and she can be seen at the side of an amused Cary Grant in *Monkey Business* (1952), directed by Howard Hawks, who was to shine the spotlight on her in *Gentlemen Prefer Blondes* (1953), with Hughes's other protégée, Jane Russell, playing second fiddle. Monroe also played the manic-depressive babysitter in Roy Ward Baker's *Don't Bother to Knock* (1952), with Richard Widmark, before setting Technicolor on fire in *Niagara* (dir. Henry Hathaway, 1953) and *How to Marry a Millionaire* (dir. Jean Negulesco, 1953), in which Betty Grable gamely passed her the torch. The legend was gathering pace.

Marilyn Monroe, born in Los Angeles on June 1, 1926, died in the same city on August 5, 1962. She synthesized all the blondes who had gone before her (and moreover brought Jean Harlow's hair colorist on set with her, at great expense) to create a child-woman, an invention both vulgar and divine, presented to the world like an angel of light, transcending both the era and the legend of Hollywood.

ABOVE, LEFT: *Gentlemen Prefer Blondes*, dir. Howard Hawks, 1953. Marilyn Monroe. Portrait.
ABOVE, RIGHT: *Sabrina*, dir. Billy Wilder, 1954. Audrey Hepburn.

TOP: *The Man with the Golden Arm*, dir. Otto Preminger, 1955. Kim Novak and Frank Sinatra.

CENTER: *From Here to Eternity*, dir. Fred Zinnemann, 1953. Burt Lancaster and Deborah Kerr.

BOTTOM: *Convicted*, dir. Henry Levin, 1950. Glenn Ford.

FACING PAGE, TOP LEFT: *The Barefoot Contessa*, dir. Joseph L. Mankiewicz, 1954. Ava Gardner.

FACING PAGE, TOP RIGHT: Gina Lollobrigida, 1958.

FACING PAGE, BOTTOM: *Houseboat*, dir. Melville Shavelson, 1958. Cary Grant and Sophia Loren.

Before her life slid into tragedy, Monroe was the symbol of the American zest and high spirits of the 1950s, as also epitomized by Lucille Ball and Bob Hope, who projected the "pinup girl" image that Jayne Mansfield parodied just as wickedly in *The Girl Can't Help It* (dir. Frank Tashlin, 1956).

At the opposite end of the scale from the Monroe sex appeal were the gamine, elfin qualities of Leslie Caron, Jean Seberg, and Shirley MacLaine. And, of course, the most elegant of all with her swanlike neck and doe eyes, Audrey Hepburn. She had been heading for a career as a dancer when the writer Colette plucked her up and put her in the Broadway production of *Gigi*, in the role later taken by Leslie Caron in the Minnelli film (1958). It was William Wyler who made the sophisticated European actress a star in *Roman Holiday* (1953), playing opposite Gregory Peck. Her princess role earned her an Oscar, the unconditional love of her fans, and an everlasting cult. Like Monroe, Hepburn sang delightfully. Through her collaboration with Givenchy, Audrey Hepburn also pioneered the partnership between fashion and film, which exploited the impact of Dior's New Look to sensational effect. When she returned from Paris transformed into a fashion plate in Billy Wilder's *Sabrina* (1954), or when Grace Kelly, that other miraculously exquisite phenomenon of the 1950s, appeared to James Stewart in *Rear Window* (1954), their outfits became characters in themselves.

Neoclassical directors, such as Billy Wilder and Alfred Hitchcock, the one defined by the quality of his screenplays, the other by his obsession with visual suspense, knew precisely how to make use of modern femininity, whether slender and swanlike or brimming over with sexuality. *Sabrina*, with Humphrey Bogart and William Holden, and *Love in the Afternoon* (1957), with Gary Cooper and Maurice Chevalier, were vehicles for Audrey Hepburn. Billy Wilder also showed off Marilyn Monroe's potential in brilliant style in *The Seven-Year Itch* (1955), containing the iconic scene of Monroe's white dress billowing up over a subway grate (which in the film lasts a fraction of a second). And, of course, in *Some Like It Hot* (1959), the best film comedy of all time on the Richter scale. Monroe didn't give a damn about the Hays Code, singing "I Wanna Be Loved by You" in a

TOP: *How to Marry a Millionaire*, dir. Jean Negulesco, 1953.
Marilyn Monroe, Betty Grable, and Lauren Bacall.
BOTTOM: *Pillow Talk*, dir. Michael Gordon, 1959. Doris Day and Rock Hudson.

sheer nude figure-hugging gown, while Jack Lemmon and Tony Curtis camped it up as musicians in drag with such relish that Wilder was nervous about whether Lemmon in particular would ever get back to "normal".

Audrey Hepburn was to have a romance with William Holden but never got on with Humphrey Bogart. Marilyn Monroe, meanwhile, was not the simple, luminous creature of *Some Like It Hot*, but a difficult and complex actress haunted by doubts.

Hitchcock at his Peak

The cinema now favored independent productions and auteurs, a trend enthusiastically embraced by Alfred Hitchcock. Unlike Billy Wilder, who alternated successes with failures and was a scathing critic of the advent of television (as well as of the illusions of cinema, revealed as a moribund world) in the masterpiece *Sunset Boulevard* [1950, see p. 27], Hitchcock adored television, even creating his own series, *Alfred Hitchcock Presents*. He gave his name prominent billing in the credits of the films in which he appeared, and constantly refined the art of suspense and his fantasy of the ice-cold blonde. After making excellent films such as *Rope* (1948) and *The Trouble with Harry* (1955), he held audiences spellbound with a series of Technicolor masterpieces that were also vehicles for Grace Kelly: *Dial M for Murder* (1954), *Rear Window*, and *To Catch a Thief* (1955).

Hitchcock resented his muse for leaving him for a prince, had little time for the unstable temperament of Kim Novak, who was nevertheless perfect in the masterly *Vertigo* (1958), and had nothing but praise for Eva Marie Saint in *North by Northwest* (1959). A stylish cinema, in step with the new design ethos of the 1950s, with perfect plots. So many lessons in the art of cinema in which Hitchcock's two alter egos, James Stewart and Cary Grant, as handsome as he thought himself ugly, presented a peerlessly elegant image of the American male.

And God Created the Actors Studio

Let us head to New York, where many production companies relocated in the face of the Hollywood debacle. With his jeans and well-muscled torso, Marlon Brando made a sensational Hollywood entrance in Elia Kazan's *A Streetcar Named Desire* (1951), in which he reprised his Broadway role.

A co-founder of the Actors Studio, which proposed a radical new model for the actor's craft based on internalization and improvisation, Kazan could boast of bringing two of the most powerful cinema legends to the screen: James Dean and Marlon Brando, whose black leather look in *The Wild One* (dir. Laslo Benedek, 1953) were so troubling to the leagues of decency.

Vertigo, dir. Alfred Hitchcock, 1958. James Stewart.

Unlike Brando, who was to explore his own genius in a range of roles that were all as emotionally and physically charged as each other (notably in Kazan's *Viva Zapata!* [1952]), James Dean was not so fortunate. Hollywood's most enduring legend survives in just three films, all released in 1955–56. It was Kazan who discovered James Dean, who trained him in the Stanislavsky method and who gave him his first great tortured role in *East of Eden* (1955). Dean followed this up with *Rebel Without a Cause* (1955)—a high-voltage collaboration with Kazan's friend Nicholas Ray—with Natalie Wood and Sal Mineo. Dean had scarcely finished filming *Giant* (1956), directed by George Stevens, billed as a Texan version of *Gone with the Wind*, when, aged just twenty-four, he died at the wheel of his Porsche on the way to Salinas, California. *Rebel Without a Cause* came out a month later. In his role as a disaffected seventeen-year-old, Dean became the first teenager and millions of confused teenagers recognized themselves in this rebellious adolescent.

It is not hard to imagine the impact on the public of these two new gods of the cinema. You can watch Marlon Brando falling to his knees in front of Kim Hunter in his ripped T-shirt, or imitating a wildcat to impress Vivien Leigh as Blanche DuBois (the only British actress to win two Oscars for playing a Southern belle) a dozen times: the impact remains the same. *A Streetcar Named Desire* garnered a clutch of Oscars—but not for Brando. He made up for this the following year with *On the Waterfront* (1954). Eva Marie Saint, for her part, won the Oscar for Best Supporting Actress at the age of thirty for a role that had been turned down by Grace Kelly. Not just a masterpiece of realism (in its depiction of longshoremen in natural settings), lyricism, and humanity, with its celebrated repartee, *On the Waterfront* was also an attempt by Elia Kazan and his screenwriter Budd Schulberg (who also wrote Kazan's *A Face in the Crowd* [1957]) to rehabilitate themselves after naming fifteen of their colleagues to the House Committee on Un-American Activities. The spirit of McCarthyism was everywhere.

Despite his masterly oeuvre (to which we shall return in the next chapter), Kazan was destined always to be seen as an informer who had collaborated with the odious Hollywood blacklist that sent some artists (such as the director Edward Dmytryk) to prison and others into exile, and destroyed many careers, including that of the actor John Garfield, who died in 1952 at the age of just thirty-nine, shortly after being blacklisted. In his acting style and looks, John Garfield was the precursor of the young bucks of the Actors Studio.

James Dean wanted to be like Marlon Brando and Montgomery Clift; Brando took his inspiration from Clift, who had arrived first with films such as Fred Zinneman's *The Search* (1948) and William Wyler's *The Heiress* (1949). Moody and sensitive, expressing more with his intense blue eyes than any words could say, Montgomery Clift was unique.

A Place in the Sun, dir. George Stevens, 1951. Montgomery Clift and Elizabeth Taylor.

Suddenly, Elizabeth Taylor

These cool, modern sex symbols, Montgomery Clift and James Dean, as well as Rock Hudson and later Marlon Brando, all had someone important in common: Elizabeth Taylor. The actress with violet eyes, who wouldn't rest until she had broken away from her image as a former MGM child star, met "Monty" on the set of George Stevens's magnificent *A Place in the Sun* (1951) and was to remain his loving confidante until the end of his life. Clift suffered terrible facial injuries when he crashed his car during the filming of *Raintree County* (dir. Edward Dmytryk, 1957). But his new, less mobile features made him even more striking as Dr. Cukrowicz in *Suddenly, Last Summer*, directed by one of the towering figures of the decade, Joseph L. Mankiewicz. Who could forget the image of Elizabeth Taylor in her white swimsuit, over-exposed in every sense on a white-hot beach, in one of the cruelest stories (adapted from the Tennessee Williams play) ever told on the cinema screen? "Maggie the Cat," as Paul Newman nicknamed her during the filming of *Cat on a Hot Tin Roof* (1958), also formed firm friendships with Rock Hudson and James Dean on the set of *Giant*. Like Montgomery Clift, Rock Hudson was forced to hide his homosexuality. And James Dean was a child.

But in the mid-1950s, the biggest stars at the box office were Marlon Brando and Marilyn Monroe. Marlon Brando gave himself free rein, appearing in a musical comedy with Frank Sinatra, who dubbed him "the mumbler"; in Shakespeare in Mankiewicz's *Julius Caesar* (1953); as a Nazi alongside Montgomery Clift in Edward Dmytryk's *The Young Lions* (1958); as a social pariah in Sidney Lumet's *The Fugitive Kind* (1959), in a role written specially for him by Tennessee Williams, with Anna Magnani getting her own back on Ingrid Bergman for stealing Roberto Rossellini from her by nailing some superb Hollywood roles. In 1956 the incomparable Magnani won the Oscar for Best Actress for her role in Daniel Mann's *The Rose Tattoo* (1955).

Monroe, weary of her self-created role as sex object, and no happier with the intellectual Arthur Miller than she had been with the sportsman Joe DiMaggio, joined the Actors Studio and demonstrated what she had learned there in devastating fashion in Joshua Logan's *Bus Stop* (1956). She was touching in *The Prince and the Showgirl* (1957), which she herself produced, under the sardonic gaze of Laurence Olivier, who gave her little help in making this romantic tale—anachronistic but not without charm—a success.

Drama in the Air

The 1950s also saw the emergence of a swathe of harrowed and harrowing roles for actresses, of girls without hope and

Ivanhoe, dir. Richard Thorpe, 1952.
Robert Taylor and Elizabeth Taylor.

TOP, LEFT: *I Want to Live!*, dir. Robert Wise, 1958.
Susan Hayward.

TOP, RIGHT: *Sweet Smell of Success*,
dir. Alexander Mackendrick, 1957. Tony Curtis.

LEFT: *Touch of Evil*, dir. Orson Welles, 1958.
Orson Welles, Akim Tamiroff, and Janet Leigh.

FACING PAGE: *Suddenly, Last Summer*,
dir. Joseph L. Mankiewicz, 1959. Elizabeth Taylor.

women on the edge of a nervous breakdown. Drink, mental health problems, they had everything thrown at them. Susan Hayward imprisoned in *I Want to Live!* (dir. Robert Wise, 1958), Joanne Woodward ruined in *The Fugitive Kind* (1959) or suffering from multiple personality disorder in *The Three Faces of Eve* (1957). These were women who were the product of corrupt or malicious men, such as the self-important "gentleman" of the press played by Burt Lancaster in *Sweet Smell of Success* (1957), directed by Alexander Mackendrick (who also made *The Ladykillers* [1955] with Alec Guinness), another vitriolic portrait of show business, which gave the slicked-back Tony Curtis one of his finest roles.

Sex and drama were in the air. Tennessee Williams put his finger on just where it hurt; on the radio, Elvis Presley revolutionized the airwaves; and thanks to Richard Brooks's *Blackboard Jungle* (1955), with Glenn Ford as a dedicated teacher, America was now as afraid of juvenile delinquents as of Communists. The film closed with Bill Haley & His Comets singing "Rock Around the Clock" and revealed a new star, Sidney Poitier, who four years later would be chained to Tony Curtis in *The Defiant Ones* (1958).

FACING PAGE: *A Streetcar Named Desire*, dir. Elia Kazan, 1951.
Vivien Leigh and Marlon Brando.
ABOVE: *Rebel Without a Cause*, dir. Nicholas Ray, 1955.
James Dean and Natalie Wood.

Hollywood meanwhile clung to its stars from earlier years. After her Italian interlude with Roberto Rossellini, which had added spice to her filmography and given her three children, Ingrid Bergman, pilloried so shabbily by Hollywood, made a triumphant return following her divorce (heralded in *Viaggio in Italia* [*Journey to Italy*], in which she and George Sanders played a couple on the brink of separating, in 1954), in *Indiscreet* (dir. Stanley Donen, 1958) and *Anastasia* (dir. Anatole Litvak, 1956).

The screen goddesses of an earlier era, for their part, were now celebrated in roles that placed them on a pedestal. Ava Gardner gave Grace Kelly and Clark Gable a hard time in the iconic *Mogambo* (dir. John Ford, 1953), but it was in *Pandora and the Flying Dutchman* (dir. Albert Lewin, 1951) and *The Barefoot Contessa* (dir. Joseph. L. Mankiewicz, 1954), playing a restless gipsy opposite the shadowy James Mason and Humphrey Bogart, that she was to inspire men most irresistibly to sacrifice themselves for her love.

Rita Hayworth, divorced from Prince Aly Khan, endeavored to revive the Gilda effect in Vincent Sherman's *Affair in Trinidad* (1952) with Glenn Ford. Her dance of the seven veils in *Salome* (1953), directed by William Dieterle after her former husband Orson Welles left to work on *Othello*, suited her better. But it was in *Miss Sadie Thompson* (dir. Curtis Bernhardt, 1953) that—as the eponymous bar girl—she showed everyone how it was done. Her tipsy, smoky, sultry rendering of "The Heat Is On" (dubbed by Jo Ann Greer), amid a group of infatuated Marines (including Aldo Ray) has entered the annals.

Giant, dir. George Stevens, 1956. Elizabeth Taylor and James Dean.

Lana Turner was herself the center of a scandal when her teenage daughter killed Turner's abusive gangster lover (she was acquitted), and played herself swathed in fabulous costumes by Jean Louis in Douglas Sirk's *Imitation of Life* (1959), alongside the teen sensation Sandra Dee. The Danish-German director Douglas Sirk, who returned to the cinema with reluctance during the war after working as a farmer in rural America, rivaled Vincente Minnelli in producing stylized melo-dramas, with an emphasis on heightened color to express inflamed emotions; the use of symbols such as mirrors, staircases, and televisions; and the choice of glamorous heroines such as Lauren Bacall (who excelled in both Minnelli's *The Cobweb* [1955] and Sirk's *Written on the Wind* [1956]). Sirk revealed the handsome Rock Hudson, who was a huge hit in romantic comedies with Doris Day, who—fine actress that she was—added the missing touch to Hitchcock's *The Man Who Knew Too Much* (1956) with her rendition of "Que Sera Sera," thus ensuring the film's success.

Contradictions

The 1950s was a decade of contradictions. On the one hand, the teen B movies aimed at young drive-in audiences, and science-fiction classics: *The Day the Earth Stood Still* (dir. Robert Wise, 1951), *The War of the Worlds* (dir. Byron Haskin, 1953), and *Invasion of the Body Snatchers* (dir. Don Siegel, 1956); on the other, an adult and mature, intellectual cinema. *The Quiet Man* (1952), directed

On the Waterfront, dir. Elia Kazan, 1954. Eva Marie Saint and Marlon Brando.

by John Ford, with his favorite actors John Wayne and Maureen O'Hara, is a marvel. But the classic directors, such as Hawks, Ford, and Lang, were now more appreciated in Europe, and America was not untouched by the new wave films by Bergman, Fellini, Truffaut, Buñuel, and De Sica. Elsewhere, there were Satyajit Ray and Akira Kurosawa. Windows on the world.

The 1950s. Striking images. Legendary scenes. Close-ups of nocturnal animals, a badly sewn rag doll, and "LOVE" and "HATE" tattooed on the knuckles of Robert Mitchum's murderous preacher in *The Night of the Hunter* (1955), Charles Laughton's only film as director. Burt Lancaster and Deborah Kerr kissing on the beach in *From Here to Eternity*, which revisited Pearl Harbor. The opening tracking shot of *Touch of Evil* (1958), Orson Welles's second masterpiece. Kim Novak and William Holden dancing in *Picnic* (1955); Holden's ripped shirt. Deborah Kerr and Cary Grant drinking champagne cocktails in *An Affair to Remember* (1957), Dorothy Malone dancing in *Written on the Wind*, all of Vincente Minnelli's *Some Came Running* (1958).

Let us pay tribute to all the supporting and character roles that have given Hollywood movies their special quality, as represented by one excellent actress who was later recognized in her own right: Thelma Ritter. This homely, wisecracking Brooklyn woman, who was an institution with Mankiewicz and stole the scene from the stars in *Rear Window*, was to attain iconic status during the decade. Let us pay tribute too to Humphrey Bogart, who passed on too early but knew it was coming. To Cecil B. DeMille, also gone while those like King Vidor and Raoul Walsh went into semi-retirement. And to James Dean, to be rediscovered on regular basis. All today's young actors owe everything to him. At the same time, still to come into the light was a certain John Cassavetes, newly married to a certain Gena Rowlands, who in 1959 made a film called *Shadows*.

TOP: *The Night of the Hunter*, dir. Charles Laughton, 1955.
Robert Mitchum.

BOTTOM: *Samson and Delilah*, dir. Cecil B. DeMille, 1949.
Hedy Lamarr and Victor Mature.

FACING PAGE: Photographs taken during the filming of *Some Like It Hot*,
dir. Billy Wilder, 1959. Marilyn Monroe.

ABOVE, LEFT: A young Douglas Sirk examining some frames.

ABOVE, RIGHT: *Imitation of Life*, dir. Douglas Sirk, 1959. Lana Turner and John Gavin.

ABOVE, LEFT: William Holden, portrait, 1959.

ABOVE, RIGHT: *Designing Woman*, dir. Vincente Minnelli, 1957.
Lauren Bacall and Gregory Peck.

Kirk Douglas

Born Issur Danielovitch in Amsterdam, New York, on December 9, 1916, the son of poor Russian immigrants (his father was a ragman), Kirk Douglas grew up with a fierce determination to be an actor, and has left an indelible stamp on American cinema. After becoming a star in *Champion* in 1949, he worked with all the Hollywood greats, including Billy Wilder, Joseph L. Mankiewicz, Michael Curtiz, William Wyler, Vincente Minnelli, King Vidor, Raoul Walsh, Elia Kazan, and Robert Aldrich. Playing characters of every type, from heroes to villains, he found his iconic role in *Spartacus* (1960). He was at the height of his fame when, in 1960, he became executive producer on this huge historical epic, based on the rebellion of Roman slaves led by Spartacus. Douglas played a pivotal part in putting an end to a shameful period in Hollywood by hiring and giving an official credit to the blacklisted screenwriter Dalton Trumbo. He also replaced Anthony Mann with the director of *Paths of Glory* (1957), then aged thirty-two, Stanley Kubrick.

This interview took place at his home in Beverly Hills, on the occasion of the tribute paid to him by the Festival du Cinéma Américain de Deauville. Not an ostentatious mansion, but a handsome residence containing a remarkable collection of modern art, including works by Chagall and Braque. Ensconced on a sofa under a Picasso painting, wearing matching silk pajamas and robe, this great survivor (of a plane crash and a heart attack) was vital, impish, and passionate. A lesson in life.

At the beginning of your film career, Lauren Bacall was a presence.

[*Smiles.*] We go back a long way, Lauren and I. We were both students at the American Academy of Dramatic Arts in New York. I knew her when she was fifteen. I was struggling to pay for my classes. I remember the jacket I used to wear, which was too light for the time of year. I was shivering. When she saw that, she took the coat from her uncle, who was with her, and gave it to me. I wore it for years.

FACING PAGE: Portrait, late 1940s.

ABOVE, LEFT: In *Young Man with a Horn,* dir. Michael Curtiz, 1950.

ABOVE, TOP RIGHT: With Ann Sothern in *A Letter to Three Wives,* dir. Joseph L. Mankiewicz, 1949.

ABOVE, BOTTOM RIGHT: With Paul Stewart in *Champion,* dir. Mark Robson, 1949.

Later she made films with Howard Hawks, and she was the one who got me my first part in *The Strange Love of Martha Ivers* in 1946, a film by Lewis Milestone with Barbara Stanwyck. Then Lauren and I worked together on *Young Man with a Horn* in 1950, with Michael Curtiz as director.

A very good film with Doris Day in a dramatic role, and you playing a trumpeter.

Yes. With the singer and composer Hoagy Carmichael and a very touching actor, Juano Hernandez. Lauren was already married to Humphrey Bogart. A good man.

What was it that made you decide to work on a particular film?

If you see eye to eye, that's all that matters. When I worked with Stanley Kubrick on *Paths of Glory*

in 1957, he was very young. I'd discovered him after seeing *The Killing* [1956]. He really looked like a kid. But his instinct for cinema was obvious.

Did you stay in touch with Kubrick?

No. I don't want to go into the details. Kubrick was an extremely gifted director who made few films, and his final film was his least successful, sadly. Our relationship was close but strange. My feelings about him are mixed.

Has taking an active part in films always been important to you?

Yes. Actors should get involved. When my company, Bryna Productions [named after his mother], produced *Spartacus,* we were responsible for getting

Laurence Olivier, Charles Laughton, and others involved, and then each of these great actors brought something to the project in their turn.

Was it the fact that you always wanted to let directors know your ideas that earned you a reputation for being difficult?
I have never asked more of anyone else on a film than myself, and I don't know where this reputation came from. Burt Lancaster, John Wayne, Lana Turner, Tony Curtis? I don't think so.

Burt Lancaster said that being demanding was your hallmark.
We were both demanding. He, too, became a producer and director quite early in his career. Yes, we were demanding. It's not a flaw.

You're remembered together in *Gunfight at the O.K. Corral* [dir. John Sturges, 1957], but you'd been acting together since the late 1940s, for example in *I Walk Alone* [dir. Byron Haskin, 1948].
We had a great deal in common. We felt the same need to be committed, to be part of society, of our time. And in Hollywood you could sometimes communicate this need. A political film such as John Frankenheimer's *Seven Days in May* [1964] suited us. Burt's opinion mattered to me. He was as subtle in his psychology as he was impressive

in his physique. He'd started off in the circus, and had to stop because of an injury. He was a real showman.

What sort of relationship did you have with Tony Curtis? He shared top billing with Burt Lancaster on Carol Reed's *Trapeze* [1956], and afterward you hired him to play a slave in *Spartacus*.
Between the two I'd made *The Vikings* [1958], with Tony Curtis and Janet Leigh. He was an actor who had more to offer than his image suggested, as he showed in *Some Like It Hot* [1959] and *The Sweet Smell of Success* [1957].

In becoming an actor-producer so early in your career, during a period still ruled by the star system, you were ahead of your time. Many other actors subsequently followed your example.
I was a pioneer in the genre. I didn't want to become a movie mogul, but for me a film should be as entertaining and exciting as possible. With the best story. But good projects were few and far between. Just before I set up my production company, MGM wanted me to film a huge production, *The Great Sinner* [1949], directed by Robert Siodmak, with Ava Gardner and Gregory Peck. I told them I'd rather make a small film called *Champion* [dir. Mark

TOP: With Lana Turner in *The Bad and the Beautiful*, dir. Vincente Minnelli, 1953.
CENTER: With Burt Lancaster in *Seven Days in May*, dir. John Frankenheimer, 1964.
BOTTOM: With Burt Lancaster and Lizabeth Scott in *I Walk Alone*, dir. Byron Haskin, 1948.

Robson, 1949]. They thought I was one of those crazy New York actors, but I've always done what felt right for me. *Champion* was my first chance to play a role that made me explore physical violence. I *felt* that part. *The Great Sinner* was a flop, and *Champion* was a hit. Clearly, it doesn't always work that way. For instance, Billy Wilder, with whom I'd just finished making *Ace in the Hole* [1951], one of his best films, wanted me to play in *Stalag 17* [1953]. I'd seen the play. Well, I wasn't so keen. Billy made the film with William Holden, who won an Oscar for the part I would have played! But hold on: I made *The Bad and the Beautiful* [dir. Vincente Minnelli, 1952], which I believe is a good film. Well, I only made it because Clark Gable had turned the part down.

Your bravura performance as an egotistical producer in *The Bad and the Beautiful*, apparently inspired by David O. Selznick, won you an Oscar nomination.

I've been nominated three times, for *Champion*, *The Bad and the Beautiful*, and *Lust for Life* [1956]. Three times I came home empty-handed! [*Smiles.*] For my third nomination, for *Lust for Life*, I was in Munich, filming I can't remember what. [*Laughs.*] What I do recall is that everyone thought I was the favorite. And I do think I made a credible Van Gogh.

With a striking resemblance to him.

Thank you. It's true that when everyone showers you with praise, you can't help believing it. I'd even written my speech and prepared my best surprised expression for

In *Spartacus*, dir. Stanley Kubrick, 1960.

when I was announced as the winner. There were about fifty-eight journalists waiting outside my hotel, waiting to climb up to my room to immortalize my reaction on the spot. It was my friend Yul Brynner who won, but the photographers didn't miss out: they got my reaction, and it certainly was surprised! [*Laughs.*] That night I was on my own and feeling low when there was a knock at my door and I was handed a box. Inside it was an Oscar, and on it was inscribed: "With us, you deserve an Oscar always." It was signed by my wife and my son Peter. It's

the only award that I keep in my study. I received another Oscar, an honorary one, in 1996, and I gave it in return to my wife Anne, who is French.

Can you pick a favorite from all your films and the parts you've played?

Lonely Are the Brave [dir. David Miller, 1962] is my favorite movie, with my favorite anti-hero. Gena Rowlands played my wife, and Walter Matthau was the sheriff. The story of a cowboy thrown into jail for wanting to help his friend. The theme of the individual crushed by society has always fascinated me. The screenplay was by my friend Dalton Trumbo.

We should mention that Dalton Trumbo had been blacklisted, and by giving him an official credit for his screenplay for *Spartacus* you became the first to signal an end to the Hollywood witch hunt.
It's hard to imagine now, but under that persecution we lived through a terrible time. Dalton had been sent to prison. The supreme irony was that he'd won an Oscar in 1956 for *The Brave One* [dir. Irving Rapper], under a pseudonym. It was time to put an end to that absurdity.

You have always tackled sensitive subjects.
That's why I love the colonel in *Paths of Glory*, who was shocking at the time, because we'd dared to make an anti-war movie. I also have a soft spot for *Spartacus*, a particularly interesting part because in an epic movie it was difficult to make the hero human. Epic movies are successful when they manage to paint an intimate portrait of a character.

You have said: "Virtue is not photogenic."
I've enjoyed playing hard-boiled, tough characters, even bad ones, but that made me appreciate even more playing a good man in *Lonely are the Brave*. A kind man, but a complex one. That's rare. I love the realism of that movie, which was way ahead of its time. It's become a cult movie. And then there were movies like *20,000 Leagues Under the Sea* [1954], and *The Vikings* [1958], both directed by Richard Fleischer. Less "serious," but honest.

Who are your favorite directors?
Impossible to choose, as I've worked with Hawks, Mankiewicz, Wilder, Minnelli, and Kazan. In the two projects we worked on together, I greatly valued the richness of Minnelli's vision, which for me was like that of a painter. The film I made with Kazan was *The Arrangement* [1969, with Faye Dunaway], a movie about adultery.

What was your first impression of Hollywood?
I'd come from Broadway and knew nothing about cinema. I'd made

the journey specially, because I'd been offered a movie with Barbara Stanwyck—the part that Lauren Bacall had got for me in *The Strange Love of Martha Ivers*—and I thought the part was automatically mine. But when I got there I was told it had been given to Van Heflin, and that in fact they wanted me for the supporting role of Barbara Stanwyck's weak, alcoholic husband, and not only that, I'd have to do a screen test! I already had something of a reputation on Broadway, so I was a little put out. I did the screen test in front of the director, Lewis Milestone, who handed me six or seven pages of the screenplay and told me that first of all we were going to rehearse it. When we'd done this, I asked him when we were going to film. He said, "Go home. It's in the can!" The cameras had actually been filming without my knowing it. Monty Clift and Richard Widmark also auditioned for the part, but I got it! I've always thought it was very generous of Lewis Milestone to give me a break like that.

Your image is one of strong-jawed invincibility. Where do your vulnerabilities lie? Do you suffer from stage fright?
Ah, the dreaded stage fright! [*Laughs.*] I get it on stage mostly, but never so badly that I can't deal with it.

With Faye Dunaway in *The Arrangement*, dir. Elia Kazan, 1969.

Michael Douglas won the Oscar for Best Producer for *One Flew Over the Cuckoo's Nest* [1975], but originally you were supposed to produce it. At first, I didn't encourage Michael in his vocation as an actor, because I know only too well how hard it can be. I'm incredibly proud of his career, but cinema can be tragically frustrating. I'd bought the film rights of the book. Initially I adapted it as a stage play, and played it during a six-month run in New York, then for ten years I tried unsuccessfully to get a movie off the ground. A low-budget movie, what's more. Michael was already quite well known from *The Streets of San Francisco*, and he suggested that he should have a go at raising the money. He did it, but then they decided I was too old for the part. I so wanted to play McMurphy on screen! As it turned out, Jack Nicholson was not only excellent in the part, but he also got an Oscar for it! Everyone got an Oscar. I was at once very happy for Michael and very hurt. It was the biggest frustration of my career. But I'm one of the exceptionally lucky ones. When you can't imagine doing anything else except acting, and millions of people give you encouragement and allow your movies to change their views, it's an overwhelming feeling. It goes way beyond the vanity of being a "star." You've made a mark. Doing good work has always been my ambition.

In *Lust for Life*, dir. Vincente Minnelli, 1956.

Interview by Juliette Michaud at Kirk Douglas's home, summer 1999.

That's
Entertainment

Judy Garland, Gene Kelly, Cyd Charisse, Fred Astaire. The gods of musicals encountered each other on a daily basis on the main MGM lot, often covered in bruises from endless rehearsals to perfect a dance routine, complex tap numbers springing as if by magic from a click of their fingers.

From the choreographed routines of Busby Berkeley to the flamboyant fantasies of Vincente Minnelli, from the contemporary zest of Stanley Donen to that of *West Side Story* (1961), via all those happy tunes sung by angels, musicals—born fully and exuberantly formed with the talkies—came to symbolize a Hollywood that had even Garbo and Brando dancing. That's entertainment!

Top Hat, dir. Mark Sandrich, 1935. Ginger Rogers and Fred Astaire.

Heaven, I'm in Heaven

An image of perfect happiness? How about Ginger Rogers and Fred Astaire gliding in harmony through the mirrored sets of *Top Hat* (1935) or *Swing Time* (1936)? Unless perfect bliss was Fred Astaire and Cyd Charisse in *The Band Wagon* (1953), both dressed in spotless white and drifting into a dreamy love duet? Or, if happiness is a synonym for pleasure, perhaps it lay in the legendary legs of Cyd Charisse, the longest and most desirable on the silver screen?

The golden age of musical comedy was split between two eras, the 1930s, and the 1940s and 1950s. These three glorious decades of musicals offer such a display of fireworks that the selection of any film lover can only be highly personal. There's Cyd Charisse in green in *Singin' in the Rain* (1952) and in yellow in *Brigadoon* (1954); there's Fred Astaire singing "Cheek to Cheek," the jewel of the Irving Berlin songbook, or doing his ceiling dance in *Royal Wedding* (1951). There's Judy Garland hurling the furniture, among other things, at Gene Kelly's head in *The Pirate* (1948); Ann Miller, the brunette who could tap "500 times a minute" to "Shakin' the Blues Away"; Louis Armstrong, Frank Sinatra, and Bing Crosby in *High Society* (1956), and music by Cole Porter so *Anything Goes* (1956). There's Marilyn Monroe as a gold digger or a Lolita whose heart belonged to Daddy; there are the aquatic ballets of Esther Williams, and the honeyed voices of Nat King Cole and Doris Day. And there were Gene Kelly, again, and Fred Astaire, still, brought together in a *Ziegfeld Follies* (1945) sketch. And—how can we not beg for an encore?—there's Judy Garland back from over the rainbow and singing the sublime "The Man That Got Away" in a nightclub at dawn, thinking that she is alone with the band, in *A Star Is Born* (1954).

The America of jazz and tap, ragtime and boogie-woogie: what should we make of the fact that the musical genre so dear to Hollywood was imported from the East Coast and Broadway? Fred Astaire, Mickey Rooney, James Cagney, Judy Garland, Vincente Minnelli—that whole clutch of extraordinary talents came from the school of vaudeville, the American music hall that performed in every key, from traveling theater to honky-tonk and from Harlem minstrels to the clowns of burlesque.

That the first talkie should be a musical seemed to go without saying in the land of swing: it was time for the movies to turn up the volume, and for all those effervescent talents to join together and banish the blues of a nation with its heart in its boots. If the stars being able to talk was good, the stars being able to sing was even better. Had the ex-chorus girl Marlene Dietrich not hit the big time by importing her Berlin cabaret? Had the Americans not gone wild for Maurice Chevalier? Yet the genre very nearly died as soon as it was born. Was it through an excess of enthusiasm? *The Jazz Singer* (1927) lit the fuse for an explosion of adaptations of Broadway hits that were lavish but derivative, mining the possibilities of Technicolor to lure in their audiences. So MGM produced *The Hollywood Revue of 1929*, Warner Bros. counter-attacked with *The Show of Shows* (1929). Films that are sadly forgotten today. Because you should see them, all the MGM stars of the day,

42nd Street, dir. Lloyd Bacon, 1933. George E. Stone.

Joan Crawford, Buster Keaton, Laurel and Hardy: all standing in raincoats in front of a rainbow and "Singin' in the Rain," the song that was already a hit.

But the market was flooded, and as early as 1930 the public was begging for mercy. Movie theaters were obliged to put up notices in their foyers promising, "This is not a musical." It was Busby Berkeley, with the spectacular musical numbers of *42nd Street* (1933) and the *Gold Diggers* series, who reconciled a public avid for escapism with the musical. Berkeley, born cinema director and choreographer, is supposed to have drawn his inspiration from the military precision he had observed as a soldier in World War I. His immediately recognizable style created an entirely new rhythm: the geometry of bodies and limbs moving in unison like dominoes to create hallucinogenic kaleidoscopes of movement; serried ranks of dancers filing past in one direction or another according to the angle of the shot; swarms of show girls in glamorous costumes; and a host of faces in close-up that fed the dreams of fame of millions of young girls. Thumbing his nose in stylish fashion at the censorship at the heart of the Great Depression. Yet even if the camera was liberated and the sets delirious, the action still took place within a rigid framework. Wildly innovative though he was, Busby Berkeley did not revolutionize musicals. It was Fred Astaire who was to take care of that.

The Fred Astaire Revolution

Like most of the masters of musicals, Fred Astaire came from music hall. From a well-to-do back-ground, he was dancing from the age of four, and for twenty-five years performed in a double act with his sister Adele. When she got married and left the country, he ended up in Hollywood. According to Hollywood legend, confirmed by Astaire himself, his screen test report read: "Can't act. Slightly bald. Also dances." This was enough for him to flex his creative muscles, losing no time in transforming the way in which musicals were filmed.

From his first steps, in *Dancing Lady* (1933), he insisted on being filmed full-length and in contin-uous sequences, so as not to interrupt the fluid and elegant movement. Suddenly, the whole of life was choreographed. Astaire's solo success was short-lived: in his second film, *Flying Down to Rio* (1933), a virtual unknown called Ginger Rogers was foisted on him. The magic was instant. Their partnership stole the limelight from the Mexican bombshell Dolores del Rio and soared away on the wings of dance. "He gives her class and she gives him sex appeal," observed Katharine Hepburn wickedly. In life, the most celebrated couple in cinema history got on each other's nerves and often said terrible things to each other through clenched teeth as they danced, smiling brightly for the camera. On screen, in the eleven films they made together, as they exchange tap sequences, the virtuoso fusion of the impetuous Ginger Rogers and the ironic Fred Astaire leaves the viewer lost for words. Ginger, skirts whirling, eyes and smile sparkling, sometimes sulky but always with her heart on her sleeve, the perfect partner. Fred, always in a tuxedo, an unlikely seducer, relaxation personi-fied, inasmuch as such an astonishing dancer can be human. When *Swing Time* came out in Europe in 1936, the American theatre critic Thornton Wilder wrote: "If you are in Austria or France go to see a Ginger Rogers – Fred Astaire movie. Watch the audience. Spellbound at something terribly uneuropean—all that technical effortless precision; all that radiant youth bursting with sex but not sex-hunting, sex-collecting; and all that allusion to money, but money as fun, the American love of conspicuous waste, not money-to-sit-on, not money-to-frighten-with. And finally, when the pair really leap into one of those radiant waltzes the Europeans know in their bones that their day is over."[1]

Dancing Lady, dir. Robert Z. Leonard, 1933. Joan Crawford and Fred Astaire during filming.

---

1. Robert Gottlieb, "Man of Letters: The Case of Thornton Wilder," *The New Yorker*, January 7, 2013.

While Europe and the rest of the world allowed itself to be dazzled by the "fun" of the American lifestyle in general and the genially abstract charm of Fred Astaire in particular, in Hollywood, musicals were about to open the dancing. Tap movies became a genre in their own right. The charming Ruby Keeler passed the baton to the prodigious Eleanor Powell, who in 1940 gave Fred Astaire a run for his money in their celebrated number "Begin the Beguine."

Many comedies, like those of the Marx Brothers, also had regular recourse to skills learned on Broadway. Closer examination reveals, moreover, that all the great Hollywood stars found themselves at one time or another in a musical, or at least singing the occasional ditty. And the singers were all taken up by the big screen. It was all in the genes. Fox, meanwhile, had found a different type of goose that laid a golden egg, or rather an adorable gosling, in the form of Shirley Temple. The little singing and dancing princess was to be the studio's muse until the end of World War II.

But let us turn the spotlight on Metro-Goldwyn-Mayer, which had lost its best men. The young mogul Irving Thalberg, the producer of musicals such as *The Great Ziegfeld* (1936), had died prematurely; David O. Selznick had become an independent producer. So the big boss of MGM, Louis B. Mayer, always inclined to surround himself with the best, engaged a new creator of magic, Arthur Freed. Universally capable and a lyricist, Freed—real name Arthur Grossman—persuaded Mayer to entrust him with a new production department at the heart of the studio, an independent unit devoted exclusively to musicals, and cut his teeth on an atypical project, *The Wizard of Oz* (1939, see chapter 5). In its wake, he produced some ten films, one after another, for young audiences, with MGM's pair of teen prodigies, the impish Mickey Rooney (another child star), who sang and danced on screen for the first time, and Judy Garland, poised to become a superstar. Arthur Freed also liked to surround himself with the crème de la crème, and lost no time in putting a team together: he poached Fred

Astaire and his choreographer Hermes Pan, imported the dancer-choreographer duo of Gene Kelly and Stanley Donen from Broadway, made sure MGM put Frank Sinatra under contract, enticed the swimming star Esther Williams, and bribed a certain Tula Ellice Finklea about whom he'd heard a good deal, although he preferred her married name, Cyd Charisse. He also brought in one Vincente Minnelli, whose impressive work and universal talents at New York's Radio City Hall he had long admired. Minnelli was put to the test with a modest budget on *Cabin in the Sky* (1943), a black-and-white fable in the vein of *Stormy Weather* (1943), with Lena Horne and a galaxy of extraordinary musicians including Duke Ellington. The director took advantage of this exercise in style to develop his own: elegant, refined, and sophisticated.

Meet Me in St. Louis (1944), Judy Garland's first film under the official direction of Minnelli, was the first Technicolor production by the Freed unit. And what colors! It was also the first time that a musical had an original screenplay. And that the musical numbers and their whirling staging formed an integral part of the storyline, rather than the narrative being reduced to an excuse for the songs.

I'm Singing in the Rain

An exuberant pirate in the colorful world of the Caribbean; an excited marine on shore leave in Manhattan. On the one hand, Vincente Minnelli's frenetically paced *The Pirate*, with music by Cole Porter.

Babes in Arms, dir. Busby Berkeley, 1939. Mickey Rooney and Judy Garland.

The Band Wagon, dir. Vincente Minnelli, 1953. Fred Astaire and Cyd Charisse.

On the other, the effervescent *On the Town* (1949), directed by Stanley Donen and Gene Kelly, with a score by Leonard Bernstein. Two films in which the true talents of Gene Kelly, his joie de vivre and energy, at once modern and romantic, shone at last, symbolizing the winds of optimism and freedom that were sweeping postwar America. It was Vincente Minnelli, less and less "factory foreman" and more and more cinema artist of genius, who first revealed the athletic qualities, comic timing, and virile persona of the reluctant MGM star (who had wanted to be a choreographer).

The Pirate, too ahead of its time, was a flop that was to cost Louis B. Mayer dear. But Gene Kelly's energy had shown Arthur Freed that he was ready to direct and perform in *On the Town*. The story of three sailors on leave, which brought together for the third and last time Gene Kelly and his infectious grin and Frank Sinatra with his velvet voice (they had made a memorable pair in *Anchors Aweigh* [1945], in which Kelly danced with Jerry the mouse). Kelly insisted that his assistant Stanley Donen should be credited as co-director. The first "realist" musical shot on location in the streets of New York, with choreography filling the screen, *On the Town* was an immediate triumph.

Gene Kelly would describe his style of dancing as "hybrid." It contained both elements of his tough Pittsburgh background and his passion for the ballet, his lessons in tap from a famous Afro-American tap dancer in New York, and those he had from Rita Hayworth's uncle, Angel Cansino. And we have Kelly's mother to thank for making him and his brothers go to ballet lessons. Because,

men dance, too. Gene Kelly was forever having to prove it by making his tap technique more athletic, so as to distinguish himself from Fred Astaire. "I used to envy his cool, aristocratic style, so intimate and contained, but I was wise enough to know it wasn't for me. Fred wears top hat, white tie and tails to the manner born—I put them on and look like a truck driver."[2] For Kelly, dance was democratic, T-shirt, muscled torso, and moccasins, more Actors Studio than dandy.

But the disciple would remain faithful to the master. It was Gene Kelly who brought Fred Astaire out of early retirement in 1947, in order to take his place in *Easter Parade* (1948) with Judy Garland—which Charles Walters was appointed to direct in place of Vincente Minnelli, a last-minute decision by the studio prompted by fears of marital friction between the Minnelli spouses. The marriage of Judy Garland, MGM's enfant terrible, to a director who found the time to make two or three masterpieces (such as *The Bad and the Beautiful* [1952]) between musicals, was soon to end in divorce, despite the birth of the future leading lady of *Cabaret* (1972) and *New York, New York* (1977), Liza Minnelli.

The Show Must Go On

And it was the wings of this world of relentless work to improve on perfection, of the demands of art in the face of "real" life and changing times, that featured in the unassailable *Singin' in the Rain* and *The Band Wagon*, produced in quick succession by Freed and both written by the famous screenwriting duo Betty Comden and Adolph Green. The first, which saw the sparkling reunion of Gene Kelly and Stanley Donen, was a direct commission by Arthur Freed as a vehicle for the famous song "Singin' in the Rain" that he had written in the 1920s. The inspired idea was to situate the film in the difficult transition from the silent era to the talkies, when in fact its real subject was the arrival of television in America. This was 1952, Americans were discovering the joys of this new medium, and the film industry was upping the stakes with CinemaScope, stereo sound, and 3D in order to win audiences back. *Singin' in the Rain*, with its producer who declares "we don't want to be left out of it," poked gleeful fun at this desperate showing off in order to keep up with the times. The contemporary and exquisitely precise rhythms of Gene Kelly and Stanley Donen; the petulant comic counterpoint between Debbie Reynolds, the delightful girl next door, and Donald O'Connor; the sex appeal of Cyd Charisse and delicious songs that were to become legendary were to do the rest. In the key scene of *Singin' in the Rain*, of disconcerting simplicity, Gene Kelly makes us believe that we too can splash through the puddles and be happy again.

It was the story of their own relationship that Comden and Green wrote in *The Band Wagon*, but this time viewed through Minnelli's nostalgic lens. To renew its inspiration, art must honor the past. And what finer lesson in humility than Fred Astaire accepting, at the age of fifty-four, the part of a faded star brought back to save an artistic fiasco? A Fred Astaire who spanned the two golden ages of musicals with his legendary grace, whom Stanley Donen had the wonderful idea of pairing with Audrey Hepburn in *Funny Face* (1957): Hollywood's two most graceful creatures dancing in unison.

FACING PAGE: *Million Dollar Mermaid*, dir. Mervyn LeRoy, 1952. Esther Williams.
ABOVE: *Singin' in the Rain*, dirs. Stanley Donen and Gene Kelly, 1952. Gene Kelly and Cyd Charisse.

2. Tony Thomas, *The Films of Gene Kelly: Song and Dance Man* (New York: Citadel Press, 1976), 10.

Singin' in the Rain, dirs. Stanley Donen and Gene Kelly, 1952. Cyd Charisse (above) and Gene Kelly (above and facing page).

Meanwhile, Gene Kelly enjoyed a huge success with *An American in Paris* (1951), which he co-directed with Vincente Minnelli. The score was by Gershwin, and the French actress Leslie Caron was a revelation in her first film role. A classic garlanded with awards, often considered the finest of all musicals. Yet Minnelli did not have the director of photography he wanted, except for the last seventeen minutes in which we are transported, in a feast for the senses, into the world of nineteenth-century French painting.

Minnelli's musical comedies were distinguished by their celebration scenes, chic or baroque parties in which he gave full rein to his perfectionist love of fashion. Did he not start out as a window dresser for Marshall Field's department store in Chicago? The magic of the costumes and the beauty of the characters were also part of the sequined magic of musicals. In Minnelli's films, moreover, there is always a point at which the plot gives way for a pure dream sequence, as though the protagonists needed to catch their breath before returning to life's cynicism and reality.

The Freed unit continued to dominate the first half of the decade, going as far as to reappropriate Busby Berkeley, who was making films featuring the Brazilian Carmen Miranda or the synchronized swimming of Esther Williams.

Elsewhere, the genre leaned on its stars. Bob Hope and Bing Crosby had started up their entertaining *Road to . . .* musical comedies with renewed vigor; Dean Martin let loose with Jerry Lewis; and the GIs who had taken down their pinups of Rita Hayworth and Betty Grable now ogled the new sex bomb, Marilyn Monroe, whose voice and looks predestined her for Howard Hawks' excellent

Funny Face, dir. Stanley Donen, 1957. Fred Astaire and Audrey Hepburn.

ABOVE: *Guys and Dolls*,
dir. Joseph L. Mankiewicz, 1955.
Marlon Brando.

RIGHT: *Ziegfeld Follies*, dir. Vincente Minnelli,
1945. Fred Astaire and Gene Kelly.

Gentlemen Prefer Blondes (1953). Glamour had reached its pinnacle. For some stars, musicals were also a way of getting away from typecasting. James Cagney, another highly talented actor born into the business, recalled his roots in the patriotic *Yankee Doodle Dandy* (1942), in which he played the Broadway pioneer George M. Cohan with brio. Yet sometimes audiences did not follow where the stars led. George Cukor's *Two-Faced Woman* (1941), with a radiant Greta Garbo dancing "la chica choca," was to be the divine Swede's swansong.

By the mid-1950s, the studio system was in decline. It was for lack of money that *Brigadoon* was not shot on location in the Scottish mists. Sensing the end was looming, MGM closed ranks, and refused to loan Gene Kelly to Joseph L. Mankiewicz for *Guys and Dolls* (1955). Fox got their own back by signing the new box office star Marlon Brando, who sang (it's his own voice we hear) and danced for the first time opposite Frank Sinatra. This major coup was a hit with the public. MGM was no longer number one. MGM let go of stars who were too expensive, such as Judy Garland. George Cukor, whose elegance transcended musical comedy, glorified her in the second adaptation of *A Star is Born*: the rise of one artist, the death of another. Judy Garland was to die aged forty-seven, victim of a system that owed her everything.

Something's Coming . . . Maybe Tonight . . .

In 1961, when the age of musicals seemed to be over, the veteran choreographer Jerome Robbins and the director Robert Wise revealed the new face of Hollywood in *West Side Story*. Ten Oscars, including Best Supporting Actor for George Chakiris, took revenge on behalf of all victims of racism and of the hypocrisy of an industry in which black artists, notably, were for so many years relegated to secondary roles. Or to no roles at all. Lena Horne, the first great "Minnelli creation," and the unforgettable *Carmen Jones* (1954) as played by Dorothy Dandridge—to mention but two—never had the careers they deserved. Although *West Side Story* broke with the tradition of the "happy ending" and was rooted in reality, this contemporary version of *Romeo and Juliet* did not revolutionize the genre.

Running against the tide, musicals clung more than ever to Broadway hits, to epics, and to family entertainment. George Cukor and Cecil Beaton transformed *My Fair Lady* (1964) into a glittering vehicle for Audrey Hepburn, but the desire to make a blockbuster is palpable. Which did not stop Julie Andrews's golden voice from sparkling in *The Sound of Music* (1965) and *Mary Poppins* (1964). Meanwhile Elvis Presley's fine films—*King Creole* (1958), *Jailhouse Rock* (1957), and *Meet Me in Las Vegas* (1956)—were directed by Freed unit veterans such as Norman Taurog and George Sidney. Gene Kelly was entrusted with the making of *Hello, Dolly!* (1969) with the new star Barbra Streisand—which sadly met a lukewarm reception. *It's Always Fair Weather* (1955), a sort of nostalgic sequel to *On the Town*, signaled the end of his friendly professional relationship with Stanley Donen, who would go on to shine in a solo career. It was a pleasure to see Kelly playing a cameo role in *Let's Make Love* (1960) with Yves Montand and Marilyn Monroe, and—in a new wave tribute to the past—in *Les Demoiselles de Rochefort* (1967).

It was Kelly once again who managed to entice his old friend Fred Astaire out of retirement in the 1970s for *That's Entertainment!* Surprisingly, this montage of clips was such a success that it gave rise to two sequels. All of Arthur Freed's players were brought back together to evoke an era when "there was too much control, but at the same time we were able to work under the best conditions until we reached perfection. The true luxury at MGM, was to give us time."[3]

An American in Paris, dir. Vincente Minnelli, 1951. Leslie Caron and Gene Kelly.

---

3. Jane Powell in *That's Entertainment*, dir. Jack Haley Jr., MGM, 1974.

The clips speak for themselves. Bravura sequences from the *Broadway Melody* series of films which shifted into emerald-green mode on Cyd Charisse's legs. A tribute to film noir with "Girl Hunt," with Cyd Charisse again, by turns brunette and blonde, magnetic and raw. Ava Gardner, in the next dressing room, had better watch out! An excited public discovered or rediscovered all the hit songs: "Make 'Em Laugh," "Singin' in the Rain," "I Got Rhythm," "The Heather on the Hill," "Love is Here to Stay," not forgetting the anthem of musicals, "That's Entertainment!"—written in half an hour by Dietz and Schwartz for *The Band Wagon*: "The world is a stage, / The stage is a world of entertainment!"

ABOVE: *Carmen Jones*, dir. Otto Preminger, 1954. Dorothy Dandridge.
FACING PAGE: *Gentlemen Prefer Blondes*, dir. Howard Hawks, 1953. Jane Russell and Marilyn Monroe.

ABOVE AND FACING PAGE: *West Side Story*, dirs. Jerome Robbins and Robert Wise, 1961.
With George Chakiris and Russ Tamblyn (above), and Natalie Wood (facing page).

Julie Andrews

The studio publicist had warned that she was feeling a bit tired, having just flown in from Gstaad a few days earlier. More importantly she wanted to rest her voice, after back to back interviews to promote her film, *Tooth Fairy* (2010), for 20th Century Fox. But there she was, looking prim in a pearl gray outfit and matching scarf, regally installed in the corner of a plush hotel sofa. At seventy-five, Julie Andrews still has an English-rose complexion. Smiling graciously, she extends a hand with the elegance of the consummate professional.

Trained in vaudeville from the age of seven in her native England, she quickly became a household name known for her unique vocal range. Broadway came calling in 1954 and two years later she became a sensation in *My Fair Lady*. Audrey Hepburn was chosen for the screen version, which must have been a blow. But in 1963, Walt Disney handpicked her to be *Mary Poppins* for which she earned the Best Actress Oscar the following year. A movie star was born. Her Hollywood career flourished, featuring iconic performances in *The Sound of Music* (1965), and *10* (1979) and *Victor Victoria* (1982), two of the seven films she made with Blake Edwards, whom she married in 1969. In 1997, an operation on her vocal cords forced her to give up singing, but, thanks to the success of *The Princess Diaries* (2001) and the *Shrek* films, she has been discovered by a new generation.

She has also become a successful children's book author in collaboration with her eldest daughter. Between sips of tea, she embarks down memory lane with her clipped accent and unmistakable voice.

What does the word Hollywood mean to you now?

Home. Because I live here. It represents a place that gave me phenomenal opportunities. And a certain kind of magic.

Do you remember the first time you visited?

I flew in to make a television special with Bing Crosby [in November 1955], which was not successful. It was just before I went to Broadway for *My Fair Lady*. I was very lonely. I felt it was a vast place. I didn't know where the shops or the grocery store were. I didn't know anything. I just landed and was taken to the hotel, but I then met with many, many kind people connected with the television special, and very quickly made friends. I was actually busy finding who I was, what I was doing, and I had no knowledge of the place. This was long before I really had the experience of being a Broadway star or when I came back to Hollywood for *Mary Poppins* in 1963. That was really what I would consider the first time I understood Hollywood.

Did you enjoy it more the second time?

Very much. I was invited by Walt Disney. He spoiled me.

In what way?

Oh my God, in every way. He came to see me on Broadway in *Camelot* and said, "Would you like to come to Los Angeles to see what I am doing with *Mary Poppins*?" And I said, "I am having a baby, I'm afraid." And he said, "That's all right, we'll wait." I didn't realize how long it took to produce a movie. I was invited to the studio to meet everybody, to listen to the songs, to see the drawings for the movie. He took me to the races. He took me to Disneyland. I went to his home. He was a kind gentleman. I think Disney made everything possible, I have to say. He really began my career in movies.

Did you sign a contract right away?

No, not then and there. But I knew from the quality of the songs and the story that he showed me that it was something I could do. I was excited about it. The songs had a kind of vaudeville quality, which I recognize because I was raised in vaudeville as a child so I thought: "I think I could bring something to this movie." And when Walt Disney asked you to do something—My God, how lucky can you be? And then, when I came back to do the movie, he made everything available to me. The house to live in, the furniture to make it pretty, a car to go to the studios, everything to make me feel at home.

Where was the house?

In the [San Fernando] valley, in Toluca Lake, near the Disney studios.

Once you started production, was Walt Disney very controlling?

He was the head of the studio, not the director. He controlled the special effects. It was his team that made all the special effects, the bird on my hand when I sing "A Spoonful of Sugar," etc. He personally developed those with his team. I was here with my first husband [Tony Walton], who designed all the costumes and some of the sets for the movie. So it was a very safe time. Disney made me feel very safe. He put me in the hands of very nice people with whom I am still friends.

Portrait, 1965.

their money back. So it was a very interesting time.

What stars impressed you when you arrived at the very end of Hollywood's golden age?

I didn't socialize that much, mainly with people I met behind the scenes on the movies. But I met quite a lot of people. Like Shirley MacLaine who was on the Fox lot making *Irma La Douce* [1963] at the same time. I met Debbie Reynolds who was doing something I don't remember, maybe *The Unsinkable Molly Brown* [1964].

How was your first meeting with Alfred Hitchcock for *Torn Curtain* [1966], his fiftieth film?

I think I went to meet him on the Universal Studios lot. He had his own bungalow there, his own office.

Did he tell you why he chose you? Apparently you replaced Eva Marie Saint, who had to drop out of the project.

I really don't know. If you are right, that is possible.

After *Mary Poppins*, you went on almost immediately to do *The Americanization of Emily* [1964], directed by Arthur Hiller? Did you screen-test for it?

Yes, I did. I did one scene for them in England. It was a terrible test. But they seemed to think it was good enough. And I am very proud of being in that movie. It is a very good movie with a phenomenal screenplay by Paddy

Chayefsky. It says so much about the stupidity of war.

Your third Hollywood movie, *The Sound of Music*, was partly shot on the 20th Century Fox lot in 1964.

They had just done *Cleopatra* [1963], which was not a big success. It used up all their money, and the lot was very quiet and not much was going on. And we made *The Sound of Music* and I think it made them all

Did he tell you that he had seen you in *Mary Poppins* or *The Americanization of Emily*?

No, we just met. So I guess I was the new girl in town. And blonde. [*Laughs.*] Maybe that's what he liked!

Were you impressed?

Are you kidding? Yes, and he was very kind to me. He had a reputation for not caring very much, but I didn't find that.

He wanted to teach me. One day he was talking about a certain kind of lens, a close-up, and his cameraman suggested one lens and he said, "Not on a woman. My God, not on a woman!" He knew his camera very well. I said, "You know, Hitch, I don't know very much about lenses or how they work." He said, "Come with me," and he took me in his trailer on the studio set and he spend maybe forty-five minutes, one hour with me drawing and saying, "Never let a cameraman use this size, do a close-up with this size, or your nose will grow long. This is what you need here and this is what you need there." It was a phenomenal education. It was the beginning of my learning about the technical side of moviemaking. And then he would say, "Come here, I want you to look through the camera. I made a Mondrian." And I knew the painter, and he had. He made such a beautiful set. Paul Newman here, me here, and beautiful red, black, and white behind us. He had made a Mondrian. And he was so happy with himself. He did not care much about the script. There was a day when Paul and I said, "This scene is difficult." We felt it didn't say what it should say and he said to us, "Say what you wish to say." And I was very surprised but he would say, "I want you to sit here in the airplane and as the door opens I want you to turn." And I said, "What do I see?" He said, "It doesn't matter. I just want you to turn." I said okay and just turned. He knew exactly what he wanted. If it wasn't necessary to fill my head with motivations, he didn't. He let me find the character. I would have liked him to have done more explaining because in those days I didn't know very much and I wasn't very good at finding it for myself but he was helpful enough really. And when I first saw the movie, I wasn't pleased with myself. I didn't think I did as good as a job as I could have. I felt I could have given more.

With Paul Newman in *Torn Curtain*, dir. Alfred Hitchcock, 1966.

In *The Sound of Music*, dir. Robert Wise, 1965.

Paul Newman had problems with Hitchcock, who apparently wanted him to play his character differently. Did you feel the tension between them?

No, I didn't. But we were friends instantly, and he was very, very nice to me. And he was much more experienced than I was.

What was the very first shot?

I think it was the love scene at the beginning under all the bed covers. I think that was the first one. He was very excited about it because he said, "I want it to be so cold outside and I want it to be so warm inside."

Did you stay in touch with Hitchcock afterward?

Yes. We exchanged Christmas cards. He sent me wine, which he was a great connoisseur of. I might have gone once to his house in Bel Air, where I met his wife and daughter. You have to remember I was very young and all of Hollywood was like an assault on my senses. So much was happening in my life at that time.

After that, you did many films back to back.

Because I was lucky to be successful. I am the lucky lady who was asked to be in a Hitchcock movie. The lucky woman who was asked to be in *The Sound of Music.* I still did not know what I was doing. I never had a career plan.

Hollywood was going through major changes at the time. Were you aware of it?

I did feel the studios changing around the time I made *Star!* [a 1968 biopic on Broadway legend Gertrude Lawrence, one of Noel Coward's favorite actresses], which was an expensive movie in those days. Suddenly big expensive movies were out and low-budget independent movies like *Easy Rider* [1969] were in. It was an interesting change. The movie was difficult for me because [the character] wasn't immediately lovable. And it was exhausting! Seventeen musical numbers, I think. I had something like eighty-nine costumes to be fitted, not just once but many times. Wigs, nails, makeup. For different ages, decades. It was very hard, and I was very tired after that movie. What I enjoyed the most was working with Michael Kidd, the choreographer. He and his wife became lifelong friends, perhaps my best friends here in Hollywood.

Do you remember having turned down some important roles?

I remember feeling that I was not right for *Hawaii* [1966]. And my agent at the time said, "No, this would be a very good movie for you to do. It's going to be a very big movie and prestigious, and I think it would be smart to take that." And I listened and I am very glad I did, because I learnt a lot from George Roy Hill. He was so very talented. And to be able to observe how he made movies, his passion for the Hawaiians, which he really felt strongly. He wanted to make that movie from the Hawaiian point of view. I met James Michener, the author. I worked with Max von Sydow, which was a joy. The filming was epic and went on for months. We had a measles epidemic, floods, hurricanes, fire. But what an unforgettable experience.

And a year later you worked with George again on the musical *Thoroughly Modern Millie* [1967].

How different. It was just such a silly, sweet movie. An adorable romp. Millie was so innocent and so green and so full of convictions and so brave. She was adorable to play. I loved it.

Can we talk about *Darling Lili* [1970]?

Blake Edwards called to say he would very much like to speak with me regarding a movie. He said it will just take fifteen minutes of my time and may he come to my house. I did not want him to come to my house, but he did! I said, "Could we meet at the Polo Lounge?" "No, no, no, I won't be that long." By the end of the evening, I wanted him to stay in my life, that's for sure. I wished he could stay for supper, he could not but we had our first date after that and the rest is history.

Interview by Jean-Paul Chaillet at the Casa del Mar Hotel, Santa Monica, Suite 637, January 9, 2010.

In *Star!*, dir. Robert Wise, 1968.

The
Legend
of the
Wild West

Barely had cinema come into existence than the newly won territories in the West gave their name to the western. *The Great Train Robbery* (1903), *The Squaw Man* (1914): Hollywood was above all cowboys and Indians. From John Ford's landscapes of Monument Valley to the ubiquitous gunfights, from John Wayne's laconic heroism to Gary Cooper's languid beauty, every director and every star would one day or another come face to face with the Wild West. Modest, low-budget movies gave way to flamboyant blockbusters, low instinct gave way to high intellect, and the differences between the good, the bad, and the ugly became increasingly nuanced. Westerns now came in a whole variety of different flavors and tastes, spaghetti above all. But in the Hollywood legend, the western—with or without a sheriff—was law.

The Searchers, dir. John Ford, 1956. John Wayne.

Sensation, Color, Action

Men with golden colts walking into the light. The sun glinting off spurs and polished rifle butts. The sangfroid of cowboys galloping their mounts through water or snow. We are in North America, but in the Far West. Sometimes even in Canada. Or in Mexico. So close to Hollywood, and yet so far.

The western is the finale of *Duel in the Sun* (1946), with Gregory Peck and Jennifer Jones dueling to the death beneath a blazing red and ocher sun, the battle between the flamboyance of producer David O. Selznick and the more down-to-earth approach of director King Vidor. A delight. The western is the wild stampedes of armies of Indians or "palefaces," both ultimately chasing the same goal: the freedom to gallop across the prairies and to hunt their herds of buffalo. The western is the gleaming blond hair of Alan Ladd as *Shane* (dir. George Stevens, 1953), the gunslinger with an unknown past who tries to bring law to the lawless isolated valleys of Wyoming. And it's his handsome pale buckskin costume, as if to distinguish him from the villainous Jack Palance, clad in black down to his gloves.

It all came down to the art of wearing a kerchief or bandana, and the costume designers on westerns—the same gifted few as on the other films of Hollywood's golden age, such as Edith Head and Sheila O'Brien—knew that the way they cut a cowboy jacket or duster coat would launch a perennial fashion. Just as the set designers were conscious of creating a myth by building ranches on a deliberately small scale so as to make the characters appear more impressive. With their convoys of mules and tractors, the production teams that set off to film on location in Arizona or Mexico must have looked like processions of Indian braves.

Rugged Features

The western was rugged, sunburned faces: the good, such as Van Heflin and Van Johnson, and the bad, such as Lee Marvin and Lee Van Cleef. It was swaggering music composed by Hollywood maestros who had returned to form: with music by Max Steiner, Victor Young, or Alfred Newman on the credits, the wagon train could hit the trail. The haunting theme of *High Noon* (1952) composed by Dimitri Tiomkin and the powerful theme of *The Magnificent Seven* (1960) by Elmer Bernstein. In cult westerns it was the use of singers: Ricky Nelson and Dean Martin in *Rio Bravo* (1959); the title song of *Johnny Guitar* (1954), sung by Peggy Lee herself in the film; and the eponymous theme song of *River of No Return* (1954), sung by Marilyn Monroe into the charmed ear of Robert Mitchum.

Duel in the Sun, dir. King Vidor, 1946. Gregory Peck.

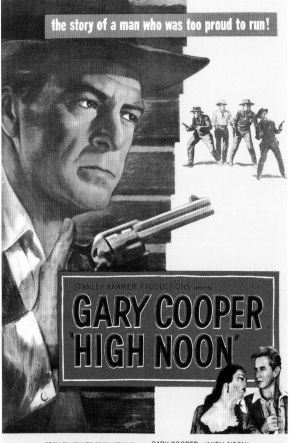

The western was Burt Lancaster as an Apache and James Stewart as a villain, while Marlene Dietrich or Joan Crawford ran the saloon. For in this male world where you had to be quick on the draw, there were many actresses who held their own. Dietrich brought her glamour to *Destry Rides Again* (dir. George Marshall, 1939). Barbara Stanwyck, in *The Furies* (dir. Anthony Mann, 1950), seemed born for the genre. Jean Arthur, who had started her cinema career in B-movie Westerns, ended it as a married homesteader, drawn to Alan Ladd's title character in *Shane*. And Shelley Winters became the embodiment of the Western's saloon girl with a heart of gold in *Winchester '73* (dir. Anthony Mann, 1950). Not forgetting Jane Russell in *The Outlaw* (1943): co-directing with Howard Hawks, Howard Hughes made the movie as a vehicle for his protégée of the moment, whose braless image on the poster caused a scandal.

ABOVE AND LEFT: Poster and still from *High Noon*, dir. Fred Zinnemann, 1952. Gary Cooper.
FACING PAGE: *Gunfight at the O.K. Corral*, dir. John Sturges, 1957. Kirk Douglas, Burt Lancaster, John Ireland, and DeForest Kelley.

Looking for an Angle

Once audiences had got over the shock of being fired on by an outlaw holding up a train, and despite the many westerns made by pioneers of cinema such as Cecil B. DeMille, the genre had not yet found its "angle," and Tom Mix was already way out of date. In 1930, Raoul Walsh made a commendable effort, putting John Wayne in the saddle in *The Big Trail*, which lasted an ambitious seventy minutes but proved a flop with the audiences.

It was in 1939 that John Ford revived a dying genre with *Stagecoach*, a magnificent black-and-white epic featuring a group of travelers riding on a stagecoach through Apache territory, and facing their own demons under attacks from Apache arrows. It was Ford's eightieth film, and it was to make him the standard bearer for American cinema. In the role of the Ringo Kid, John Wayne became an international superstar. Between them, these two buddies who had started their careers together were to notch up a total of 290 films together. That is an awful lot of panoramic shots of wide-open prairies and Indian ambushes (as in the sudden Apache attack in *Stagecoach*). American classicism was born.

The style that made John Ford a legend was one of simplicity on every level: stylistic, narrative, physical, verging on the lyrical. John Wayne, restrained to the point of minimalism, was in the same mold: the ideal Ford hero, a lone and courteous outsider. And upright. In the beginning, at least.

The Magnificent Seven, dir. John Sturges, 1960. Charles Bronson, Yul Brynner, Horst Buchholz, James Coburn, Brad Dexter, Steve McQueen, and Robert Vaughn.

A pillar of Hollywood, or rather a monument in himself, Ford was one of the creators of genre cinema. Meaning that he shrank the world to a highly specific universe, by offering audiences characters that were timeless and familiar, by magnifying his actors and the situations in which they found themselves. But he also opened up this imaginative world to new frontiers, new horizons and new legends, by inventing a new way of dreaming.

The Dream of America

In westerns, the dream was always the same: the American dream. And if America can claim a genre that is truly its own, then it must be the western. With its moral codes, parched landscapes, and quest

ABOVE: *Stagecoach*, dir. John Ford, 1939.
RIGHT: *Shane*, dir. George Stevens, 1953.
Jean Arthur, Van Heflin, and Alan Ladd.

for identity, its heroes and renegades, its cattle ranchers and rustlers, its illustrious figures, such as Davy Crockett and Buffalo Bill, and its outlaws, such as Billy the Kid and Jesse James. But also, along the way, its growing doubts about having meted out rough treatment to all the peoples who had preceded the "palefaces," and about having eradicated the Native Americans: now American history met American mythology face to face, for their own showdown.

The Ford Adventure

For John Ford, the adventure began when he left his native Maine to join his brother Francis, who had gone with Gaston Méliès (brother of Georges) to try his luck in Hollywood. The family name was really O'Feeney, but John changed his name to follow the example of his brother, who was already an actor, screenwriter, and director at Universal Studios, where he quickly found small jobs for his brother. In return, John would make his brother the official mascot of all his films.

John Ford's silent westerns included the celebrated *Iron Horse* (1924), which told the story of the conquest of the railroad. In 1939, the same year as *Stagecoach*—the plot of which was inspired by the Maupassant short story "Boule de suif" ("Butterball")—he also directed *Drums Along the Mohawk*, featuring a young and plucky Claudette Colbert. After the war came the immortal classics. First was *My Darling Clementine* (1946), in which Ford worked again with his hero of *The Prisoner of Shark Island* (1936), Henry Fonda, to tell the story of the friendship between Wyatt Earp (Fonda) and Doc Holliday (Victor Mature). Then came his trilogy celebrating the US Cavalry (even if they were always late): *Fort Apache* (1948), *She Wore a Yellow Ribbon* (1949), and *Rio Grande* (1950).

Deeply American and liberal, in other words giving voice to all his country's contradictions, Ford was to deliver westerns that were increasingly somber in tone. In a return to fundamentals, and a calling into question of the benevolence of his compatriots' intentions, he created another milestone of cinema in 1956 with *The Searchers*, an archetypally laconic and lyrical Western that for film lovers is one of the all-time greats. The plot

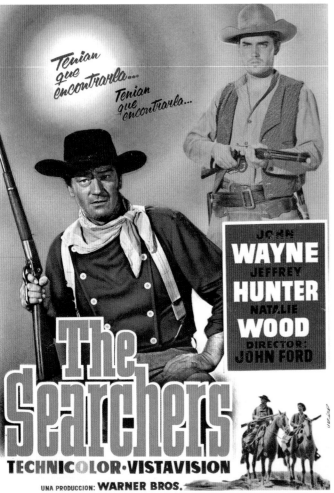

TOP: *My Darling Clementine*, dir. John Ford, 1946. Henry Fonda.

BOTTOM: Poster for *The Searchers*, dir. John Ford, 1956.

concerns the search, pushed to extremes over five years, for a young girl, Debbie (Natalie Wood), who has been kidnapped by Comanche Indians. Her uncle (John Wayne) is no longer the just and charismatic hero, but instead is racist, wild, ready to kill his niece because she has become "one of them," and condemned—like the Indian whose body he has defiled—to wander in the wind.

Along the way, Ford applied himself to erasing the image of Indians as violent and intent on killing at any cost. In *Fort Apache*, Cochise and his Indian warriors are depicted as dignified and courageous, and Ford's last Western, *Cheyenne Autumn* (1964), paid tribute to the Native Americans confined on reservations. It was the least he owed them.

A story relates that one day a producer complained to the great gruff man who affected an eye patch that they had lost three days on the production schedule. Ford took the script, calmly ripped out a few pages and replied: "Now we're three days *ahead* of schedule."[1] Cool and commanding, both behind the lens and in front of it, an attitude that was also part of the fascination of the western: a cool and macho persona that all the girls fell in love with and all the boys wanted to have. A sangfroid that concealed an inevitable resignation (prompted in Ford's case by his giving in to the system). The self-assurance of all those Marlboro Men, from Gary Cooper's killer "yup" to John Wayne's "that'll be the day" in *The Searchers*.

The Tough Guys

The director Raoul Walsh, who first worked as an actor with D. W. Griffith (who also made his fair share of westerns), was another great Hollywood figure who wore an eye patch, along with John Ford, Raoul Walsh, André De Toth, and Fritz Lang

TOP: John Wayne, portrait, 1956.
BOTTOM: *The Searchers*, John Ford, 1956.
Jeffrey Hunter.

1. Gerald Peary, ed., *John Ford: Interviews* (Jackson: University Press of Mississippi, 2001), 66.

JOAN'S GREATEST TRIUMPH

HERBERT J. YATES
presents

JOAN CRAWFORD

in

"JOHNNY GUITAR"

TRUCOLOR CONSOLIDATED

starring

STERLING HAYDEN · SCOTT BRADY
MERCEDES McCAMBRIDGE

with BEN COOPER · ERNEST BORGNINE · WARD BOND · JOHN CARRADINE
Screen Play by PHILIP YORDAN · Based on the novel by ROY CHANSLOR

Associate
Producer-Director NICHOLAS RAY

A REPUBLIC PICTURE

(not forgetting Nicholas Ray). All of them sported this intimidating accessory; all of them were tough guys.

Walsh had lost his right eye while working on *In Old Arizona*, the first western talkie, in 1928. Even when he wasn't making westerns, such as *High Sierra* with Humphrey Bogart in 1941, he might almost have been. Walsh loved soldiers, gangsters, and pirates as much as he loved cowboys, but the heart of the director who made *Pursued* with Robert Mitchum in 1947 belonged to the western. The same was true of André De Toth, the Austro-Hungarian director who was married to Veronica Lake, master of the B-movie for some, and for aficionados such as Martin Scorsese and Bertrand Tavernier—who have battled to bring the director of *Day of the Outlaw* (1959), a black-and-white rarity with a heartrending performance from Robert Ryan—a film-maker of essential importance.

As soon as he arrived in Hollywood, Fritz Lang, meanwhile, asked to spend some time with Indian tribes. If he was to shoot a western—and the studio handed out projects to directors according to their availability—he wanted to be sure of his ground. His first two westerns, *Western Union* (1941) and *The Return of Frank James* (1940), were conventional. *Rancho Notorious* (1952), written especially for Marlene Dietrich, heralded the strong female roles in *Johnny Guitar*.

Which brings us to Nicholas Ray. It was precisely because he did not seem destined for westerns that the subversive and poetic director of *They Live by Night* (1949)—who had not yet made *Rebel Without a Cause* (1955)—that he so excelled at them. Or at least in his masterpiece, *Johnny Guitar*. Ray, who

Poster and scenes from *Johnny Guitar*,
dir. Nicholas Ray, 1954.

towards the end of his life wore an eye patch almost as an extra sign of rebellion, was to make two other westerns, *Run for Cover* (1955) with James Cagney and *The True Story of Jesse James* (1957) with Robert Wagner, but it was *Johnny Guitar*, unrealistic, flamboyant, over the top, and almost fairytale-like, that was to be a landmark in the history of the western, tipping it over into the modern era.

Johnny Guitar reversed all the roles. The heroes were two strong and capable women who were rivals on screen and detested each other off screen: the fierce saloon keeper Vienna, played by Joan Crawford, then in her early fifties and finally, after decades of work, the recipient of an Oscar; and Emma, the vengeful owner of the saloon, played by Mercedes McCambridge, an actress who was not afraid of overacting to make sparks fly and who had won an Oscar for Best Supporting Actress with her first big film (*All the King's Men*, 1949). Between the two was the conciliatory tall blond of post-war cinema, Sterling Hayden, playing the ex-lover Johnny, who carries his guitar slung on his back (a bit like Marlon Brando in *The Fugitive Kind* [1959]. All the leitmotifs of the western are here: fist fights, gun fights, jealous lovers, power struggles, lynching, and craggy features (Ernest Borgnine and John Carradine). Even the arrival of the railroad. But the visceral movie filmed in Trucolor (which favored green and blue shades), with its dramatic costumes—Crawford's brilliant yellow blouse, her fairytale white dress as the noose is placed around her neck—and its almost eerie sets, is in fact a parable making a stand against the extremist views of the 1950s.

Stagecoach, dir. John Ford, 1939. John Ford on set.

The Witch Hunt

The start of the decade was marked in Hollywood by two new developments: McCarthyism, the witch hunt that drove artists to "confess" their alleged Communist sympathies and drew up a black-list that would ban ten "red" screenwriters from the business, and psychoanalysis, now all the rage in America. Nicholas Ray, protected from the House Un-American Activities Committee (HUAC) by the producer Howard Hughes, and his screenwriter Philip Yordan poured all these blind passions and more into *Johnny Guitar*. The supreme irony was that the actor Ward Bond (the whipping boy of Ford's films), who played the leader of the posse, was a leading light off-screen in the rabidly anti-Communist Motion Picture Alliance for the Preservation of American Ideals. Sterling Hayden, for his part, "cracked" in front of the committee and named names.

Destry Rides Again, dir. George Marshall, 1939. Marlene Dietrich and James Stewart.

The classic western was succeeded by what has sometimes been called the "meta-western." More even than in film noir, screenwriters short-changed by the studios took their revenge on the system by using genre films as vehicles for ideas that were taboo, right under the noses and in full view of the censors. It was one of the most legendary of all westerns, Fred Zinnemann's *High Noon* (1952), that opened the way to this new type of western. For the first time, the hero was brought low. Sheriff Will Kane (Gary Cooper) is let down by everyone on whom he counts and awaits his death, while two rival women, his impossibly pretty young wife (Grace Kelly) and his sexy former lover (Katy Jurado) have both laid down their arms. Here once again, screenwriter Carl Foreman had simply transposed his own problems with Senator McCarthy and the HUAC into the world of the western. Was Gary Cooper, who off-screen was harshly supportive of the persecutors, aware that in *High Noon* he was delivering an allegory of the witch hunt? Whatever the case, he was majestic, as at ease in the existential western as he had been in his earlier performances in *The Virginian* (dir. Victor Fleming, 1929) and *The Westerner* (dir. William Wyler, 1940). And he was just as brilliant in the cynical *Vera Cruz* (1954), directed by another guerrilla filmmaker who was to rub salt in America's wounds: Robert Aldrich.

If you'd so much as mentioned westerns with a message to John Ford, Howard Hawks, or Raoul Walsh, of course, they'd have had you tarred and feathered in a flash. John Wayne and Howard Hawks's riposte to *High Noon*, moreover, was the straight down the line *Rio Bravo* (1959).

Just another John Wayne western, people then thought. In fact, it was to prove a gem and a huge success. With *Rio Bravo*, the indefatigable Hawks delivered a new rite-of-passage narrative, in the footsteps of *Red River* (1948), in which audiences witnessed an extraordinary transmission of knowledge from John Wayne to a young Montgomery Clift. The old guard and the new brought together.

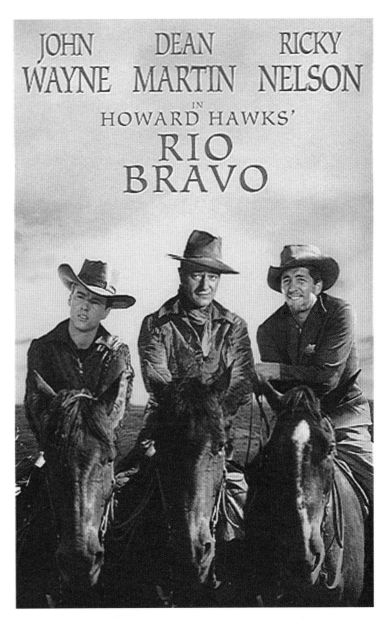

Rio Bravo, dir. Howard Hawks, 1959. Poster and still from the film.

The Psychological Western

The year 1952 was a golden one for the socio-psychoanalytical western. They were everywhere: George Stevens' *Shane*, in which everyone, including a young boy, was attracted to the lonesome hero and righter of wrongs with a troubled past; *High Noon*; Anthony Mann's *Bend of the River*, which dealt with the exploitation of poor homesteaders and men's greed for gold; and Howard Hawks's *The Big Sky*, in which two men loved the same woman.

Meanwhile, the public image of "Indians" had begun to change: 1950 saw the release of *Broken Arrow*, directed by the former screenwriter Delmer Daves, and Anthony Mann's *Devil's Doorway* with Robert Taylor. In 1954 Robert Aldrich delivered an impassioned indictment of the treatment of conquered Native Americans in *Apache*. Thanks to the talents of the most anti-American Hollywood directors and its most individualist and humanitarian star, Burt Lancaster, the political western managed to avoid the pitfalls of white actors "blacked up" as Indians, at a time when the fashion was tending increasingly towards antiheroes, as in *3:10 to Yuma* (dir. Delmer Daves, 1957), with Glenn Ford and Van Heflin. With *The Unforgiven*, John Huston's 1960 western with Burt Lancaster and Audrey Hepburn, times were changing. From 1953, Native Americans were finally considered full citizens. This new political climate gave artists permission to rehabilitate a people who until then had been depicted as a threat. A whole new wave of directors, following the example of John Ford, now denounced the genocide of the Indians. The Native American tribes were not

portrayed in soft focus, but the honor of the "white man" versus the "redskin," as preached in the classic Western, was now questioned as trickery. Perhaps General Custer was not the heroic figure of *They Died with Their Boots On* (dir. Raoul Walsh, 1941), but rather a bloodthirsty warrior.

In 1962, another giant, Henry Hathaway, directed the most iconic sequences, in Cinerama, of *How the West Was Won*, co-directed with John Ford and George Marshall, a western anthology that recalled the early joys of riding across the plains and pitting your strength against the forces of nature. With *True Grit* in 1969, Hathaway secured an Oscar for John Wayne (wearing a black eye patch), who was to die in 1979, but not before being savagely beaten one last time in Don Siegel's *The Shootist* (1976).

Red River, dirs. Howard Hawks and Arthur Rosson, 1948. John Wayne, Montgomery Clift, and Joanne Dru.

For the big chiefs and generals of the westerns—Ford, Hawks, Vidor, Walsh—were to grow old alongside their favorite actors—Wayne, Cooper, Stewart—whose craggy features would never surrender, while young cinema audiences thronged to see Paul Newman as Billy the Kid, handsome as a silver mine and solving Freudian problems in Arthur Penn's *The Left-Handed Gun* (1958). Cinema was entering the age of the *film d'auteur*.

Everyone in Hollywood Makes a Western

In 1960 westerns came from Japan. John Sturges, who had directed *Gunfight at the O.K. Corral*, with Burt Lancaster and Kirk Douglas, and *Last Train from Gun Hill*, with Kirk Douglas and Anthony Quinn, remade Akira Kurosawa's *Seven Samurai* (1954) as *The Magnificent Seven* (1960), played by the new gunslingers of CinemaScope: Yul Brynner, Steve McQueen, James Coburn, Charles Bronson, Horst Buchholz, Brad Dexter, and Robert Vaughn. Seven mercenaries hired to protect a Mexican village, each with his own reasons.

The 1970s saw the Vietnam War and a return to nature, while Robert Altman and Warren Beatty, or Dustin Hoffman and Arthur Penn (*Little Big Man*, 1970) offered their own liberated version of the Wild West. Robert Redford and Paul Newman attracted female audiences to the western. By this stage on the western's journey, the golden age of Hollywood had long ago bitten the dust. Perhaps partnerships such as that formed by Anthony Mann and James Stewart heralded the end of an era. Perhaps this was why James Stewart appeared so haunted as he put his intense, now taciturn, features at the service of *The Naked Spur* (1953) or *The Man from Laramie* (1955): dark, vengeful roles that in some cases should originally have been played by Richard Widmark in psychotic mode. (The two actors were to work together on a John Ford Western, *Two Rode Together* [1961]; sadly the film was not a success and they did not hit it off.)

Another partnership of the last days of the western was that of director Budd Boetticher and his great dry cowboy Randolph Scott, who were to make seven cult westerns with insignificant plots and impassive but garrulous characters, in

TOP: *Winchester '73*, dir. Anthony Mann, 1950.
James Stewart.
BOTTOM: *A Fistful of Dollars*, dir. Sergio Leone, 1964.
Clint Eastwood.

NOW IT WAS 3:05....

...in a few minutes a man scared but brave would run an outlaw gauntlet... ...to put his prisoner on gallows-bound train to Yuma!

time for another great one... *3:10 to YUMA*

starring

GLENN FORD · VAN HEFLIN · FELICIA FARR

Screen Play by HALSTED WELLES · Based on a story by ELMORE LEONARD · Directed by DELMER DAVES · Produced by DAVID HEILWEIL · A COLUMBIA PICTURE

which heroes and villains played poker with the same cards. Westerns infused with a strange metaphysical aura, such as *Seven Men from Now* (1957) or *The Tall T* (1957). And on the fringes, the incendiary Samuel Fuller, with *Run of the Arrow* (1957) and *Forty Guns* (1957), should also inspire a little fire dance.

Sooner or later, everyone in Hollywood came up against the western. Even Marlon Brando, who directed himself in the fiasco that was *One-Eyed Jacks* (1961). Even a sophisticated director such as Joseph L. Mankiewicz, who scored a hit with *There Was a Crooked Man* (1970). Not forgetting all the comedies, right from the silent era, that sent up the genre in such light-hearted fashion.

The legend was strong enough to absorb any blows. In an atypical Ford masterpiece, *The Man Who Shot Liberty Valance* (1962), James Stewart does the washing up, while John Wayne shyly offers flowers to Vera Miles. Stewart's character becomes a senator after killing the bad guy, Liberty Valance (Lee Marvin), but we learn that in fact it was John Wayne who set it up. "This is the West, sir. When the legend becomes fact, print the legend," explained the editor of the *Shinbone Star*.

It was the Italian director Sergio Leone who exploded the myth in *For a Fistful of Dollars* (1964), with a then-inexpensive television actor, Clint Eastwood. *Once Upon a Time in the West*: in 1968, it was Henry Fonda's turn to become an ill-shaven brute who shoots before he speaks.

America's answer to Spaghetti westerns and Zapata westerns (set during the Mexican revolution) was Sam Peckinpah. Peckinpah didn't so much make films as break them. For him the last frontier was violence, which he aestheticized in order to debunk any romantic notions, in images that are now normal to us: the impact

TOP: *Little Big Man*, dir. Arthur Penn, 1970. Dustin Hoffman.

BOTTOM: *Apache*, dir. Robert Aldrich, 1954. Burt Lancaster and Jean Peters.

FACING PAGE, TOP LEFT: Tom Mix and his famous horse Toni, c. 1920.

FACING PAGE, TOP RIGHT: *Butch Cassidy and the Sundance Kid*, dir. George Roy Hill, 1969. Paul Newman and Robert Redford.

FACING PAGE, BOTTOM LEFT: *Lonely Are the Brave*, dir. David Miller, 1961. Kirk Douglas.

FACING PAGE, BOTTOM RIGHT: *3:10 to Yuma*, dir. Delmer Daves, 1957. Van Heflin and Glenn Ford.

of bullets and spurting blood filmed in slow motion, repeated close-ups, and salvos of curses. In 1969, with *The Wild Bunch*, led by a veteran Hollywood hero, a whisky-bloated William Holden, magnificent and pathetic, a film disparaging the myth, restricted to over-18s and torn to shreds by the critics, the cinema had a new outlaw.

And you would have to be above the law to keep the western alive. Doomed by its very nature to sink into the sand and to emerge periodically, trigger-happy with nostalgia. But dead and buried? That'll be the day!

The Man Who Shot Liberty Valance, John Ford, 1962.

TOP, LEFT: *Comanche Station*,
Budd Boetticher, 1960.
Randolph Scott and
Nancy Gates.

TOP, RIGHT: *Decision at Sundown*,
Budd Boetticher, 1957.
Randolph Scott.

BOTTOM: *The Left Handed Gun*,
Arthur Penn, 1958.
Paul Newman.

Ernest Borgnine

He jovially welcomes you at home with his trademark gap-toothed smile. At ninety, he has a robust laugh, and contagious energy. What a presence. He has lived here since 1965, in the large English country-style estate built in the 1930s and perched on a quiet knoll, just off Mulholland Drive. He starts by gladly showing off the Oscar he received in 1956 for his performance in *Marty*. It sits on a shelf in the spacious dark wood-paneled den with several other shiny awards and plaques. And he insists his visitors hold the heavy golden statuette, still very proud, all these years later, to have won over James Cagney, James Dean, and Spencer Tracy.

In a sixty-year career, he has made around 140 films. Westerns, comedies, war dramas, Biblical epics, horror films, and science fiction. Some classics, some B movies, and quite a few more forgettable ones along the way. "Clinkers," as he amusingly calls them. He isn't ashamed of anything he did. The list of his most memorable films is impressive, including *From Here to Eternity* (1953), *The Vikings* (1958), *The Dirty Dozen* (1967), *The Wild Bunch* (1969), and *The Poseidon Adventure* (1972). He played every sort of character, but was often typecast as the bad guy or the heavy. He didn't mind. And he worked with some of the best filmmakers: Robert Aldrich, with whom he made six pictures; Richard Brooks; Sam Peckinpah; Nicholas Ray; John Sturges; and Fred Zinnemann. In the 1960s, television gave a new boost to his career, thanks to the popularity of the series *McHale's Navy*.

With genuine generosity and infectious enthusiasm, he talks about his memories. He died on July 8, 2012, and will forever be remembered as one of the last Hollywood giants.

"I spent ten years in the Navy and when the war was over, I said, 'That's it. I'm not going to be a sailor anymore.' I went home to Connecticut and after two weeks my mother asked me what I was going to do. I didn't want to work in a factory. So I thought I would go back in the Army for another ten years and get a pension. And out of a clear blue sky my mother said: 'Have you thought of becoming an actor? You always like to make a damn fool of yourself in front of people. Why don't you give it a try?' [*Laughter.*] And I went to drama school.

I did my first screen test in New York with Robert Siodmak in 1951 for *The Whistle at Eaton Falls*. I went over to Schrafft's and opened the door and there were about 147 people ahead of me. I was told to come back in three hours. I had a dime in my pocket, just enough to get back to my house on the subway, so I walked along Fifth Avenue and I went into Saint Patrick's Cathedral to sit down. And I saw the man on the cross and said, 'Please help me. I am a bad Catholic but I need the work!' When I went back, I was the last one to be put in front of the camera. Robert Siodmak told me to sit on a chair and say one word. I said, 'Sir, what do you want me to say?' He said, 'Just say the word 'shit'!' [*Laughter.*] And I said it. And he said, 'When you say it, it makes you smile, and you've got a good smile.'

I first went to Hollywood to do *The Mob* [1951], directed by Robert Parrish at Columbia. I found a place as close as possible to the studio in Culver City. I didn't have a car to go around. It was ten dollars a day and one block away, and I would walk every morning. Money is money.

FACING PAGE: Portrait, 2006.

BELOW: With William Holden and Warren Oates in *The Wild Bunch*, dir. Sam Peckinpah, 1969.

I only met Harry Cohn, the head of the studio, after my second film there—*China Corsair*, where I played a Chinaman! He wanted to offer me a 50-week contract at 150 dollars a week. I said, 'Thank you, Sir, but I don't think I can take it.' 'What do you mean?' 'Well, my wife can't stay away from her family that long.' 'Is she Jewish?' he asked. 'Yes, as a matter of fact, Sir, she is.' 'Goddam Jews, they are all the same' was his comment! And I didn't get the contract. [*Chuckle.*]

I went home to New York for two and half years during which time I read a book called *From Here to Eternity*. Nobody knew me, but I said to myself, 'Holy mackerel, I am going to play that character Fatso Judson.' Around Christmas time, my agent called me and told me I had to go back to Hollywood: they wanted me for the part of Fatso! And I went. Fred Zinneman, the director, took one look at me and said 'Yeah, yeah, yeah. Get a haircut.' So I went to the barbershop right around the corner. I had to go back nine times before he was satisfied!

I had never met Frank Sinatra, Montgomery Clift, or Burt Lancaster before we did the rehearsal of the scene where I was playing the piano and almost get into a fight. It broke the ice. And I thank Frank with all my heart because from then on we were friends. I really got to know Monty when we had to prepare for our fight where he kills me. Two professionals did it first in front of us and Fred Zinneman. And then we did it ourselves, starting at 4 p.m. on a Saturday and finished about 5 o'clock on Sunday morning!

I made six movies with Robert Aldrich and my first was the western *Vera Cruz* [1954] with Gary Cooper. He was the greatest actor I have seen work besides Spencer Tracy. He listened to what the other fellow was saying and he'd answer as if he really meant it, like a real exchange. That is acting.

You never saw him prepare. He walked on set, he knew his lines. It was perfect. Quiet. Easy. No strain. He played Gary Cooper. In Mexico, he became a Mexican himself! He would take his lunch and give it to the kids and then buy his own lunch from the locals. We were riding together one day and I told him: 'I wish I could act like you, Mr. Cooper. You got two Oscars'. And you know what his answer was? 'I just got them for saying, "Yep."' Just beautiful.

And that's when I first met Charles Bronson, who at the time was still called Charles Buchinsky. We were friends. At one time, we almost got killed together. We were on horseback in our costumes on location in Mexico and we had run out of cigarettes. We had some time between setups so we decided to go to the cantina to get some. And we were dressed up as desperadoes and we passed some soldiers in uniforms who were there to protect some visiting political official. They said '*Halto*,' stop, and had their guns drawn on us. They thought we were some bandits trying to attack them!

I was doing *Ice Station Zebra* [1968] with Rock Hudson at the same time as I was filming *The Legend of Lylah Clare.* Bob [Robert Aldrich] hated old man Harry Cohn! Kim Novak was quite a gal. She was into her purple binge at the time! Everything had to be purple. So one day she says, 'I am not going to wear that wig anymore.' But she had to as it was essential to the picture. So over the weekend, her trailer and makeup room were all painted purple. But Robert Aldrich never complained. He was the most wonderful guy in the world. He never asked his actors to do something he would not try himself first. He was like a brother and a father to me. I was up to his house many, many times. On his boat. In one scene during *Flight of the Phoenix* [1965] with that wonderful guy who played the doctor, [Christian] Marquand, I started to cry and when we finished I looked over to Bob and he had tears coming down.

Joan Crawford was Joan Crawford: a star in her own right. What are you going to say? During the filming of *Johnny Guitar* [1954], she used to come in at 4 a.m. to get made up. What she looked like before I didn't know, but when she walked on set, she was Joan Crawford. She likes a cold set, making everything chilly and invigorating, and we and all the crew were cold as hell! Nic [Nicholas Ray] was a womanizer and he had a little something with Mercedes McCambridge, which made her a little mad. He was a wonderful director. Never said a word to the gang I was in. He let us do our things, just making sure we were in the right position.

I made a couple of pictures with Burt Lancaster. Never said too much to anybody. Always thinking and doing his work. James Stewart was the opposite. After we finished a scene, boom he sat down. He never left the set. Stayed right there. He was a sweetheart. After we made *The Flight of the Phoenix* together, I always called him the General!

Richard Brooks could eat his actors alive for breakfast, you know. On the very first day for *The Catered Affair* [1956], for the first scene in the picture, where I come home and our daughter comes home and says she is going to get married, somehow a thing was happening that could not get worked out. We tried to rehearse and still to no avail. So Richard Brooks told us to work it out by ourselves! And I said, 'Miss Davis, let's try it this way. I think I know what's wrong. It's a matter of timing.' She said, 'Well, let's try it.' So we did this, bim bam boom, and it worked fine. And when he came back to the set, she said to him, 'Ernie

In *Ice Station Zebra*, dir. John Sturges, 1968.

figured it out.' 'Goddam thinking actor,' he said. Then we moved to the next set. I was supposed to get into bed after driving all night long and we are still talking about the wedding and everything else. I am on one side of the bed and Bette on the other and Brooks has everybody around us and he looked at me and he said: 'All right Mr. Borgnine, what have you got in mind for this scene?' Oh my God, what have I done?

Bette Davis was one of my favorites. She was just wonderful to work with. She knew not only her lines but everybody's lines. I remember when I won the New York Screen Critics' Award for *Marty* when we were filming. She gave me a beautiful horseshoe arrangement of roses and there was a ribbon across it that said: 'Congratulations, Ernie. Why don't you Italians go home?' [*Laughter.*] Because Anna Magnani had also won for *The Rose Tattoo* [1955].

When I stop to think about Sam Peckinpah's *The Wild Bunch*, I only had about fifteen lines, and it seems I'm talking all the time, doesn't it? Sam would say to us, 'I want you fellows to ride out by yourselves with a cameraman and shoot.' So we ride out in the sunset without saying too much to anybody, filming all the time. Sam just loved constant improvisation. When my horse stumbled he said, 'Great, keep going,' and you heard [William] Holden say to me, 'Come on, get up out of there you dumb son of a b—.' These kinds of things to keep the action rolling, so I rolled out there and bam bam bam with my guns. That's the kind of work we did on *The Wild Bunch* and we all just loved it.

I remember what Lee Marvin once told me when we were making *The Dirty Dozen* in 1967. He said, 'Believe it or not, we are the end of an era.' I said, 'What do you mean?' He said, 'Well, after us comes a different kind of world in this picture business.' You never know when you are making a film if it will become a classic. You are just working, attempting to bring things—the words—to life. And if you can make them true to life, then, oh my God.''

Interview by Jean-Paul Chaillet and Juliette Michaud at Lake Glen Drive, Beverly Hills, November 21, 2007.

FACING PAGE: With his Oscar for *Marty*, 1955.

Something's Got to Give

The 1950s invented it all: rock and roll, American beauties, television. The first half of the 1960s brought *Lawrence of Arabia* (1962), *Psycho* (1960), *Lolita* (1962), *Breakfast at Tiffany's* (1961), and James Bond. The films were powerful, daring, delightful. They were to leave their mark on culture. Yet there was a sour taste. The 1960s had Kennedy, but not for long. They lost Marilyn Monroe, Montgomery Clift, Clark Gable, and Spencer Tracy. No wonder there were so many misfits. Like *Bonnie and Clyde* (1967). A film hated by virtually everyone—except the public. The revolution had begun. Preferably on a motorcycle. A new dream, a new cinema, stars who were anti-stars. But Dennis Hopper had started out with James Dean; Peter and Jane Fonda owed everything to the great Henry. The last movie moguls were disappearing, the curtain was falling on Hollywood, but the legend lived on.

Something's Got to Give, dir. George Cukor, 1962. Marilyn Monroe.

Marilyn is No More

How could things ever be normal again without her? She left a harrowing performance in *The Misfits*, written by her husband Arthur Miller. She left some nocturnal scenes filmed by the veteran George Cukor. A cinematic requiem. Another film left unfinished. *The Misfits*, released in 1961, was more than a long poem by John Huston on a group of outsiders adrift in their own lives. The film became a symbol of the end of the legend of the Wild West and of Hollywood's golden age. Marilyn Monroe had only to delve into the failures of her personal life in order to identify with a role that was cruel, but that allowed her to display her immense complexity. Montgomery Clift played a former rodeo rider with a bruised soul. After three last films—Stanley Kramer's *Judgment at Nuremberg* (1961), John Huston's *Freud* (1962), and Raoul Lévy's *L'Espion* (*The Defector*, 1966), a forgotten co-production—the inimitable Clift succumbed to a deadly cocktail of alcohol and despair at the age of forty-five. Clark Gable, who played one of the last cowboys in *The Misfits*, died of a heart attack a few days after the end of filming. Marilyn Monroe, with her legendary lateness, would have had his hide. She adored him, seeing him as a father figure. Monroe would never complete the filming of *Something's Got to Give*, begun by George Cukor in 1962. A prophetic title.

In the early 1960s, something did indeed have to give. Hollywood was in crisis. Production had more than halved over the previous decade, ticket prices had gone up, and audiences had plummeted. The big studio bosses, if any remained, had lost the "knack," and had to recognize that they understood nothing about the younger generation who needed to feel they were represented on screen. Ever more extravagant productions left audiences cold and bank accounts drained. Badly managed, Hollywood made more and more errors of judgment.

International co-productions made everyone believe miracles were possible. Everyone wanted to be Sam Spiegel. The producer of *The Bridge on the River Kwai* (1957) enabled David Lean to surpass himself, revealing his astonishing epic inspiration to the world at the same time as resurrecting a forgotten hero of World War I, T. E. Lawrence, and making a star out of a young English stage actor with piercing blue eyes, Peter O'Toole.

Lawrence of Arabia, an Undisputed Masterpiece

Lawrence of Arabia, which won the Oscar for best picture in 1963, was a mirage in the desert. Three and a half hours of masterly filmmaking in 70-mm Super Panavision to a haunting score by Maurice Jarre, with a melody that instantly brings tears to the eyes with its promise of unforgettable cinematic moments, with Omar Sharif and Anthony Quinn. The combination of new foreign talents, ambition, money, and multinationals, under the aegis of a Hollywood studio (Columbia), which acted as distributor, set new records.

In Spain, the producer Samuel Bronston had set up a major infrastructure that was responsible for large-scale productions such as *El Cid* (dir. Antony Mann, 1961) with Charlton Heston and Sophia Loren, and *The Fall of the Roman Empire* (dir. Anthony Mann, 1964) with Loren and Stephen Boyd. But what could Bronston have been thinking of when he gave *55 Days at Peking* (1963, with Charlton

Lawrence of Arabia, dir. David Lean, 1962. Peter O'Toole and Anthony Quinn.

Heston, Ava Gardner, and David Niven) and the biblical epic *King of Kings* (1961) to Nicholas Ray to direct? The mad dog of American cinema excelled as much in his use of color as in his portraits of outsiders (which is how he saw Jesus in *King of Kings*), but there was nothing he could do with these unwieldy giants. He collapsed with a heart attack on the set of *55 Days at Peking*. Sailing close to the wind in his life as in his art, one of the great *poètes maudits* of the cinema was never again to get a viable project off the ground.

And what was Fox thinking of when it signed its own death warrant by having Joseph L. Mankiewicz, Hollywood's intellectual, whose genius lay in the power of words, not in moving pyramids, direct *Cleopatra* (1963)? The nightmare production process kicked off on September 28, 1960. Love at first sight for Elizabeth Taylor and Robert Burton, and a last-minute change of director (originally Rouben Mamoulian, who wouldn't have been a much better choice). Delays and scandals piled up (the stormy affair between Taylor and Burton, both married, marked the demise of Hollywood's strict moral code), and so did costs. Taylor's fee of $1 million—unprecedented, and the start of the inflation of stars' fees—was dwarfed by a budget of almost $40 million. Filming took two years, and on its release in 1963 the film received a lukewarm reception.

While Fox showered gold upon Elizabeth Taylor, it penalized Marilyn Monroe and threatened her with lawsuits every time she caused a delay on *Something's Got to Give*. As the production process veered uncomfortably close to a bad version of *Hellzapoppin'* (the cult parody of a film shoot released in 1941), the newspapers fell upon events on set with glee. Fox wanted to replace her. Dean Martin took her side, declaring in the press, "No Marilyn, no film." Cyd Charisse threatened to sue Dean Martin for loss of earnings. But what was Marilyn, at the height of her powers, doing in this insipid affair anyway? *Something's Got to Give* was a remake of an old-fashioned comedy starring Irene Dunne (to be made again the following year with Doris Day). Neither George Cukor nor Monroe, who had been at daggers drawn since *Let's Make Love* (1960), thought much of it. She had to do screen tests to prove that she was back on form and under control.

She celebrated a lonely thirty-sixth birthday on set, then fell ill, and stopped turning up. Despite this disastrous soap opera, the images that were filmed, the night scenes with Monroe naked in the pool, are magic. A few weeks later, everything was sorted out, and Cukor had been replaced by Jean Negulesco, who had directed Monroe in *Gentlemen Prefer Blondes* (1953). But there was the drinking, the sleeping pills, the Kennedys, the Cuba missile crisis, the Mafia. Did Marilyn know too much? Was this the final act in a suicide that had started long before? When she died, her

TOP: *Judgment at Nuremberg*, dir. Stanley Kramer, 1961. Maximilian Schell and Richard Widmark.

BOTTOM: *The Misfits*, dir. John Huston, 1961. Clark Gable and Marilyn Monroe.

hair was so badly damaged by years of peroxide that it was covered up with the same platinum-white wig that she had worn for *Something's Got to Give*. Her spirit took wing, her image stayed forever.

Audrey Hepburn could make everyone forget everything. After *My Fair Lady* (1964), she proved she was capable—though not an ideal choice for Truman Capote's heroine—of showing a darker side in the bittersweet *Breakfast at Tiffany's*, directed by Blake Edwards. Her look, that croissant moment in front of the Tiffany's window display, her singing of "Moon River," her way of twisting George Peppard round her little finger, and her chic had their unforgettable effect. She worked with Stanley Donen again on *Charade* (1963) with Cary Grant, just to show that the veteran stars still held their value.

Meanwhile Jerry Lewis, Hollywood's master of slapstick, now directed his own comedies. He was the first to use a monitor on set as he was filming, a technique that was adopted on every film set. His popularity waning by the late 1960s, he was rediscovered abroad. The hilarious comic with rubber limbs was one of the first, as early as the 1950s, to use his talents to raise money for charity, in the famous Jerry Lewis telethons.

Television was no longer the enemy. It produced new heroes, or rather antiheroes. It created new stars, such as Clint Eastwood, the pedigree Californian Robert Redford, and the ultra-modern Steve McQueen in *Wanted: Dead or Alive*. Clint Eastwood attracted attention playing opposite Natalie Wood in *Inside Daisy Clover* (1965), which denounced the exploitation by the Hollywood studios. For the heroine of *West Side Story* (1961), who was to develop brilliantly into adult roles (until her tragic death in 1981), and who had been pushed relentlessly by her mother from the beginning, this was a topic she knew well.

Steve McQueen was to make a string of hit films. In 1963, he exploded on to the screen in *The Great Escape*, directed by John Sturges, with whom he had made *The Magnificent Seven*

Breakfast at Tiffany's, dir. Blake Edwards, 1961.
Audrey Hepburn and George Peppard.

(1960). Two hours fifty minutes in a prison camp, an escape on a motorcycle (McQueen's idea), music by Elmer Bernstein, and the naturalness of a laidback rebel of an actor who could be demanding: the public was captivated.

Economic Changes

In 1963, when television contracts were still included in actors' packages, the music company MCA, led by the agent Lew Wasserman, bought Universal Studios and changed everything. The government was to intervene to bring order to what was viewed as a new monopoly (asking Lew Wasserman to cease representing his clients, who included Alfred Hitchcock), but the reign of the agents had begun.

Hitchcock was always shrewd. In 1960 he found the means (the ridiculously small budget of a minor horror movie) to give audiences a cold shower and relaunch his career with *Psycho*. The film radically changed the image of Janet Leigh, known until then as the uncontroversial wife of Tony Curtis, but was to typecast Anthony Perkins as a psychopathic killer.

Psycho set new standards for horror-thrillers. Once again, an essential part was played by the music, composed by Hitchcock's faithful collaborator Bernard Hermann. But if the audiences of the Swinging Sixties who went to see beach films such as *Beach Blanket Bingo* (1965) and *How to Stuff a Wild Bikini* (1965), with sound tracks by the Beach Boys, applauded Hitchcock's masterly skill, to be reproduced again in *The Birds* (1963), in a troubled period a young and sophisticated public also needed to be represented on screen.

Stars and Society

With the (still) unexplained death of Marilyn Monroe, the assassinations of President John F. Kennedy, Senator Robert Kennedy, the Reverend Martin Luther King, and Malcolm X, and the Vietnam War, American optimism and the winds of freedom took a battering. In 1968, a former actor under contract to Warner, Ronald Reagan, stood for the presidency of the United States for the first time. He lost to Richard Nixon. For the time being.

There were many films espousing tolerance, such as *To Kill a Mockingbird* (dir. Robert Mulligan, 1962) with Gregory Peck as Atticus Finch, a lawyer who defends a black suspect. There was also Stanley Kramer. He had introduced Sidney Poitier, who was a revolution in himself. Awarded an Oscar in 1963 for *Lilies of the Field*, he was shown—as detective Virgil Tibbs—slapping a white man in *The Heat of the Night* in 1967. The tide was turning.

That same year *Guess Who's Coming to Dinner* was released. The last of the "battles of the sexes" between Katharine Hepburn and Spencer Tracy features the pair as parents flabbergasted by their daughter's engagement to a doctor played by Sidney Poitier. Less than a month after the end of filming, Spencer Tracy, former drinking buddy of Humphrey Bogart, died. Admired for the dignity

The Errand Boy, dir. Jerry Lewis, 1961. Jerry Lewis.

with which she dealt with this loss (Tracy was still married), Hepburn became a national treasure. Her successes continued both on stage and on film—*The Lion in Winter* (1968), *On Golden Pond* (1981). She won a record four Oscars, though she never attended a ceremony to accept them. But if *Guess Who's Coming to Dinner* touched a nerve with middle-aged white audiences, the student generation found it all rather passé.

Like the rest of America and the world, Hollywood was ready for a real revolution. In a film from the 1970s, the screen would split in two. On one side, Robert Benton and David Newman, two authors who tried in vain to find a buyer for their first screenplay entitled *Bonnie and Clyde*, although Jean-Luc Godard had shown an interest; on the other, Bob Rafelson, a director from the worlds of television and pop music (the Monkees were his creation), and his associate producer Bert Schneider, who wanted to inject the energy of the counterculture into the cinema. They were taken under Columbia's wing. The studio was aware it needed to put its faith in young talents. *Bonnie and Clyde* took off when Warren Beatty announced that he wanted to play the title role and produce the film. Presented by Elia Kazan as a new James Dean, Beatty had already lit up tortured films such as *Splendor in the Grass* (1961) and *The Roman Spring of Mrs. Stone* (1961) with his screen presence. But for the moment he was regarded as a "pretty boy," not to be taken seriously.

"They're not scared of you. They're scared of what you represent to them. . . . What you represent to them is freedom," says Jack Nicholson to Dennis Hopper in *Easy Rider* (1969). The band of creative hippies that formed around Bob Rafelson, who was to make a series of seminal films that were beacons of the "new Hollywood," including *Easy Rider* and *Five Easy Pieces* (1970), a breeding ground for desperadoes like Jack Nicholson and Dennis Hopper, discovered alongside James Dean in *Rebel Without a Cause* (1955) and *Giant* (1956). Hopper described how *Easy Rider* came about: "One day, Peter Fonda called me in Canada, at three in the morning, to suggest an idea for a movie. It was about two bikers on Harley Davidsons smuggling drugs into the United States from Mexico. I agreed straight away. I liked the idea. So then we talked about this and that and worked out a plot. We filmed it in a few weeks without being able to view the rushes, thirty-two hours of images. Then I spent a year and a half on the editing. In addition to its groundbreaking style, it was also the first time that a film didn't have its own specific music, but instead we introduced rock music and a song specially written by Bob Dylan."[1]

Meanwhile, Warren Beatty had implored Jack Warner to let him produce *Bonnie and Clyde*. With the then virtually unknown Faye Dunaway and three other New York actors who didn't need to be paid much, Gene Hackman, Estelle Parsons, and Gene Wilder, *Bonnie and Clyde* brought into existence one of cinema's most legendary couples. It was shocking. Never had so much violence been seen on screen. But seen through the lens of the intelligent Arthur Penn, sex and violence were never gratuitous. Jack Warner detested the film. So did the

Cleopatra, dir. Joseph L. Mankiewicz, 1963.
Richard Burton and Elizabeth Taylor.

1. Brigitte Baudin, "L'Amérique insolite de Dennis Hopper à la Cinémathèque," *Le Figaro*, October 16, 2008.

critics—except for Pauline Kael. In the good old days, the gossip writers of Hollywood could make or break a film. From now on, it was to be the New York critic Pauline Kael who was the arbiter. *Bonnie and Clyde* turned out to be a social phenomenon. Warren Beatty became a legend just as he was acquiring the maturity to become one of the great American directors.

In 1969, *Easy Rider* came out. Against a background of rock and roll and Woodstock, *Easy Rider* was a success that surpassed all expectations. And the person who was to benefit most was Jack Nicholson. A star was born.

The time was long gone when Carroll Baker could outrage the puritan establishment by sucking her thumb for Karl Malden and Eli Wallach in Elia Kazan's *Baby Doll* (1956). Now everything that Hollywood had worked so hard to hide for all those years was put on show. In private showings it was no longer three-olive martinis that were handed around, but joints. The classic Hollywood narrative, with action that always had to drive the action, had been broken. Music became a new feature in films that now found their own phrasing.

The last film to cause a scandal, in 1962, was *Lolita*. Sue Lyon as the forbidden fruit, Shelley Winters unleashed, James Mason more remarkable than ever and a little incredulous at the improvisations of a freewheeling Peter Sellers. The perfectionist Stanley Kubrick exploded and left the country for England (like many of his compatriots before him, including Joseph Losey). Two years after his adaptation of Nabokov, he directed the finest anti-atom-bomb film in the hilarious *Dr. Strangelove, or How I Learned to Stop Worrying and Love the Bomb* (1964). But with Kubrick we hadn't seen anything yet. In 1968 he produced his monolithic science-fiction film *2001: A Space Odyssey*. Cinema had entered another dimension.

This was also an era that loved parodies, producing a wealth of lighthearted romps with a galaxy of stars. Bond, James Bond. *Dr. No* (1962) was the first in a long string of successes, initially starring Sean Connery. The new Venus was Ursula Andress. Bond didn't take himself completely seriously, and allowed himself to be gleefully caricatured in *Casino Royale* (1967), made by several directors with a cast of stars of several

Psycho, dir. Alfred Hitchcock, 1960.
TOP: Janet Leigh.
BOTTOM: Anthony Perkins.

generations. A pastiche that featured a little man who went by the name of Woody Allen. Who would then have imagined that he would transform the image of the American male?

This delirious comedy shone the spotlight on the English actor Peter Sellers, who the following year would play Inspector Clouseau in *The Pink Panther* (1963), with its unforgettable theme tune by Henry Mancini, which was to launch another string of successful films. *Casino Royale* could also boast of introducing the English actress Jacqueline Bisset. Anxious not to let this gorgeous and talented brunette slip through its fingers, Fox made her sign an old-style contract that ensured that she filmed with all the Hollywood legends, before she became an international film icon.

Freed from constraints, many stars gave their best. Ava Gardner had never before projected such potent sensuality as in *The Night of the Iguana* (1964), in which John Huston had the brainwave of bringing together his love of Mexico, Richard Burton, Deborah Kerr, and Ava Gardner in the love-hungry world of Tennessee Williams. Marlon Brando, undeterred by

2001: A Space Odyssey, dir. Stanley Kubrick, 1968.

TOP, LEFT: *In the Heat of the Night*, dir. Norman Jewison, 1967.
Sidney Poitier and Rod Steiger.

TOP, RIGHT: *Midnight Cowboy*, dir. John Schlesinger, 1969.
Jon Voight and Sylvia Miles.

BOTTOM, LEFT: *The Great Escape*, dir. John Sturges, 1961.
Steve McQueen.

BOTTOM, RIGHT: *Splendor in the Grass*, dir. Elia Kazan, 1961.
Warren Beatty and Natalie Wood.

the costly failure of *Mutiny on the Bounty* (1962), in which he discovered his love of island paradises, gave one of his finest performances in John Huston's *Reflections in a Golden Eye* (1967). Elizabeth Taylor and Robert Foster were equally powerful. Huston made one cult film after another. Burton and Taylor were incendiary in the exemplary *Who's Afraid of Virginia Woolf?* (1966), directed by another new prodigy, Mike Nichols. With *The Graduate* (1967), Nichols left his audiences in no doubt that his subject was the 1960s, in a comedy that was a pretext for rebellion against parents and society, with a soundtrack by Simon and Garfunkel and a revelation in its young leading man, Dustin Hoffman.

The Oscars, 1969. The Academy Award ceremony, last eternal vestige of the golden age, consecrated two radically opposed cowboys. On the one hand, John Wayne, with his Oscar for *True Grit* (dir. Henry Hathaway, 1969); on the other, John Schlesinger's *Midnight Cowboy* (1969). Contrary to all expectations, it was John Wayne who, in co-directing *The Green Berets* (1968), was to be the first to venture into the quagmire of Vietnam.

So yes, on a creative level Hollywood had undergone a revolution. The film industry ushered in the magnificent wave of movies by directors such as Schlesinger and Altman, followed by Spielberg, Lucas, Scorsese, and Coppola, which was to transform the film world and head at full tilt towards the "new Hollywood," and the Hollywood we know today. But it should not be forgotten that this takeover happened with the consent of the studios themselves (with their backs to the wall, admittedly), and in many cases was carried out by the sons and daughters of the status quo. Bert Schneider, who with Bob Rafelson was behind the success of *Easy Rider* and *Five Easy Pieces*, was the son of a big shot at Columbia. And however much Jane Fonda, whose career ascended gently with *Barefoot in the Park* (dir. Gene Saks, 1967) before taking off properly in the late 1960s with *Barbarella* (dir. Roger Vadim, 1968) and *They Shoot Horses, Don't They?* (dir. Sydney Pollack, 1969), and her "born to be wild" brother Peter suffered from the coldness of their famous father Henry,

Guess Who's Coming to Dinner, dir. Stanley Kramer, 1967. Katharine Hepburn and Spencer Tracy.

they gave new life to both the legend and the aura. As for Richard D. Zanuck, the edgy young man who introduced Steven Spielberg and *Jaws*, he was the son of the movie mogul Darryl F. Zanuck, who had spent some time in self-imposed exile in Europe. In 1962 the elder Zanuck demonstrated that he still had what it took by releasing *The Longest Day*, chronicling the American contribution to the Normandy landings, directed by Ken Annakin and starring John Wayne. Three hours long, with a glittering array of stars and an easy to whistle marching song by Maurice Jarre, it launched the vogue for war films with armor-plated casts.

Hollywood. Constantly starting over, constantly returning to its roots. Antiheroes were not born in the late 1960s. They have always existed; they were there a decade earlier in the "fantastic" *Marty* (dir. Delbert Mann, 1955), in which none of the characters was especially good-looking or even interesting. Independent filmmakers have always existed. Roger Corman, king of the B-movie and always on the fringes of the system, likes to recall that he was only doing what the pioneers of movies had done, making movies on a shoestring. For the big stars it has always been harder. In the 1960s, they had to push the envelope ever further in order to survive. Proof came in the form of *What Ever Happened to Baby Jane?* (1962), in which Robert Aldrich embarked on the most prolific phase of his career with a cruel but exhilarating (and not unfeeling) depiction of the grueling battle between the two sacred monsters Bette Davis and Joan Crawford, rivals from the beginning of their careers.

But film actors also benefited from the newly democratic climate. Home movies made in 1965 by the former child star Roddy McDowall reveal the famous barbecues—friendly and unpretentious—that he used to host at his Malibu cottage. There the Hollywood elite would gather together, bronzed and relaxed, stars of the golden age and the new wave mixing happily at a period that was caught in the crossfire but full of promise. Among the guests are old friends such as Kirk Douglas and Lauren Bacall, George Cukor and the lovely Jennifer Jones, with her husband David O. Selznick. Jones had recently filmed *Tender Is the Night* (dir. Henry King, 1962), with Joan Fontaine and Jason Robards, Bacall's second husband. Selznick was no

Bonnie and Clyde, dir. Arthur Penn, 1967. Warren Beatty and Faye Dunaway. Poster (top) and still from the film (bottom).

longer working. Reduced by his abuse of amphetamines to doing little more than crosswords, he
died of a heart attack later that year.

Kirk Douglas was the iconoclast at these little
gatherings. With Burt Lancaster, he had spear-
headed the movement toward engagé actor-
producers. Lancaster distinguished himself in this
period with *Elmer Gantry* (dir. Richard Brooks, 1960)
and *The Swimmer* (dir. Frank Perry, 1968). And of
course in Luchino Visconti's *The Leopard* (1963),
as Hollywood royalty was increasingly attracted by
international productions. Kirk Douglas had discovered Stanley Kubrick and broken the malevolent
stranglehold of the blacklist. His athletic physique
on display in bathing trunks, he is shown deep in
animated discussion with John Frankenheimer,
director of his highly political thriller *Seven Days
in May* (1964). Frankenheimer, with his actor's
looks, also chats with Rock Hudson, soon to act
in the avant-garde *Seconds* (1966) and ready to
break away from his string of delightful sentimental
comedies with Doris Day.

Also present is Judy Garland, who had just
finished filming with Burt Lancaster on the little-
known *A Child Is Waiting* (1963), directed by John
Cassavetes. The future leading light of independent cinema, who had been out of step with the
studios from the beginning, would continue his
acting career in cult films such as *Rosemary's Baby*
(dir. Roman Polanski, 1968) and *The Dirty Dozen*
(dir. Robert Aldrich, 1967). Cassavetes and Gena
Rowlands were preparing to move to Los Angeles.
Faces would be released in 1968. New rhythms,
new phrasing, new inspiration.

Another guest in the Malibu films is Simone
Signoret, who had won an Oscar in 1960 for *Room
at the Top*, directed by Jack Clayton. Her husband
Yves Montand's affair with Marilyn Monroe was in
the past. She was in Hollywood to film *Ship of Fools*
(1965), directed by Stanley Kramer. And there is Ben
Gazzara, star of the Actors Studio. And Lee Remick.
And over there is the Greek god of the 1960s, Paul
Newman. With *The Hustler* (dir. Robert Rossen, 1961),

TOP: *The Graduate*, dir. Mike Nichols, 1967.
Dustin Hoffman.

BOTTOM: *Dr. No*, dir. Terence Young, 1962.
Sean Connery and Ursula Andress.

TOP, LEFT: Poster for *The Pink Panther*,
dir. Blake Edwards, 1963.

TOP, RIGHT: *Reflections in a Golden Eye*, dir. John Huston,
1967. Elizabeth Taylor and Marlon Brando.

Cool Hand Luke (dir. Stuart Rosenberg, 1967), and *Hud* (dir. Martin Ritt, 1963), time had been good to Paul Newman. He had managed to rival his "master" Brando, whose political commitment he shared. And there is Robert Redford, who also supported the stands taken by his future co-star in *Butch Cassidy and the Sundance Kid* (1969) and *The Sting* (1973) by George Roy Hill, and encouraged him to become a director.

Actor-directors such as Paul Newman (*Rachel, Rachel*, 1968, starring his wife Joanne Woodward) found their niche at United Artists, given new life by a pair of movie-buff lawyers who kept the business interests of Mary Pickford afloat (Chaplin had sold his shares) until they were eventually sunk by Michael Cimino's *Heaven's Gate* (1980).

What is striking in these snatched images of beach parties is that even when they were *au naturel*, the combined beauty, charisma, and personality of these stars was just as dazzling, if not more so. When she arrived in Hollywood (where Cary Grant wanted to marry her), Sophia Loren said that that when she saw the actors' faces they were like an "army of heroes."

Sometimes these heroes rebelled against the system, standing shoulder to shoulder. But even stronger sparks flew between artistic control and expression, welding together the extraordinary teamwork that enabled everyone to excel, and to reach for the same dream, whether shaped in glossy black and white or in colors worthy of an old master.

Every particle of light that went to make up its glamour was choreographed, naturally. The former furrier Adolph Zukor and the former glove salesman Sam Goldwyn were the first to exploit the sensual lines of art deco to increase the luster of their stars. A wink from Jean Harlow required every bit as much orchestration as a stunt in a swashbuckling action movie. And then there were the private lives of the stars, which had to be orchestrated for public consumption in order to prolong the fantasy. Hollywood's golden age would not have existed without the Hays Code, and it crumbled with it. But however grandiose Hollywood's reinvention of its past may be, the legend was real. Was it not already trailing along in the wagons of those pioneers who were prepared to do anything in order to make movies? Movies that were beautiful, imaginative, fast-paced, pithy, pertinent, and funny, and whose tradition of attention to detail and quality ensures that we can watch them over and over again, without ever growing weary of them. Hollywood. A world fascinated by its own vision. A vision that continues, in turn, to fascinate us.

Among the stars pictured relaxed and united in those Malibu home movies, we catch a glimpse in a corner, finally, of a youthful Dennis Hopper, then aged twenty-nine. For that moment, the *Easy Rider* director and actor was able to enjoy the normal face of a Hollywood whose magic, in that great summer of the 1960s, was written in the sand.

FACING PAGE, BOTTOM LEFT: *Dr. Strangelove*, dir. Stanley Kubrick, 1964. George C. Scott and Peter Sellers.

FACING PAGE, BOTTOM RIGHT: *Lolita*, dir. Stanley Kubrick, 1962. Sue Lyon.

RIGHT: *Easy Rider*, dir. Dennis Hopper, 1969. Dennis Hopper, Peter Fonda, and Jack Nicholson.

TOP: *Lawrence of Arabia*), dir. David Lean, 1962.
Peter O'Toole and Omar Sharif.

BOTTOM: *Doctor Zhivago*, dir. David Lean, 1965.
Julie Christie and Omar Sharif.

Mutiny on the Bounty, dir. Lewis Milestone, 1962. Marlon Brando.

TOP: *Who's Afraid of Virginia Woolf?*,
dir. Mike Nichols, 1966. Elizabeth Taylor and
Richard Burton.

CENTER: *What Ever Happened to Baby Jane?*,
dir. Robert Aldrich, 1962. Joan Crawford and
Bette Davis.

BOTTOM: *Seconds*, dir. John Frankenheimer,
1966. Rock Hudson and Salome Jens.

FACING PAGE, TOP: *The Hustler*,
dir. Robert Rossen, 1961. Paul Newman.

FACING PAGE, BOTTOM LEFT: *The Swimmer*,
dir. Frank Perry, 1968. Burt Lancaster.

FACING PAGE, BOTTOM RIGHT: *A Child Is Waiting*,
dir. John Cassavetes, 1963. Burt Lancaster
and Judy Garland.

CLOCKWISE, FROM TOP LEFT:

Filming *Charade*, dir. Stanley Donen, 1963.
Cary Grant and Audrey Hepburn.

Filming *Elmer Gantry*, dir. Richard Brooks, 1960.
Richard Brooks and Burt Lancaster.

Filming *In the Heat of the Night*, dir. Norman Jewison, 1967.
Sidney Poitier and Norman Jewison.

Filming *Cool Hand Luke*, dir. Stuart Rosenberg, 1967.
Paul Newman and Stuart Rosenberg.

Filming *My Fair Lady*, dir. George Cukor, 1964.
George Cukor and Audrey Hepburn.

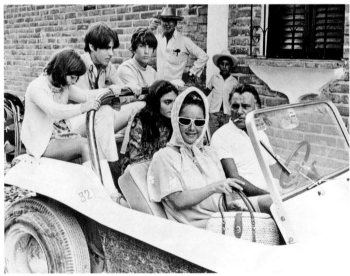

TOP: Marilyn Monroe in a bar with Arthur Miller, Yves Montand, Simone Signoret, and Frankie Vaughan during filming of *Let's Make Love*, dir. George Cukor, 1960.

BOTTOM, LEFT: Elizabeth Taylor and Richard Burton, 1969.

BOTTOM, RIGHT: Filming *This Property Is Condemned*, dir. Sydney Pollack, 1966. Robert Redford, Natalie Wood, and Sydney Pollack.

Jane Fonda

I have interviewed Jane Fonda several times. At every new development in her career, I would ask to meet her, conscious of the privilege of being able to speak to an exceptional woman who is completely modern, an activist icon of the twentieth century (and still today), and an integral part of the Hollywood legend.

Jane Fonda has published engrossing memoirs. How could a young woman who was so magnificent—*Barbarella* (1968) turned her into the sex symbol of the 1960s—and yet, by her own account, so deeply damaged, both change the world and create performances such as those in *They Shoot Horses, Don't They?* (1969), *Klute* (1971), *Julia* (1977), *Coming Home* (1978), *The China Syndrome* (1979), and *The Morning After* (1986).

The interview starts with a look back to the 1960s, when the career of the great American actress began—with a little help from Marilyn Monroe.

Some Like It Hot

"When I was nineteen, my dad asked me to move out
to be independent. I didn't want to be an actress, but
I became friends with Susan Strasberg when she was
playing with my father in *Stage Struck* [1958], directed by
Sidney Lumet. Susan kept insisting that I try her dad's
acting class. Lee Strasberg was known for teaching The
Method, the American adaptation of a Russian method
of acting invented by Konstantin Stanislavsky. At the
Actors Studio, Lee was teaching Paul Newman and
Joanne Woodward, Marlon Brando, Anne Bancroft,
Geraldine Page, and, of course, James Dean and Monty
Clift. Marilyn Monroe was also a student of Lee's.
That summer, she was shooting *Some Like It Hot* [1959]
in Santa Monica. Paula Strasberg, Lee's wife, was
Marilyn's personal coach. The Strasbergs had rented a
house near the one my dad was renting, so I was seeing
a lot of Susan. She took me to see her mother on the set
of *Some Like It Hot*. I knew studio sets because I visited
my dad on his films, but this time it felt different, I was
more observing, interested. I said hello to Billy [Wilder]
and Jack Lemmon. They were shooting a scene in
the train with Marilyn, Tony Curtis, and Jack. Susan
pointed out her mother.

Paula Strasberg was a large woman, all dressed in
black with big glasses, focused on Marilyn's needs. At
the end of each take, Marilyn would turn to Paula,
instead of a very frustrated Billy, to ask how she was.
When the scene was over, I saw Marilyn come out from
the light. Her body was walking before her. I saw her
face, with those eyes of a terrified child. At that moment
I was really happy that she had the nurturing Paula
to take care of her. She whispered hello to Susan and
me. She was very nice, but she needed to have Paula's
attention back on her quickly. This encounter somehow
convinced me to go meet Lee Strasberg. This very blunt
man accepted me in his class because, he said, 'I saw in
your eyes something other than the well-behaved, well-
brought up girl.'

To find the courage to go on stage at the Actors
Studio, to show the emotions that my dad had taught
me to hide all my life, was liberating. By then, I was
modeling to pay the rent and for those classes. I was
often seated behind Marilyn at the Actors Studio. She

never did a scene in front of people, her stage fright
was too overwhelming. She was wearing a trench, scarf,
and no makeup. One day I followed her outside. She
just hailed a cab, nobody recognized the most beautiful
woman in the world. I wanted to hold her hand. I wish I
had done that.

Insecurity

At an audition with Elia Kazan for *Splendor in the Grass*
[1961]: he asked me if I was ambitious. My answer,
in a high-pitched voice, was 'No.' He let me continue
but I knew it was over. I bet Natalie Wood, who got the
part, said 'Yes.' I was so insecure. I often feared, even
later in my career, being exposed as an overpaid fraud.
Being an actor is nerve-wracking. But if things are easy,
what's the point? I remember Faye Dunaway becoming
a sensation in *Bonnie and Clyde* [1967]. Those kinds of
women who were able to assume their sensuality and
who seemed to own their destiny were role models. I
was the opposite.

I got a part with my godfather, the director Joshua
Logan, in *Tall Story* [1960] with Anthony Perkins. A
college student story. Joshua had revealed Marilyn's
true talent in *Bus Stop* [1956]. He was not so helpful
with me. He said I should have my jaw broken,
some teeth removed. He said that with my nose, I
would never be a dramatic actress. They put hideous
makeup on me, suggested I wear fake breasts. All the

confidence I had gained at the Actors Studio vanished. For three years I got into a vicious circle of insecurity, eating disorders. Awful.

My break was to play the prostitute Kitty in *Walk on the Wild Side* [dir. Edward Dmytryk, 1962] with Barbara Stanwyck. I think my dad and Barbara had had an affair. She was fabulous. Because I saw Marilyn with Paula, I also brought my own coach, which helped me tremendously.

Sense Memory

The first time I enjoyed making a film was *Barefoot in the Park* [dir. Gene Sacks, from a Neil Simon play, 1967]. I was a little in love with Robert Redford and could not wait to be on the set, but he was always late! [*Laughs.*] He had just bought his land in Utah. Bob is the most decent person I know. When we were filming *The Electric Horseman* [dir. Sydney Pollack, 1979] in Las Vegas, a woman threw herself at him, trembling, hysterical. She almost had a seizure. He hated that aspect of fame.

To do a film that really said something, like *They Shoot Horses, Don't They?* [dir. Sidney Pollack] was a key factor in my need to follow the waves of protest that had erupted everywhere in the country. It was also the first movie in which I could practice what I had learned from Lee Strasberg. Sense memory. My mother killed herself when I was a kid: when Gloria asks Michael Sarrazin's character to kill her, I could relate. Sydney Pollack had the perfect balance between technical and psychological approaches. One of my favorite directors.

When I got the Oscar for *Klute*, I realized I had won, but my father never had. That was not right. It was wonderful to be able to produce *On Golden Pond* [1981], which finally gave him an Academy Award, and to play his daughter in the film. But even then I did not know what he thought, he did not talk. He had always made fun of the Actors Studio Method, but he was supportive. He even suggested at the very beginning that I could play James Stewart's daughter—Jimmy was one of his good friends—in *The FBI Story* [dir. Mervyn LeRoy, 1959]. But that felt too much like a setup. I needed to prove that I was more than Henry Fonda's daughter. Katharine Hepburn, for me, was a legend, and working with her was not easy. She was very competitive. When I see that movie now, I just sob and sob.

The French Touch

In 1964, I did *Joy House*. René Clément, Alain Delon, not bad! Shooting on the French Riviera. I had visited France for three months when I was younger, to be as far as possible from my dad's shadow. But everybody loved him so much in France that I was actually very proud to be his daughter. I met so many legends in France: Greta Garbo, swimming in the Mediterranean, who told me that I should be an actress. Simone Signoret and Yves Montand, who became very good friends. Simone was my mentor. I had no idea that the French liked classic American cinema, like Hawks or Hitchcock, so much. In the US, we were opening up to films from all the new waves, French, Swedish, Japanese, British, Italian.

I met Roger Vadim on that trip to France, dancing at Maxim's. Dangerously attractive. When I was told later that he wanted to work with me, my first reaction was, 'No!' [*Laughs.*] I lived with him in France for six years. We did *La Ronde* [1964] and *The Game Is Over* [1966] together, but people remember *Barbarella*, a part that Brigitte Bardot had turned down. For the striptease scene in space, I drank a lot of vodka to overcome my shyness. I thought it would be bad, and it became a cult

Jane and Henry Fonda on the set of *Tall Story*, dir. Joshua Logan, 1960.

movie. *Barbarella* is my trump card: if a young actress makes me feel like a grandma on set, I pull out a sexy photo of myself in that film. [*Laughs.*]

Malibu, Summer 1965

During the summer of 1965, I shot the fun western *Cat Ballou* [1965] and *The Chase* [dir. Arthur Penn, 1966] back to back. *Cat Ballou* was a departure, and my first success. It was a very low-budget film, they asked us to work really late hours. Lee Marvin, so sweet, taught me that I could say no. Do you remember Nat King Cole in that film? If not, you have to rent it, it's delightful.

The Chase was appreciated in Europe, but it was not very good, which I had not felt on the set. It allowed me to get to know Marlon Brando better. He is the one who turned me on to activism. Shirley MacLaine also started to work for the Democratic Party because of Marlon Brando. He was focused, calm, and it was almost impossible for women to resist Marlon. But you didn't want to fall in love with him! [*Laughs*] As an actor, Brando seemed to belong in another reality. He had his own inner rhythm, you had to adjust.

That summer Vadim and I were renting a house in Malibu in front of the beach. The actor Roddy McDowall was a very good friend of mine. He was known for his casual beach parties at his Malibu cottage, where everybody from Hollywood met. We really had a great time that summer. There was really a *désinvolture* in the air.

Around the same time I gave a party for the Fourth of July. I asked my hippie brother: 'I am going to put a big tent up on the beach and give a big party. Who should I get to come and play? What musicians?' And he said, 'The Byrds.' It was David Crosby's band. I invited all my friends: George Cukor with whom I had done *The Chapman Report* [1962], Danny Kaye, William Wyler, Roddy McDowall, Sharon Tate, Warren Beatty, Tuesday Weld who was in *The Cincinati Kid* [1965], Paul Newman, Joanne Woodward, maybe even Frank Sinatra and Mia Farrow. My dad was in charge of roasting a huge pig on the beach.

There was also Sam Spiegel, Jack Lemmon, Dennis Hopper, Romain Gary and his wife Jean Seberg,

Portrait, c. 1960.

Lauren Bacall, Sidney Poitier, Gene Kelly, and Natalie Wood. The buffet line was the best cast you ever saw. I'll never forget this woman with a tie-dye dress and one enormous breast feeding her baby while she was serving food. Danny Kaye was right behind her, panting. Darryl Zanuck was about to have a heart attack. [*Laughs.*] When the hippies left, all the medicine cabinets had been emptied! It was really the first time that these two worlds—old time Hollywood and the new hippiedom—came together. People still talk to me about that party. So yes, at the end of the 1960s, Hollywood was changing [*Laughs*].

Easy Rider

When Peter showed us *Easy Rider* [1969], I was puzzled. I loved some scenes, but I thought it was too much for the audience. At this time, I was still very conventional. My dad did not know what to think, but he was proud of Peter. Only Vadim understood at that screening that this film my brother did with Hopper, would actually entirely change our approach to filmmaking."

Interview by Juliette Michaud at the Four Seasons Hotel, Beverly Hills, April 26, 2007, at the Cannes Film Festival, May 2007, and at the Hollywood Foreign Press Association, West Hollywood, May 2, 2012.

Index of Films

Title, director, release date

Bibliography

America Lost and Found: The BBS Story. Blu-ray box set. New York: The Criterion Collection, 2010.

Arce, Hector, and Vincente Minnelli. *I Remember It Well*. New York: Doubleday, 1974.

Bergman, Ingrid, and Alan Burgess. *Ingrid Bergman: My Story*. Thorndike, ME: Thorndike Press, 1984.

Black, Gregory D., and Clayton R. Koppes. *Hollywood Goes to War: How Politics, Profits and Propaganda Shaped World War II Movies*. Berkeley: University of California Press, 1990.

Brooks, Louise. *Lulu in Hollywood*. New York: Knopf, 1982.

Brown, Peter Harry, and Patte Barham. *Marilyn: The Last Take*. New York: Dutton, 1992.

Brownlow, Kevin. *The Parade's Gone By . . . .* Berkeley: University of California Press, 1976.

Cahiers du Cinéma. Made in USA, no. 334/335. April/May 1982.

Gardner, Ava. *Ava: My Story*. Thorndike, ME: Thorndike Press, 1992.

Goodman, Ezra. *The Fifty-Year Decline and Fall of Hollywood*. New York: MacFadden Books, 1962.

Graver, Gary, Orson Welles, and Ricki Franklin (prod.). *The Silent Years*. Twelve-part television series. Public Broadcasting Service (PBS), 1971.

Haver, Ronald. *David O. Selznick's Gone with the Wind*. New York: Wings Books, 1986.

Hayne, Donald. *The Autobiography of Cecil B. DeMille*. Englewood Cliffs, NJ: Prentice-Hall Inc., 1959.

Hepburn Ferrer, Sean. *Audrey Hepburn, An Elegant Spirit*. New York: Atria Books, 2003.

Hepburn, Katharine. *Me: Stories of My Life*. New York: Ballantine Books, 1996.

Katz, Ephraim. *The Film Encyclopedia*. New York: Harper Perennial, 1994.

Lawton, Richard, and Hugo Leckey. *A World of Movies: 70 Years of Film History*. New York: Random House Value Publishing, 1985.

Legrand, Jacques, ed. *Chronique du cinéma*. Boulogne-Billancourt: Chronique, 1992.

MacPherson, Don. *Leading Ladies*. New York: St. Martin's Press, 1986.

Malraux, André. *Esquisse d'une psychologie du cinéma*. Paris: Gallimard, 1939.

Maltin, Leonard. *The Great Movie Comedians*. New York: Bell Publishing, 1978.

Mandelbaum, Howard, and Eric Myers. *Screen Deco*. New York: St. Martin's Press, 1985.

Masson, Alain, ed. *Hollywood 1927–1941: La Propagande par les rêves ou le triomphe du modèle américain*. Mémoires series, no. 9. Paris: Autrement, 1991.

Moguls and Movie Stars: A History of Hollywood. Seven-part television series. Turner Classic Movies, 2010.

Passek, Jean-Loup. *Dictionnaire du cinéma*. Paris: Larousse, 2001.

Porfirio, Robert, Alain Silver, James Ursini, and Elizabeth Ward, eds. *Film Noir: The Encyclopedia*. New York: Overlook Duckworth, 2010.

Ray, Nicholas, and Susan Ray. *I Was Interrupted: Nicholas Ray on Making Movies*. Berkeley: University of California Press, 1995.

Rooney, Mickey. *Life Is Too Short*. New York: Villard Books, 1991.

Sennett, Ted. *Hollywood's Golden Year 1939: A Fiftieth Anniversary Celebration*. New York: St. Martin's Press, 1989.

Studio magazine. Cent ans de cinéma, no. 96 S. March 1995.

Taylor, John Russell. *Hollywood 1940s*. New York: Gallery Books, 1985.

Thomas, Tony. *The Films of Gene Kelly: Song and Dance Man*. New York: Citadel Press, 1976.

Truffaut, François, and Helen Scott. *Hitchcock*. New York: Simon & Schuster, 1985.

Weinberg, Herman G. *The Lubitsch Touch: A Critical Study*. New York: Dutton, 1968.

Wray, Fay. *On the Other Hand: A Life Story*. New York: St. Martin's Press, 1989.

Photographic Credits (t: top; b: bottom; l: left; r: right; c: center)